ONE LONG WAR

ONE LONG WAR
ARAB VERSUS JEW SINCE 1920

Netanel Lorch

KETER
BOOKS

ILLUSTRATION CREDITS

Tel Aviv, Labour Archive, p. 12.
Photo Matson, Alhambra, California, p. 18, 19, 22, 31, 32, 34.
Washington Library of Congress, p. 18, 19, 22, 31, 32, 34.
Jerusalem, Central Zionist Archives, p. 20.
Tel Aviv, Haganah Historical Archives, p. 23.
Keren Hayesod, United Israel Appeal, p. 41, 58.
Photo K. Mayerowitz, p. 41.
Associated Press, p. 56, 117.
Tel Aviv, Government Press Office, p. 69, 72, 86, 97, 118, 123, 126, 129, 196.
Tel Aviv, Israel Sun Ltd., p. 162.
Israel Air Force, Public Relations Department, p. 177.
Photo Vered, p. 190.
Photo Morris, p. 203.
Ba-Maḥaneh, Israel Ministry of Defense, p. 203.

MAPS:

Based on *Historical-Geographical Atlas of Eretz Israel*, p. 49, 64, 68, 75.
Based on *Atlas of Israel*, p. 92.

Cat No. 251514
ISBN 0 7065 15455

Set, printed and bound by Keterpress Enterprises Jerusalem
Printed in Israel.

In memory of my father
Dr. Max Mordekhai Lorch
1895–1972
witness to violence and veteran of war
whose vision of peace never dimmed.

Glossary

Aliyah: literally "ascent"; immigration to the Land of Israel; specifically, one of the waves of immigration within the last century; e.g., the Second Aliyah of 1904–1914, consisting mainly of pioneers from Eastern Europe.

Eretz Israel: the Land of Israel.

Halakhah: traditional rabbinic law.

Kibbutz: a mainly agricultural communal settlement.

Ma'apilim: literally "trail-blazers" or "daring pioneers"; the so-called "illegal" refugees; immigrants to Mandatory Palestine.

Moshav: smallholders' cooperative agricultural settlement.

Mussaf: additional prayer service for Sabbath and Festivals.

Naḥal: an Israel Defense Forces unit of pioneering youth.

Shofar: ram's horn sounded on certain religious occasions.

Tefillin: small parchment scrolls encased in leather capsules, worn during prayer.

Waqf: a Moslem charitable pious foundation; state property held in trust by such a foundation.

Yishuv: the Jewish community of Eretz Israel.

Contents

List of Maps

Preface

ERETZ-ISRAEL was the birthplace of the Jewish people. Here their spiritual, religious, and political identity was shaped. Here they first attained to statehood, created cultural values of national and universal significance and gave to the world the eternal Book of Books.

After being forcibly exiled from their land, the people kept faith with it throughout their Dispersion and never ceased to pray and hope for their return to it and for the restoration in it of their political freedom.

Impelled by this historic and traditional attachment, Jews strove in every successive generation to re-establish themselves in their ancient homeland. In recent decades they returned in their masses. Pioneers, *ma'apilim* and defenders, they made deserts bloom, revived the Hebrew language, built villages and towns, and created a thriving community, controlling its own economy and culture, loving peace but knowing how to defend itself, bringing the blessings of progress to all the country's inhabitants, and aspiring towards independent nationhood.

In the year 5657 (1897), at the summons of the spiritual father of the Jewish State, Theoder Herzl, the First Zionist Congress convened and proclaimed the right of the Jewish people to national rebirth in its own country.

This right was recognized in the Balfour Declaration of the 2nd November, 1917, and re-affirmed in the Mandate of the League of Nations which, in particular, gave international sanction to the historic connection between the Jewish people and Eretz-Israel and to the right of the Jewish people to rebuild its National Home.

The catastrophe which recently befell the Jewish people—the massacre of millions of Jews in Europe—was another clear demonstration of the urgency of solving the problem of its homelessness by re-establishing in Eretz-Israel the Jewish State, which would open the gates of the homeland wide to every Jew and confer upon the Jewish people the status of a fully-privileged member of the comity of nations.

Survivors of the Nazi holocaust in Europe, as well as Jews from other parts of the world, continued to migrate to Eretz-Israel, undaunted by difficulties, restrictions and dangers, and never ceased to assert their right to a life of dignity, freedom and honest toil in their national homeland.

In the Second World War, the Jewish community of this country contributed its full share to the struggle of the freedom- and peace-loving nations against the force of Nazi wickedness and, by the blood of its soldiers and its war effort, gained the right to be reckoned among the peoples who founded the United Nations.

On the 29th November, 1947, the United Nations General Assembly passed a resolution calling for the establishment of a Jewish State in Eretz-Israel; the General Assembly required the inhabitants of Eretz-Israel to take such steps as were necessary on their part for the implementation of that resolution. This recognition by the United Nations of the right of the Jewish people to establish their State is irrevocable.

This right is the natural right of the Jewish people to be masters of their own fate, like all other nations, in their own sovereign State.

ACCORDINGLY WE, MEMBERS OF THE PEOPLE'S COUNCIL, REPRESENTATIVES OF THE JEWISH COMMUNITY OF ERETZ-ISRAEL AND OF THE ZIONIST MOVEMENT, ARE HERE ASSEMBLED ON THE DAY OF THE TERMINATION OF THE BRITISH MANDATE OVER ERETZ-ISRAEL AND, BY VIRTUE OF OUR NATURAL AND HISTORIC RIGHT AND ON THE STRENGTH OF THE RESOLUTION OF THE UNITED NATIONS GENERAL ASSEMBLY- HEREBY DECLARE THE ESTABLISHMENT OF A JEWISH STATE IN ERETZ-ISRAEL, TO BE KNOWN AS THE STATE OF ISRAEL.

from the Declaration of Independence
of the State of Israel, 14 May 1948

The Declaration of Independence goes on to state:

"WE APPEAL to the United Nations to assist the Jewish people in the building-up of its State and to receive the State of Israel into the comity of nations.

WE APPEAL—in the very midst of the onslaught launched against us now for months—to the Arab inhabitants of the State of Israel to preserve peace and participate in the upbuilding of the State on the basis of full and equal citizenship and due representation in all its provisional and permanent institutions."

When the Partition Resolution had been adopted by the General Assembly of the United Nations, a few months before, there had been a euphoric outburst of joy and satisfaction amongst Jews, in Palestine and abroad. After decades of obstinate construction, of bitter political struggle, of tenacious fighting—here finally was the verdict of the supreme World Organization expressing the collective conscience of mankind which awarded the Jewish people this small piece of territory to call its own. The Partition Resolution had been a compromise. It excluded dozens of Jewish settlements from the Jewish State; above all, it excluded Jerusalem, in spite of the tremendous significance of that city in the history, the thought, and the lore of the Jewish people. Zionism had taken its name from that city—Zion. Jews had constituted a majority of its population for well over a century. However, the Resolution was accepted by the Jews, in the hope that the Arab population of Palestine would consider it as a fair compromise, one it could live with and which would be implemented peaceably. That was not to be. On the very morrow of the Resolution, violent outbursts began, and a war started, bloodier and costlier than any previous confrontation. The hand which (in the words of the Declaration of Independence) was "extended in friendship" was rejected.

★ ★ ★

Theodor Herzl, founder of political Zionism, and visionary of the Jewish State, had forecast the establishment of the Jewish State with remarkable precision. "In Basle I founded the Jewish State," he had written in his diary at the close of the First Zionist Congress; "perhaps in five, certainly in fifty years everyone will realize it." The entry was dated 3 September 1897; the Declaration of Independence quoted above was signed fifty-one years later. In his Utopian novel, *Altneuland*, he described certain physical features of the State-to-be with prophetic foresight. He was wrong, however, in one basic aspect. Not only did he envisage the establishment of the State as a process carried out without bloodshed; he assumed, as a matter of course, that the State would live in peace with its neighbors. The Jewish State, he declared, being neutral, would not require more than a garrison army. In this he proved mistaken.

Palestine—although neglected for centuries, full of malarial swamps in the plains, and barren rocks in the mountains, underpopulated by

any standard—was not an empty land: at the turn of the century
there were about 400,000 Arabs living in the country. Notwithstanding,
Zionist leaders have been accused of "blindness", of deliberately
ignoring their existence. Herzl, for example planned to transplant
a "people without a land" to "a land without a people." However, even
if that may be true of certain leaders living in the Diaspora, it is certainly
untrue of most of those who lived in the country. In fact, the problem
of relations with Arab neighbors in Palestine and beyond came to
occupy a central place in Zionist thinking and action. There were
those who expected Palestinian Arabs, whose national consciousness
had only recently been aroused, to become equal citizens of a Jewish
State, which would be exemplary in its conduct towards minorities.
There were likewise expectations that the Arabs, who within a few
decades were to gain sovereignty in some twenty countries, covering
twelve million square miles, would not begrudge the Jewish people
its sovereign existence in one corner of the Middle East.

As these and related issues were increasingly debated, the Zionist
Movement gave rise to a variety of schools of thought. There were
political Zionists, who emphasized diplomatic action aiming at
international recognition of Zionist aims and enterprise, and practical
Zionists, who attached priority to the work of development and
construction in Palestine itself. Spiritual Zionists considered the
creation of a center for Jewish cultural and scientific creativity in
Palestine as the ultimate objective and *raison d'être* of the political
framework. The revival of the Hebrew language took pride of place
for many of them. Religious Zionists envisaged the Jewish State
as the framework in which a fully Jewish life could be lived, a State
whose public and private law would be based on ancient codes enshrined in the *Halakhah*. To Socialist Zionists a Jewish State would
justify its existence by creating a model society based on social justice.
It is significant that among all the different schools of thought and
political action there was none that envisaged the application of
violence to the existing Arab population, or its displacement by the
force of arms. It was when Palestinian Arabs came to consider the
Zionist Movement as a danger to their own national aspirations
that violence became a factor in Zionist history.

The ideology of utilizing violence in order to thwart the Zionist
enterprise, prevent its expansion, destroy its accomplishments, and
weaken international support for its claim and confidence in its chances
of success originated, as will be seen, among Palestine Arabs early
in this century. When, in 1964, the Palestine Liberation Organization

was founded, and its Charter, the Palestine Covenant, was signed, it merely reiterated principles that had been laid down several decades before: "Armed struggle is the only way to liberate Palestine. It is the overall strategy, not merely a tactical phase" (Article 9). "Commando action constitutes the nucleus of the Palestinian popular liberation war . . . " (Article 10).

Jewish military organization, from the outset, came as a reaction to the Arab resort to violence, in self-defense against attacks from both irregular and regular military forces. The very names of the successive organizations—Hashomer ("The Watchman"), Haganah ("Defense"), I.D.F. ("Israel Defense Forces")—denote their basic mission. It may thus be paradoxical that a movement, and subsequently a State, which had never envisaged violence as a means for the achievement of its objectives, has been engaged almost continuously in violent struggle, and more than any other liberation movement or nascent state has had to devote its energies and resources to the development, maintenance and activation of its military capability.

Yet it is a fact: Violence has been endemic in the history of the Zionist enterprise in Palestine, and subsequently of Israel, almost since its inception. This book is an attempt to survey that violence, to describe the role, the very central role, of armed force, violence and war in that history. It is not a history of Jewish-Arab relations in Palestine, which—side by side with eruptions of violence, and in between them—has other facets which may be of crucial importance for the future. Nor is it another history of the Israel-Arab conflict. Although political developments have perforce been outlined, the emphasis is on the violent outbursts which have occured at almost regular intervals, since the early 1920s. These outbursts have not been viewed in isolation, as has been customary, but as one continuum, with peaks and valleys; as one long war with more or less prolonged periods of truce, armistice, cease-fire or otherwise regulated tranquility. And each time, after attempts by administrative, political or diplomatic means to find a "lasting solution" to the conflict, or, at least, a *modus vivendi*, the pendulum is seen swinging back towards war.

The Israel-Arab conflict has not been terminated; hostile emotions towards the Jewish State are still extant, and where there are such emotions, there are hostile intentions. Moreover, there are parties not immediately concerned that find it in their interest to keep the conflict alive. Thus it is impossible to sum up—and the final chapter is merely an attempt to compare the five major "wars" that have taken place since 1947 from different aspects—participants, casualties, duration, origins and results, and to offer some reflections and conclusions.

The chapters dealing with the wars of 1947–9, 1956 and 1967 are based primarily, with the kind permission of its editors, on the relevant items in the *Encyclopaedia Judaica*. The rest of the book is based on a great variety of sources; since they are mostly secondary, and in order to avoid cumbersome references, it has been decided in general to omit references.

The author is deeply obliged to Prof. Marie Syrkin, Dr. Zalman Abramov M.K., Prof. Martin Gilbert, Mr. Jacob Tsur and Dr. Geoffrey Wigoder for their valuable suggestions and observations. I do hope that they will find the finished product an improvement over the draft. Needless to say, they are not responsible for any shortcomings. The assistance of Mrs. E. Yeshayahu and Dr. C. Dresner of the Knesset Library is gratefully acknowledged. Last but not least, my gratitude goes to Erika, who has patiently typed and retyped the manuscript.

Knesset 15 February 1976   Netanel Lorch

1

The Pre-State Period

"Rashid Bey is a member of our new society," declares David Litwak in Theodor Herzl's visionary novel *Altneuland*, which appeared in 1902. "He is one of those who immediately realized the advantage inherent in Jewish immigration. He participated in our economic prosperity, and became rich." Rashid Bey was Herzl's prototype of an Arab, and his expectation was for the peaceful coexistence of Jew and Arab within the Jewish state. He anticipated that the enlightened humanitarian and liberal régime of this State, its religious tolerance (Herzl speaks proudly of synagogues, mosques and churches, and even Buddhist temples to be found side by side in the Jewish State), its economic wealth and technological progress would be more than sufficient to overcome any resentment toward the Jews, and any unwillingness, on the part of the Arabs, to live as a minority in a Jewish State. Although Herzl's blueprint did include a modern army, it would be a garrison army only to maintain law and order. The Jewish State would be neutral, and would not engage in wars. So, too, one of Herzl's precursors as visionary of a Jewish State, an Orthodox Hungarian Jew by the name of Akiva Joseph Schlesinger, envisaged an army composed of the Guardians of God—*Shomrei-El*—the infantry, and the Soldiers of God—*Lohamei-El*—the cavalry, all of whom would be relieved on Saturdays by their servants "from among the sons of Noah." Such an army was clearly intended to be a symbol of sovereignty, rather than an effective fighting force.

While Herzl's Utopia has in many ways come surprisingly close to the truth, it is a fact of history that conflict—mostly armed conflict—with Palestinian Arabs, and later with neighboring Arab states, has been endemic in the history of Zionism and Israel, and a constant counterpoint to the themes of building the Jewish National Home, the State of Israel, the ingathering of exiles, the conquest of the desert, the development of a new society, and the revival of an old culture. At certain times it has, in fact, become the leitmotif—overshadowing those other themes in terms of human and material efforts and sacrifices, and as measured by the interest aroused in the country and abroad.

To a certain extent, *Altneuland* reflected reality in Palestine at the time it was published. Relations with the neighboring Arab population were, on the whole, tolerable. "Moslem Arabs," wrote the Hebrew journalist and lexicographer Eliezer Ben-Yehuda in 1882, "are not really the enemies of the Jews. They probably hate them less than they do any other non-Moslems, but they despise them more than the most despicable lowly creature. They call Jews 'Children of Death,' lowly cowardly beings, who do not have the courage to stand up to any Arab tyrant, be he the most revolting and repulsive." This was still true in 1902. Although Jewish settlements and quarters existing in the country at the time were frequently exposed to theft, robbery or ambush, or involved in conflicts with their Arab neighbors over land, water, and grazing rights which led to violent clashes from time to time, these were quite normal in the country, and Jews may even have suffered less than certain other property owners, on account of the protection afforded them by foreign consuls (whose subjects they were) under the Capitulations System in existence at the time. Watchmen, mostly Arab, were also hired for protection, and contracts with neighboring sheikhs, potential enemies turned allies, were solemnly entered into.

There were some, however, who realized that the present did not augur well for the future. Already some years before, in 1891, the Zionist philosopher Aḥad Ha-Am had written in his *Truth from the Land of Israel*: "We abroad are accustomed to consider all Arabs as savages from the desert, a people who, like a donkey, do not understand what goes on around them—but that is a grave error. The Arabs, and particularly the town dwellers, see and understand our deeds and desires, but they hold their peace and pretend to know nothing because they do not consider our activities at this time as endangering their future . . . but if the time comes when the life of our people in Eretz Israel develops in a way which would displace the natives to a greater or lesser extent, they will not easily give up." In February 1905 Negib Azoury, a precursor of Arab nationalism, wrote in his *Awakening of the Arab Nation*: "Two important phenomena, of the same nature and nevertheless opposed, which have not yet attracted anybody's attention, manifest themselves at this time in Asiatic Turkey: they are the awakening of the Arab nation and the latent efforts of the Jews to reconstitute the ancient monarchy of Israel, on a very large scale.

These two movements are destined to fight each other continually, until one of them prevails over the other. Upon the final outcome of that battle between these two peoples, representing two opposed principles, the fate of the entire world will depend."

As an Arab nationalist, Azoury and his friends did everything possible to make his prediction come true, and the Young Turk Revolution of 1908 provided them with their opportunity. The central government in Constantinople was weakened. The Ottoman Empire was tottering. Arab delegates in the Majlis (Parliament) accused Zionists of the mortal sin of separatism, thus embittering their relations with the Turkish authorities. The nascent Arabic press in Syria and Palestine, first and foremost amongst which was *El Carmel* (published in Haifa), incited daily against the "Zionist enemy whose aim was to conquer Palestine and displace its inhabitants." Although illiteracy was widespread among Palestinian Arabs, this agitation had considerable effect. Relations between Jews and Arabs deteriorated. There is no evidence yet of politically inspired violence, but incidents which continued to occur, and indeed increased as a result of the weakening of Ottoman governmental authority, were broadcast and exaggerated as a means of inciting the Arab population against Jewish settlers. When an Arab youngster, who had stabbed a Jew in Tel Aviv early in 1914, was detained for a few hours in the Herzlia High School until the police came to fetch him, protest cables were dispatched to Constantinople about "Jewish jails in which Arabs were tortured"—clearly part of the plot of a Jewish government preparing to overthrow the Ottoman Turk. Similar incidents occurred at the time, directed by Arabs against German Templar colonists; but when one of their number was killed in Haifa in 1910 the German Government dispatched a gunboat to Haifa, compelling the Turkish authorities to take strong countermeasures.

It was around that time that the first Jewish self-defense organization in Palestine, Hashomer ("The Watchman"), was founded. Its aim was stated simply: "to develop in our country an element of Jewish watchmen worthy of the task." Its foundation must be viewed primarily against the background of the struggle to develop Jewish labor in the settlements; the attempt of the newcomers of the Second Aliyah (during the decade before World War I) to break the monopoly of Arab labor in Jewish settlements. Michael Halperin, one of the founders, was fired by the example of the Circassians, a small group of Moslem immigrants from Russia, who had made a name for themselves throughout Palestine for their valor. Why, he asked, cannot Jews do the same? Initially, the Hashomer was not, on the whole, well received by Jewish settlers. They wanted peace and quiet, and found that Arab watchmen, particularly from the neighborhood, were better qualified to achieve them. The young people of the Second Aliyah were suspect, in any case, for their revolutionary ideas and socialist aspirations. Whenever incidents occurred they were accused of provoking Arabs, of using arms without strict necessity; in sum, of stirring up trouble rather than assuaging it. Only gradually did Hashomer obtain the "contract" for watching over existing settlements; in some of them—notably Rehovot and Hadera—it was compelled to leave after some time, partly because of the higher cost of Jewish watchmen as compared with their Arab counterparts. As late as 1914, a considerable number of Jewish settlements were guarded by Arab watchmen, or by mixed teams. In the larger mixed cities, the centers of nationalist and anti-Zionist agitation, there was no Jewish self-defense organization.

By that time the Jewish population of Palestine had reached 85,000. About 60,000 belonged to the Old *Yishuv*, the veteran Jewish community of Palestine, who were concentrated mainly in Jerusalem, Hebron, Tiberias and Safed, the four Holy Cities of the Jews. This element had no Zionist identification and some of them were in fact opposed to Zionism. The rest had come into the country as a result of the Zionist—and pre-Zionist—awakening, starting with the foundation of the Mikveh Israel agricultural school in 1870. By 1914 there were 44 new Jewish settlements in the country, as well as the embryo of the first wholly Jewish city, Tel Aviv. Their foundation and development had encountered difficulties of many kinds—some deriving from the nature of the terrain and the primitive conditions, others from the attitude of the Ottoman Government, which fluctuated between neutrality and hostility *vis-à-vis* the progress of Jewish settlement.

Arab nationalist agitation was rife in the country at the time. Politically it was aimed both against the Ottoman Government and the Zionist movement. Publicly, however, the Zionist movement was its principal target, often its only one. However weak, the Ottoman Government was still in authority, and it was not safe to come out into the open against its suzerainty. On the other hand violence was rampant, and bloody incidents, claiming an increasing number of victims, were widespread. These incidents and the Arab victims they inevitably claimed, were politically exploited, *post factum*, but there is no evidence to show that they were politically inspired. A direct link between journalistic and political incitement to violence, and the clashes that did, in fact, occur during the decades preceding World War I, cannot be proved. It is true that in 1914 Hajj Bey al 'Azm wrote that the only way to deal with Zionists was "by means of threats and persecutions . . . through pushing the Arab population to destroy their farms and to burn their colonies, through forming gangs to carry out these projects . . . and then maybe those who are there will emigrate to save their lives." This, though, was a prescription for the future, not a description of the present. Indeed, side by side with violent clashes there were attempts, in the event unsuccessful, to bring about a harmonization between the two antagonistic movements.

Indeed, an Arab-Jewish alliance, based on a common interest in separation from the Ottoman Empire, or at least autonomy within it, was proposed by a Syrian Arab "decentralist". "You will have to work with us," he stated in a letter to a Zionist emissary in Constantinople in 1913. "Would it not be right to fight now? Now is the time to foresee the future." Thus it was that following initial contacts in Paris, Egypt and Syria, a secret meeting was scheduled for July 1914 near Beirut, between the leaders of both sides, including the ultra-nationalist editor of *El Carmel*.

The outbreak of World War I served as the reason—or pretext—for the cancellation of that meeting. There were mutual recriminations, certain Arabs accused Jewish representatives of relying on the Turkish authorities for political support, and one of them is reported to have said: "Zionists, do not rely too much on governments. Governments pass, but the people remain."

Thus the political motivation, expanded by personal grievances often exaggerated out of all proportion; the ideological and moral justification for violence; the tradition of violence itself—were all there. The seed had been sown; the harvest would follow in due course.

The years of World War I were a period of uneasy calm, almost of suspended animation, in the relations between Jews and Arabs in Palestine. The Ottoman Government was basically suspicious of the Jewish population in Palestine, and many Jews, primarily those with Russian passports, were deported. For a while there was a real danger that the massacres inflicted upon the Armenians further north would be repeated against Palestine Jewry; this in spite of the often demonstrative show of loyalty on the part of some of the leaders of the *Yishuv*, many of whose sons joined the Ottoman army. While Jews were suspect, Arabs were only a little less so. As the war progressed and the tide turned increasingly toward the Allies, both sides stepped up their efforts at co-operation with the prospective winners.

Following a great deal of complicated political manoeuvring, the British Government agreed to recruit Russian and stateless Jews resident in Great Britain, the U.S.A. or expelled by the Turkish authorities from Palestine, into special units. Starting with the Zion Mule Corps, which saw action during the illfated invasion of the Gallipoli peninsula in 1916, the 38th, 39th and 40th Batallions of the Royal Fusiliers were established, as part of the Jewish Legion. Simultaneously in Palestine, which was still under Ottoman rule, a handful of Jewish settlers led by Aaron Aaronsohn organized Nili, an intelligence network operated by the British Army HQ in Cairo. In the Arabian peninsula, T.E. Lawrence organized Bedouin tribesmen into loose fighting units, which harassed Turkish garrisons and lines of communications, with the blessing of the Sherif Hussein of Mecca.

These activities signified for both sides the establishment, for the first time, of "national" military organizations; they were not, however, intended for use in any prospective Arab-Jewish conflict; their mission was to fight against the "common" enemy, the Turk. To the extent that they had any meaning in the Arab-Jewish context, it was rather to create or strengthen a political claim in anticipation of the end of the war and subsequent post-war arrangements. "Let them see," wrote Vladimir Jabotinsky, one of the prime movers of the idea of a Jewish fighting force, early in the war, "that the Jews love Eretz Israel and are prepared to sacrifice themselves for its sake. If the Russian government will ask why they do not go to Russia, we shall reply: 'We do not wish to fight for Russia, but we are prepared to sacrifice ourselves for the Land of Israel.'" And on the Arab side: "What we want is a government which speaks our own language of Arabic, and will let us live in peace. Also, we hate those Turks." These are the words Lawrence, in his *Seven Pillars of Wisdom*, puts in the mouth of Feisal, in describing the aims of the revolt.

The semi-autonomous military efforts of both sides were thus not directed against each other; they were directed against the Turk. Even politically, they did not necessarily appear antagonistic. Feisal's territorial horizons were much wider than just Palestine. In order to gain Jewish support for his global aims, he was even prepared to concede Zionist claims to Palestine. It is no coincidence that it was Feisal, leader of the Arab revolt, and Weizmann, an active supporter of the idea of the Jewish Legion, who signed the first (and so far the only) political agreement between the two movements. In this agree-

ment of 3 January 1919, signed near Aqaba, both sides declared their
conviction that "the safest way to ensure the achievement of their
national aspirations is in the closest possible co-operation in the development of the Arab State and of Palestine." Colonel Joyce's opinion that
Feisal fully realized the future possibility of a Jewish Palestine, and
would probably accept it if it assisted Arab expansion further North,
is today generally recognized to be a measure not only of the breadth
of Feisal's vision, but also of his remoteness from the mood of Arab
nationalists in Palestine and in Syria. There, opposition to Zionism was
dormant, not dead. The Balfour Declaration, although assuring
that "nothing shall be done which may prejudice the civil and religious
rights of existing non-Jewish communities in Palestine," far from
lulling Arab fears, stirred them up.

★ ★ ★

Just one month after the capture of Damascus by Allied Forces,
in November 1918, a leaflet signed "Arab Nationalists" was dis-
tributed in Syria and in Palestine in which, under the title of *Falastin
Biladna* ("Palestine is our Land"), Zionists were warned not to covet
"one of our lands," since otherwise "the Arab sword will be un-
sheathed." Agitation was directed at Christians as well as Moslems.
"Guard the Christian Sepulchre, guard the Mosque of Omar; all
Jews are Zionists; the rivers will flow with blood—and Palestine will
not belong to the Jews," said the leaflet. The religious overtones of the
document were to become another permanent feature in anti-Zionist
and anti-Israel agitation. The *Yishuv* was as yet unaware of the dire
consequences of that agitation. Although incidents were multiplying,
particularly in the north, the Jewish community was still living in the
euphoric aftermath of the Balfour Declaration and the Allied victory.
Its confidence in the willingness and the ability of the British military
government to maintain law and order, and to facilitate the establishment of the National Home remained intact, evidence to the contrary
notwithstanding. It was only late in 1919 that Jewish activists, including
leaders of Hashomer, and soldiers of the Jewish Legion still stationed in
Palestine awaiting a decision concerning its fate, gave serious thought to
the establishment of a nationwide Jewish self-defense organization;
if possible—with the sanction of the British military authorities, if
necessary—without.
Strangely enough the first major outburst, which was to become a
symbol of Jewish heroism, had little to do with anti-Zionist agitation,

and nothing to do with the attitude of the British authorities. The attack on the settlement of Tel Ḥai on 1 March 1920 was organized and executed by local Arab chieftains who were unwilling to accept French rule in Upper Galilee. It was encouraged by the lawlessness in the region and preceded by bloody attacks against Christian villages which abounded in the area. It was motivated largely by the suspicion that the handful of Jewish settlers in the four settlements in the area were French loyalists, and as well by the hope for booty. Although anti-Zionism may have been an element—directed against the strangers as opposed to the Palestinian Jews—it was by no means paramount.

On the Jewish side, the plight of Tel Ḥai evoked the first of many similar debates. Whether Tel Ḥai should be reinforced and defended, in the face of overwhelming odds, became a question of profound principle. It was Jabotinsky who said during the debate of 22 February 1920 that "those who are in the French zone should come back to Palestine . . . should we try to defend these places alone, nothing will come of it." And it was Ben-Gurion who then replied: "Some say that this is an Arab problem, a diplomatic problem. It is neither. It is only a Zionist problem . . . it is clear to us that we have to defend every place in which a Jewish laborer works . . . If we run away from Arab robbers, we shall have to leave not only Upper Galilee, but the whole of Eretz Israel." It was decided that the *Yishuv* would mobilize to reinforce Upper Galilee, but the help in men and arms was too little and too late. Tel Ḥai fell, and Metulla and Kfar Giladi were evacuated a few days later. Ultimately the desperate yet unsuccessful stand of the handful of defenders of Tel Ḥai paid a political dividend. Contrary to previous arrangements, the final boundary between the French Mandatory Territory of Syria and that of British Palestine was drawn so as to include the "finger of Upper Galilee" in the latter. This was the first and so far the only instance of military failure bringing political benefit to the Jewish side in the conflict.

The news of the fall of Tel Ḥai spread quickly throughout the country and contributed to outbursts further south, which were far more indicative of coming events—the Jerusalem riots of Passover 1920. These were preceded by a series of Arab demonstrations in various cities, held with the consent of British military authorities, against the "Zionists who wish to conquer the country." "Palestine is our land and the Jews are our dogs" was the motto which originated at that time and was to accompany similar demonstrations in coming decades. More important, the impression was created that British military authorities did more than acquiesce reluctantly in these manifestations. At least some of their prominent members tacitly encouraged them, as proof of their own assessment that the Balfour Declaration (which in any case had already achieved its war-time purpose) as a policy for Palestine would be detrimental to British Imperial interests. *Ad-daula ma'ana*—"the Government is with us"— was to become a premise for Arab activity in years to come.

That year the feast of Nebi Mussa (i.e., the Prophet Moses; ironically, of all Moslem festivals the one most deeply anchored in Jewish lore) coincided with Passover. The annual procession—en route from the shrine near the Dead Sea—usually passed round Jerusalem, but in that year it went through the Old City. Although forewarned by Jewish leaders including Dr. Chaim Weizmann, who was in the country at the head of the Zionist Commission, the Military Governor of Jerusalem, Sir Ronald Storrs, did not ban the procession nor take any precautions beyond the removal of Jewish policemen from the Old City of Jerusalem, to avoid friction and provocation. The result was a pogrom— Jewish shops and homes in the Old City looted, women raped, Jewish passersby attacked—leaving six killed and 200 wounded. The impact was profound. The pogrom was taken as the first indication that British policy was wavering, especially when during the following days it was Vladimir Jabotinsky and other members of the Jewish Self-Defense organization, that had been hurriedly organized to rescue the Jewish Quarter, who were jailed. Whereas the instigators of the pogrom, many from Hebron, were soon released, Jabotinsky was condemned to 15 years in jail. Hajj Amin al-Husseini, the firebrand nephew of the then mayor of Jerusalem, who headed the demonstration, was shortly thereafter appointed Mufti of Jerusalem by the British High Commissioner. It was the debut of a long career which was to influence the fate of Palestine for many years, bringing bloodshed and sacrifice for both sides, and tragedy to Palestinian Arabs.

The Passover riots of 1920 set a pattern for future decades during which the fate of the country ultimately depended upon the British Government. Force, employed by Arabs against Jews, was designed primarily to influence British policy by demonstrating to the British authorities, some of whom were only too eager to be convinced, the futility, and indeed, the dangers, of the Jewish National Home. No military decision was hoped for as a result of the application of violence, merely a demonstration of force as an earnest of political determination, which would strengthen the hand of those—in London and in Jerusalem—who had disagreed with the Balfour Declaration in the first place, or were prepared to renounce it in view of subsequent events.

All that was far from obvious at the time. Sir Ronald Storrs, in his *Orientations*, while conceding that "our dispositions might perhaps have been better (though they had been approved by higher authority)," blames the bloodshed on "the narrow and winding alleys within the Old City," as well as on "that nervous quality to which the altitude of Jerusalem undoubtedly contributes." This "nervous quality" found expression in the weapons chosen—butcher knives and swords.

In the course of the pogrom six Arabs were also killed, and in an official Arab memorandum Zionists were blamed for initiating the outbreak in order "to spread lies and thus collect funds"—an argument which was often to be repeated subsequently.

This time Arab political gains were meager. Great Britain required Jewish support at the San Remo Conference, taking place at the time, to obtain the Palestine Mandate; without such support and without an express undertaking to facilitate the establishment of the Jewish National Home, the British government would not have succeeded. In the wake of the mishandled Passover riots, the Military Government was superseded by a civilian one, headed—in spite of General Allenby's protests from Cairo—by a British Jew, Sir Herbert Samuel, "because his authority with the Zionists coupled with his well-known sympathy for the Arabs, will enable him to hold scales even."

The events of March 1920 were important in another respect also. They helped deal the deathblow to the idea that the Jewish Legion, some hundreds of whose soldiers were still on active service in Palestine, would be permitted by the British authorities to undertake, legally, the defense of Jewish settlements. The handful of soldiers who, on their own initiative, went to Jerusalem, and took part in the defense of the Jewish Quarter, were among the first to be arrested and sent back to their base. Additional impetus was thus given to the further development of the nucleus of the Haganah, the autonomous Jewish self-defense force which, as an illegal organization, could, if necessary, operate without British permission, motivated by Jewish interests alone. Thus, unwittingly, the unreliability of the British in the defense of Jewish settlements contributed to the establishment of an organization which, in days to come, would prove vital to the establishment and defense of the Jewish State.

The March 1920 riots were followed by a Commission of Inquiry, whose report was never published, its publication not being considered in the public interest.

In March 1921 the new Secretary of State for the Colonies, Winston Churchill, visited Palestine. Even before his visit it was decided that

Transjordan should be constituted as an Arab province of Palestine, under an Arab governor responsible to the High Commissioner. In other words, it was to be developed as an Arab state as opposed to the west bank which would continue under the Mandate. The official report of one of his conversations states that the Emir Abdullah (King Hussein's grandfather) "after full consideration agreed to undertake the responsibility for Trans-Jordania for six months." At that time Zionist leaders were assured that Jewish settlement east of the Jordan was to be permitted.

Although this curtailing of the Mandatory territory was considered by the British authorities as primarily a matter of political and administrative convenience unrelated to the riots of the previous year, Palestinian Arabs may be excused for thinking that it was a direct result of their resort to violence. Moreover, as one senior British intelligence officer pointed out at the time, an additional impetus was given to "Moslem and Christian opposition to and hatred of the British Zionist policy by the realization of the injustice of self-government being given to nomadic savages in Trans-Jordania and refused to Palestine."

Churchill, in his conversation with Jewish leaders, while reaffirming the principle recognized in the Balfour Declaration, also dwelt on the importance of preventing the immigration of people suspected of "introducing Bolshevik doctrines." British sensitivity on this count no doubt contributed to Arab rioting which broke out anew following the 1921 May Day procession, in Jaffa. It was described in a cable from the Zionist Commission to the Foreign Office, as follows:

> On first May a riot broke out in Jaffa (Old City) resulting in serious casualties. The Jewish labour procession sanctioned by the authorities was absolutely peaceful notwithstanding the attempt of a handful of communists to cause disturbances. Advantage was taken of the occasion for attacks on the Jews in the streets and shops were pillaged. The most terrible attack was the storming of the immigrants house by a gang of rioters who attacked men, women and children. There is general testimony to the participation of the Arab Police in the riots and of the fanaticism of the murderers. The Arab crowd was stirred up by parties opposing the British Mandate and the Jewish National Home. These rioters used knives, pistols and rifles, 27 Jews were murdered and about 150 wounded. Deedes and Bentwich [Chief Secretary and Legal Secretary of the Palestine Government] took charge reestablishing order today.

After the Massacre at Immigrants House during the Arab riots in Jaffa, May 1921.

The city is under the control of the military. The protection of Tel Aviv is given over to Jewish demobilised soldiers under Jewish officers.

In fact, the total killed was 43 in two days. The open participation of Arab policemen in the killing and looting (it was they who utilized firearms) which was allowed to pass without impunity, the lack of preparedness of the Haganah, whose improvised last-minute efforts were inadequate, and the impotence or callousness of British authorities, directly encouraged rioting elsewhere. On 5 May a mass attack took place against Petaḥ Tikvah, evidently planned by former Turkish officers; in the following days Haderah, Rehovot and Gederah were attacked. In some cases, particularly in Petaḥ Tikvah, British Armed Forces came to the rescue. In others the brunt of the attack was borne by the Haganah, by now alerted by the Jaffa riots, and on the whole better organized in the settlements than in the mixed cities.

It was T.E. Lawrence, at the time Arabian Affairs Adviser at the Colonial Office, and who was not considered a friend of the Zionist movement, who commented:

I think the Jewish colonies are at present insufficiently defended. Our troops are already a good deal parcelled out, and yet do not cover half of them. In case of a serious row the British troops would not do much more than defend themselves, and my impression is that a serious row (a general rising of the Arab neighbours of the colonies against the colonists) is possible at no very distant date. It does not seem to be important whether it is our policy or the Zionists who have caused this state of affairs; in either case it is a state of affairs which we cannot afford as a permanency. The final success of Zionism will end it, but this may be fifty years hence. The right course today would seem to be to allay the local discontent by a beginning of popular government (Sir H. Samuel has proposed a means of this by changing the method of choice for the Advisory Council). If this proposal is approved and succeeds, it should prevent any general rising: and by giving the colonists the means of defence we can ensure that any *one* will be able to resist in case of local trouble until the British troops can be moved to its support.

All the same, it was following the 1921 riots that the Jewish Legion was finally disbanded. Some of its soldiers, headed by Col. Margolin, the C.O. himself, had—though belatedly—participated in the defense of Jaffa Jews and, without the permission of the British military commander, had paraded through the streets of Jaffa with fixed bayonets. The military authorities considered the possibility of court-martialling the mutinous Jewish soldiers, but thought better of it. Instead, the remnants of the Legion were demobilized; Margolin returned to Australia.

A Commission of Inquiry under the Chief Justice of Palestine, Sir Thomas Haycroft, set up to investigate the riots, had this to say about their origins:

> The disturbances raged for several days with intensity where ever Arabs came into contact with Jews, and spread into the surrounding country, where Jewish colonies, having nothing whatever to do with Bolshevism, were attacked with ferocity. The Bolshevik demonstration was the spark that set alight the explosive discontent of the Arabs and precipitated an outbreak which developed into an Arab-Jewish feud.
>
> It has been said to us by Jewish witnesses that there was no essentially anti-Jewish question at that time, but that a movement against the Jews was engineered by persons who, anxious to discredit the British Government, promoted discontent . . . It is argued by them that all the trouble is due to the propaganda of a small class whose members regret the departure of the old regime, because British admin-

istration had put an end to privileges and opportunities of profit formerly enjoyed by them . . . These witnesses asseverate that Zionism has nothing to do with the anti-Jewish feeling manifested in the Jaffa disturbances. They declare that the Arabs are only anti-Zionist or anti-Jewish because they are primarily anti-British, and that they are merely making use of the anti-Zionist cry in order to wreck the British Mandate.

We are satisfied that this is not the case . . . the feeling against the Jews was too genuine, too widespread and too intense to be accounted for in the above superficial manner. That there is discontent with the Government has appeared during this inquiry; but we are persuaded that it is due partly to the Government policy with regard to a Jewish National Home in Palestine, partly to Arab misunderstanding of that policy, and partly to the manner in which that policy is interpreted and sought to be applied by some of its advocates outside the Government. It culminates in a suspicion that Government is under Zionist influence, and is therefore led to favour a minority to the prejudice of the vast majority of the population . . . We consider that any anti-British feeling on the part of the Arabs that may have arisen in the country originates in their association of the Government with the furtherance of the policy of Zionism . . .

The suspicions of Bolshevik inclinations are here mentioned for the first time in an official document. When previously mentioned at a private meeting of the Eastern Committee by the Director of Military Intelligence, Lord Robert Cecil had retorted: "Yes, I can conceive the Rothschilds leading a Bolshevist mob." Yet this cry was to be a weapon for anti-Zionists until the early 1950s. The irony is that only a few months earlier a petition presented to Churchill by the Palestine Arab Congress had warned: "If Great Britain does not listen [to the cause of the Arabs] then perhaps Russia will take up their call some day, or perhaps even Germany. For though today Russia's voice is not heard in the council of nations, yet the time must come when it will assert itself."

As a result of the tensions, and the disturbances of 1921, an Arab delegation headed by Musa Kazim al-Husseini, former mayor of Jerusalem, visited London to confer with the Colonial Secretary, Winston Churchill, his staff, and leaders of the Zionist Organization. During their visit, on 2 November 1921, the anniversary of the Balfour Declaration, new disturbances broke out in Palestine which were

clearly designed to strengthen the hands of the delegation in its negotiations. Four Jews and an Arab were killed. Notwithstanding,
it was in the same month that one of the few direct meetings between
representatives of Palestinian Arabs and the Zionist movement took
place. The Arabs insisted on the revocation of the Balfour Declaration;
Weizmann took his stand on the Draft Mandate, which incorporated the
Declaration, though with certain changes. Weizmann, according to the
official Colonial Office report, offered to "enter into direct discussion
with the Arabs on limitation of Jewish immigration and constitutional
safeguards against Jewish political ascendancy." The report notes
that "the results of the meeting are rather negative in character, but
it is at least something to have brought the two sides together."

* * *

It has been found necessary to cover the years 1917–1921 in some
detail because it was then that some of the patterns emerged which
were to dominate the Palestine scene for many years to come. The
policy of the National Home was not accepted by the most vociferous
Arab leadership, which tried, with the active help of some senior
British officials in Palestine, to prevail on the British Government
to rescind it. Agitation and violence were used as a means of pressure
in this campaign. The British Government, divided within itself,
was wavering, and thus (in the words of Col. Meinertzhagen) helping
to "increase Arab contempt for us, and destroy Jewish confidence."
In the event, the philosophy of the use of force crystallized on both
sides. On the Arab side—which did not then, nor much later, fear
Jewish attack—violence against Jews was the means of expressing
dissatisfaction with British policy, in addition to its aim of exerting
pressure on British policy-makers. It was thus stepped up whenever
negotiations or discussions were about to take place. While not un-
equivocally successful, enough success was achieved on the political
level and in prestige on a personal level to encourage further attempts.
On the political level, soon after the riots of May 1921 Sir Herbert
Samuel had suspended Jewish immigration. The Churchill White
Paper of 1922 finalized the exclusion of Transjordan from the National
Home, contrary to the San Remo decision of 1920, and for the first
time introduced the concept that Jewish immigration must be re-
stricted in accordance with the "economic absorptive capacity"
of the country. Although the White Paper was rejected by Arab
representatives, and reluctantly accepted by the Zionists who were

concerned that otherwise the Mandate would not be approved, it incorporated the first of a series of formal and official limitations imposed on the Balfour Declaration, and thus constituted an Arab diplomatic success rightly attributed to the use and threat of violence. On the personal level, the extremist Husseini family, under its leader Musa Kazim al-Husseini who had been dismissed as mayor of Jerusalem because of his role in the riots of 1920, emerged as the leading Moslem family in the country. For the Husseinis, so far, violence and extremism had paid off. On the Jewish side, in view of the unreliability of the British, force was found necessary as a means of defense for Jewish settlements. It was at that time that the "Hagonah" was first mentioned in an official British document.

The information available regarding an admittedly illegal association whose promoters, so far from making an attempt to legalise their position have done all they could to keep their activities secret, is necessarily scanty . . .

The originator of the idea of Jewish Self-Defence Organisations in Palestine in March or April 1920 was believed to be Vladimir Jabotinsky aided by Rutenberg . . . The reasons for such a proposal were the refusal of the Military Administration to allow a permanent Jewish battalion in Palestine and its alleged antipathy to the Zionist policy . . .

About the time of the feast of Nebi Musa, 1920, bodies of young Jews began to parade the streets of Jerusalem for self-defence, which can hardly have helped to conciliate the Arabs, and quite possibly precipitated the Jerusalem disturbances of April 1920. However, after these disturbances, Jabotinsky was tried and imprisoned, but, being subsequently pardoned, went to America, where he has never ceased to reiterate in the American press and elsewhere the necessity for Jewish armed defence forces in Palestine . . .

It is believed that there was about this time [May 1921] a Jewish Self-Defence Organisation . . . On 10th January 1922, it was reported that the 'Hagonah' had taken over the Bab Hatta Synagogue as a defence position.

Up to this time there was no evidence of the 'Hagonah' as an organised body anywhere but in Jerusalem, but early in 1922 there are indications that the subject of the 'Hagonah' in Jaffa and Tiberias was being freely discussed among Jews . . .

The Zionist Commission are . . . guarded in their statements,

and while admitting the existence of the 'Hagonah' and cogniz-
ance of its aims and activities, Mr Sacher, representing Dr Eder at
a conference held on 27th February 1922, said that his knowledge
was purely unofficial . . .
By now it is thought that every town with any considerable Jewish
population has its 'Hagonah' and that large numbers of arms have
entered the country for the use of Jews . . .

Seven quiet years followed. The first High Commissioner, Sir
Herbert Samuel, thought he had hit on the saving formula. "The
Zionist Movement," he stated, "must rely on its own means, its own
enthusiasm. The establishment of the National Home is not the task
of any government; it is not an artificial creation of any law nor of
official encouragement. It is the result of the energy and the action
of the Hebrew people itself." At the same time, British gendarmerie,
the forerunners of the British Palestine Police, were recruited for
service in the country. And as far as Samuel's successor, Field-Marshall
Lord Plumer, was concerned, his military fame was popularly considered the equivalent of a battalion of soldiers. British "evenhand-
edness" seemed indeed to be a saving formula as a policy for Palestine.
    In the course of these quiet years, Hajj Amin al-Husseini, the main
instigator of the 1920 riots, who had been sentenced *in absentia* to ten
years' imprisonment, but was soon pardoned and appointed Grand
Mufti, seemed to have made his peace with the British authorities. The
villagers responsible for attacks had been heavily fined. British policy
had been circumscribed, and Jewish immigration, although rising to
almost 13,000 in 1924, dwindled in the following years of crisis,
so much so that in 1926 Jewish emigration from the country exceeded
immigration by over 2,000. Zionist policy had not changed, but even
the most extreme Arab nationalist would realize that the specter
of a Jewish majority in the country, if real, was still in the distant
future.
    In 1928 a new Arab leadership, in which the more moderate oppo-
sition to the Husseini clan was preponderant, negotiated with the
British Administration concerning a Representative Legislative Council, composed of Moslems, Jews and Christians in proportion to
their respective strength within the population. The Resolutions
of the Seventh Palestinian Conference, held in Jerusalem in June
1928, tacitly accepted the Mandate and the Balfour Declaration
which it enshrined, and assumed the possibility of political co-operation with the Mandatory Government. And then quite suddenly,

British troops marching in Jerusalem during the 1929 riots.

in a year of little immigration, a slack year for the National Home, came the riots and pogroms of 1929.

The pretext for the outburst was the situation of the Wailing Wall. Moslem scholars had discovered that this tiny area, at which for many centuries Jews had assembled for prayer, was a holy place also for the Moslems, since it was from here that the Prophet Mohammed's horse, Burak, had taken off for Heaven. Accordingly, early in 1928, a systematic campaign began to limit the Jewish rights which had been recognized under the status quo from Turkish times. It gained open support from Charles Luke, the Acting British High Commissioner, who—on the Day of Atonement in 1928—ordered the removal of the temporary partition between men and women, and thereby prevented the holding of prayer services at the Wailing Wall. Thus, the motivation once more was religious in character, and it was now exploited at the instigation of Hajj Amin al-Husseini, Mufti of Jerusalem, Head of the Supreme Moslem Council.

Political rivalry between his clan and the opposition and personal rivalry between himself and his cousin, head of the Arab Higher Committee, no doubt played their role in the initiation of the riots. The feeling that once Lord Plumer had gone the government was again "with us" served as a catalyst. Just a few weeks previously British authorities had ordered the removal of sealed boxes containing arms—which had been kept in Jewish settlements ever since 1922— "since they were no longer necessary." The weakness of Jewish leadership at the time, and the disarray of the Haganah, also facilitated initial Arab successes and thus acted as incentives for further actions.

The riots of August 1929—evidently well planned—began following Friday prayers at the Mosque of Omar, accompanied by inflammatory sermons. The crowds, equipped with nailed sticks, broke into Jewish houses and streets in the Old City of Jerusalem, stabbing and killing passers-by. The British police force, which though small, might have prevented deterioration of the situation, was passive for lack of instructions. Soon after began the attacks (primarily of small arms fire) of gangs from neighboring Arab villages against all outlying Jewish quarters in Jerusalem—to the north, Sanhedria; to the south, Ramat Rahel and Talpiot; to the west, Beit Hakerem and Bayit Vegan. Haganah outposts, miserably armed, assisted by Jewish police, were able to stem most of these attacks until British forces arrived. A group of non-Jewish students of theology from Oxford, hastily armed, and organized as a militia, earned the gratitude of the *Yishuv* for their uncompromising assistance. The riots spread like wildfire throughout most of the country. In Hebron, where the age-old Jewish community, relying on its good neighborly relations with Arabs, had refused to accept a Haganah detachment, a pogrom took place reminiscent of Kishinev and the Ukraine. Fifty-nine died, the rest were evacuated. This was the end of Jewish presence in Hebron until after the Six-Day War of 1967. A similar pogrom took place in Safed, some days later, when British reinforcements had already arrived by air and train from bases in Egypt and Transjordan. Settlements were attacked by neighboring Arabs throughout the country.

Jewish families flee the Old City of Jerusalem, at Jaffa Gate, August 1929.

Some were captured and destroyed; others evacuated by order of the British authorities. The prime mover was the rumor assiduously spread by the Mufti concerning Jewish designs against the Moslem holy site Haram al-Sharīf—a motif to be repeated in 1969, following an incendiary attempt by an unbalanced Australian Christian visitor. In addition, the anticipation of loot came to occupy an increasingly central place in the mass violence that took place.

Funeral of victims of the 1929 riots, Tel Aviv.

Only some of the larger settlements—considered impregnable by their neighbors—were immune. Attacks directed against Tel Aviv, by now a budding city, were determinedly repulsed with British help and soon ceased. The High Commissioner, Sir John Chancellor, who arrived in the country some time later, expressed his sense of horror at the cruel deeds perpetrated against members of the Jewish population regardless of age and sex, and promised that the perpetrators would be punished. A Parliamentary Commission of Inquiry under the chairmanship of Sir Walter Shaw, sent to investigate the riots and their causes, blamed the Arabs for their initiation, but concluded that their cause was to be found in Arab hostility toward the Jews because they were frustrated in their political and national aspirations and because of concern for their economic future. The Commission recommended closer supervision of Jewish immigration and the examination of the economic potential. The subsequent economic report of Sir John Hope Simpson (1930) concluded that there was hardly any land left for Jewish settlement, that the "economic absorptive capacity" had been exhausted, that there was no more room to swing a cat. A League of Nations Commission despatched to look into the matter of the Wailing Wall recommended certain rules for approach to the site, primarily limiting Jewish rights. These recommendations were accepted by the Mandatory Government. Soon after, in 1930, the Passfield White Paper incorporated the conclusions of Shaw and Hope Simpson, and without even mentioning the Balfour Declaration implied that it was no longer binding. Further Jewish immigration and land sales to Jews would depend on the country's absorptive capacity, which for all practical purposes had been exhausted. Moreover, a legislative council with an Arab majority was to be established.

The impact of the White Paper was eventually mitigated by the letter sent by Prime Minister Ramsay MacDonald to Dr. Weizmann on 13 February 1931, which reiterated that the Mandate constituted a commitment to the Jewish people, and not only to the Jewish population of Palestine, and that the British Government had no intention of stopping Jewish immigration. However, the Mufti of Jerusalem had good reason, on the whole, to be satisfied. The use of force in 1929 had resulted in the further limitation of Jewish rights under the Mandate (particularly of immigration), in curtailment of Jewish religious rights, in the augmentation of his personal prestige and recognition of his leadership of Palestinian Arabs. It had halted the expansion of the Jewish population in Arab cities (Tulkarm, Jenin, Nablus had had small Jewish communities now liquidated), and had brought a setback to the Zionist enterprise, including the abandonment—in some cases permanent—of a number of Jewish settlements.

Immediately following the 1929 riots, when the memory of the barbarity and horror of the attacks was still fresh, Palestinian Arab leaders dissociated themselves from these events, claiming that they would damage the Arab cause, and blaming them on the Jews, who had "attacked the Arabs." However, the tone soon changed. Following the execution of three of the leaders of the Hebron and Safed pogroms, the Palestine Arab Executive published a manifesto claiming that they were "innocent martyrs . . . pioneers of freedom and independence." The riots were praised for having "revived the momentum, strengthened the will, and awakened sleeping souls." Moreover, since the theme chosen had been Islamic, they did more than anything so far to enhance the solidarity of Moslems outside Palestine, who were henceforward to contribute politically and financially to the Palestinian Arab cause.

The 1929 riots resulted in the deaths of 133 Jews, out of 150,000 in the country at the time, and a similar number of Arabs. Arab "forces" were mainly fanatical mobs, and locally organized gangs equipped with small arms. On the Jewish side was the Haganah, with some hundreds of members throughout the country, armed with pistols, some rifles and a few light machine guns. Once a battalion of British forces arrived to supplement Palestine Police, they were able to stop the rioting without undue difficulty.

The years following the 1929 riots were not blessed with complete tranquillity. Sporadic outbursts occurred, particularly in the north of the country. A group of Moslem youngsters, organized in 1931 by Sheikh 'Izz al-Dīn al-Qāsim, a Syrian-born teacher and preacher in Haifa, undertook the first organized terrorist attacks against members of Kibbutz Yagur in 1931. The Sheikh was killed by the British police in November 1935 near Jenin, after refusing to surrender. His funeral turned into a demonstration of national feelings. Even his adversaries admitted that here was a new phenomenon—an Arab leader who practiced what he preached. "These are not robbers," wrote a prominent Jewish journalist, "this is a group of political terrorists." (Leila Khaled, incidentally, mentions the Sheikh, in her memoirs as the hero of her modern Arab terrorist movement.)

Arab demonstrations routed by police in Jaffa, October 1933.

Dispersing Arab riot near New Gate of the Old City of Jerusalem, 13 October 1933.

These outbursts, accompanied by journalistic agitation which became increasingly violent, did not, however, prevent the phenomenal progress of the *Yishuv* during these years of the "Fifth Aliyah" which began in 1930 and gained momentum following the accession of Hitler to power in Germany in 1933. Whereas the Jewish population of Palestine numbered 175,000 at the end of 1931, it reached close to 400,000 in May 1935. There was a growing feeling among Arab leaders that it was "now or never" if they wished to prevent the formation of a Jewish majority in Palestine and ultimately the establishment of the Jewish State. The Jews had gained a certain victory when the British House of Commons voted against the proposal to establish a Legislative Council for Palestine which, by reflecting the proportion existing at the time, would have given a majority to the Arabs. The discovery in Haifa of arms smuggled into the country by the Haganah increased Arab suspicions. The Italian invasion of Ethiopia and the impotence of Western powers to prevent it did nothing to increase the latter's prestige. In spite of all this, when the Arab rebellion (as it was called) started in April 1936, it came as a surprise to all three parties—British, Arabs, and Jews alike.

The tactics used by the instigators were similar to those of 1929. "A local incident," writes Col. Frederick H. Kisch, for many years Chairman of the Palestine Zionist Executive, in a postscript to his diary, "was in each case seized upon as the means of arousing among Moslem masses fear of an impending calamity . . . The freedom which throughout the period of the Mandate had been allowed to the Mufti in opposing the Government's measures for implementing the policy of the Mandate was now extended to the self-constituted Arab Higher Committee."

The beginning came on 16 April, when a number of cars passing through Nablus (at the time still the only artery to the north, since the coastal road had not been completed) were stopped by armed Arabs. Jewish passengers were forced out at rifle-point and two, one aged 70, were murdered in cold blood. The funerals in Tel Aviv turned into a violent demonstration and some Arab passers-by were beaten up. Three days later an organized onslaught took place in Jaffa which, though no longer a mixed city, was still the only port in the south of the country, and many Jews had to go there daily in connection with their work. Nine were killed, and 60 wounded. Soon riots spread throughout the country. They were carried out by semi-military gangs, politically or religiously motivated. Although the desire for loot was still in evidence, it was no longer a dominant feature. Accompanying the riots, which were directed both against the Jewish population and the Mandatory Government, was the general strike proclaimed by the Arab Higher Committee, which though unevenly observed (Haifa, for example, refrained from striking, as did most Arab government officials) lasted for 175 days. For a while Arab leaders managed to put aside their differences; the Husseinis, Dajanis, and Nashashibis were all represented in the higher echelons of political leadership. Abd-el Kader Husseini, son of Fahmi al-Husseini, a former mayor of Jerusalem who had been relieved of his post because of his responsibility for the outbursts of 1921, came to the fore as the leader of one of the gangs, and was taken prisoner by British forces. He was to find his death fighting on the Kastel near Jerusalem in 1948. A generation later, his son would be apprehended on terrorist activities by Israeli authorities.

The main thrust, a feature ominous for the future, was the Arab attack against vulnerable communications, most of which had to pass through Arab-populated areas. It started, innocently, with the spreading of nails to puncture tires. When simple broom attachments nullified that stratagem, primitive bombs were hurled through windows. Wire netting took care of that to a large extent. Bullets came next—and home-made steel plates were attached to motors to prevent them from being damaged. The heroes of 1936 were the Jewish drivers who went about their task relentlessly, unarmed or armed with pistols, maintaining communications with every settlement, without exception. The main burden in the active defense of communications, however, fell on British police, most of whom— on this occasion—took their duty of preserving law and order seriously. Their most dangerous task was patrolling roads ahead of convoys, and railway lines before trains were to pass. "Suicide squads" were established for these tasks.

Simultaneously, Arab attacks against individual Jews took place throughout the country, particularly in mixed cities and outlying quarters and settlements. Particularly outrageous was the murder of two Jewish nurses on their way home from Government Hospital in Jaffa, where they had been treating Arab patients; likewise the attack against a school in a Jewish quarter near Jaffa; and the attempt to set fire to a babies' nursing home in Jerusalem. Unlike previous riots, only one attempt took place to capture a Jewish settlement—Tel Joseph, and that failed. "For the first time," declared Eliyahu Golomb, recognized leader of the Haganah, "we did not lose any settlement." He rightly attributed this to the progress achieved by the Haganah during the years past, the organizing of the static defense of Jewish settlements, and the attitude of British authorities, who turned a blind eye, but subsequently permitted the legal arming and training of 3,000 Jewish supernumerary policemen.

As the riots spread, whole areas of the country came under virtual Arab control, particularly in the Triangle—Nablus, Jenin, Tulkarm—and the Hebron area. A supreme commander of the Arab rebellion was appointed: Fawzi al-Kaukji, who had led the rebellion against the French in Syria, and after his escape from there had taught at a Military College in Baghdad. Gang leaders from all over the country swore allegiance to him. He had come into the country with a handful of Syrian, Iraqi and Druze volunteers from neighboring countries, whom he employed as bodyguards and mobile reserves—the first non-Palestinian Arabs to fight in an organized way in Palestine. To combat this force the British rapidly increased their military contingent in Palestine to three and subsequently to six brigades—two divisions—a considerable force at a time of military weakness, which weighed in the balance of imperial military dispositions. The few pitched battles resulted in defeat and many casualties for Kaukji, but that did not decrease his prestige, particularly since he succeeded in shooting down a number of light observation planes, symbols of British superiority. Kaukji was to return to Palestine in 1948.

Throughout 1936 the Haganah practiced restraint—in Hebrew, *havlagah*. It understood its mission in the strictest sense of its name—literally, defense: to shoot when attacked, but not before. No offensive, no initiative. So much so that even fields of well-established settlements in the Valley of Jezreel were allowed to burn, as long as the settlements themselves were not attacked. Naturally this aroused a great deal of criticism. In the words of Eliyahu Golomb: "We do not go out to defend our fields without permits from the Government, and thus we support the feeling among Arabs that all the stories about Jewish strength are a lie. This will boomerang against us." Voices were heard, particularly that of Yizhak Landover, subsequently known as Yizhak Sadeh, first commander of the Palmah, demanding that the settlers "go beyond the fence," to protect settlements by means of ambushes beyond their perimeter, to wait for potential attackers along their probable routes of approach. The concept was only sporadically applied, in the vicinity of Jerusalem. The first primitive mobile units also came into being—a taxi without license-plates to protect laborers in an orange grove, a pick-up truck in Jerusalem. These were isolated instances. On the whole, anything beyond the perimeter was considered the responsibility of the British forces.

In October 1936, the strike came to an end. The Palestine Royal Commission—better known as the Peel Commission—was about to arrive in the country, and an unofficial truce was declared between Arab rebels and British authorities. Kaukji removed himself to the east bank of the Jordan River, whence, prodded by the Emir Abdullah, he returned to Iraq. From April to October 1936, 80 Jews had been killed by Arab terrorists and 396 wounded. Almost 2,000 attacks against Jews had taken place, as well as 900 assaults on Jewish property. Some 200,000 trees had been burned or uprooted, and over 4,000 acres of crops destroyed. There had been 380 attacks against buses and trains, 305 attacks by Arabs against Arabs, 795 against British police and the military, and 1,369 bombs had exploded. This was no longer a series of pogroms or riots. Although loosely organized and indifferently planned and supported, it was a countrywide rebellion against British rule, or at least against British policy, in which both the Jewish *Yishuv* and the British authorities were the target.

The uneasy truce—with sporadic terrorist activities continuing throughout, claiming Arab and Jewish victims—did not last long. In July 1937 the Royal Commission published its report. Following a lengthy historical analysis, the Peel Report stated that the Commission, having found the Mandate to be unworkable, recommended (for the first time in an official document) the partition of Palestine—into a Jewish state, to include the coastal belt from Be'er Tuviyyah to the Carmel, the Jezreel Valley and Galilee; an enclave (in addition to Nazareth) which would remain under British protection, and which would include Jerusalem, Bethlehem, and a corridor from Jerusalem to the sea at Jaffa (including Latrun, Ramle and Lydda); and an Arab state, which would comprise all the rest of the country (Samaria, Judea, and the Negev), and which would be merged with Transjordan. The Jewish state would pay a subvention to the Arab state. The plan as a whole was based on demographic reality at the time, with the exception of western Galilee, which was to be included in the Jewish state as a reserve, having a common boundary with Christian Lebanon. The two non-Moslem political entities in the Middle East would thus be linked territorially.

In the interim period, until the implementation of partition, land sales to Jews would be prohibited within the area allocated to the Arab state, and Jewish immigration would be determined in accordance with the absorptive capacity of the Jewish state alone. While the Commission considered partition to represent the only possible "lasting settlement," it suggested certain "palliatives" in case the British Mandate would be upheld. First and foremost among these was the limitation of immigration to a maximum of 12,000 per annum, to include all categories of immigrants, including capitalists and skilled workers.

The Report was received with mixed feelings by the Jewish side. While the Revisionists rejected it out of hand, the Zionist Movement—in fact, even the Haganah—was split on the issue. Weizmann and Ben-Gurion considered the establishment of a Jewish state even in a part of Palestine as a political achievement whose advantages would outweigh its disadvantages. Anything that might come instead of partition would mean the freezing of the National Home, stated Weizmann. Others led by Menahem Ussishkin, head of the Jewish National Fund, objected violently, some on the grounds that in view of anticipated Arab objections, all that would remain of the plan would be Jewish renunciation of rights to one part of the country. Golomb, leader of the clandestine Haganah, was willing to agree to partition provided that a Jewish army be established forthwith, and that control of immigration into the envisaged Jewish state be vested in Jewish authorities from the beginning of the interim period.

The British Government declared that "partition was the best solution, promising hope in the crisis which had been created," and announced that a commission would soon leave for Palestine to determine the precise boundaries of the three units. This in spite of violent opposition, among others from Viscount Samuel, who had been the first British High Commissioner in Palestine, and who warned against the creation of "a Ruhr belt, a Polish corridor, and half a dozen Danzigs and Memels in a state the size of Wales."

On the Arab side, the Emir Abdullah tacitly rejoiced at a plan which was to give him a kingdom on both sides of the Jordan—a dream he was to realize in 1948—and planned a triumphant entry into Nablus, the proposed capital of the future Arab state. The Nashashibis, aware of the bloodshed and frustration of the preceding two years, were willing to accept it as a basis for negotiations. The extremists, however, headed by the Mufti, considered partition as a blow to their aspirations. They insisted on the stoppage of immigration and of land sales, and the establishment of representative institutions with an Arab majority. A Jewish state with its back to the sea and open to unlimited immigration might be a jumping-board for further expansion. Moreover, the Mufti's personal position was in danger as a result of the pivotal role envisaged for his archrival, the Emir

Abdullah. Early in September 1937 the Mufti presided at a pan-Arab meeting for Palestine at Bludan, near Damascus, at which the political guidelines (for the future struggle) were laid down.

On 26 September 1937 the signal for the renewed rebellion was given by the murder of Louis Andrews, British District Commissioner of Galilee, on his way to church in Nazareth. Never before had a British official of his rank been murdered in Palestine—and the act was taken by the British government not only as an indication that this time force would be used directly, rather than through the Jewish proxy, but also as an outright challenge to the Mandatory Government. This time the British authorities reacted swiftly. The Arab Higher Committee was disbanded, and five of its members were exiled to the Seychelles Islands. On 11 October the Mufti was dismissed, and the management of the considerable Waqf funds at his disposal vested in a committee of officials. The Mufti himself, however, after hiding for two weeks in the Mosque of Omar, was able to escape to Lebanon, from where, only slightly hampered by restrictions imposed by French authorities, he directed the uprising.

Once more, the rebellion was conducted by gangs. At their peak, in October 1938, they numbered about 15,000 members, with a periphery of villagers who joined one operation or the other. The gang-leaders—some of whom were well-known robbers and criminals, while others, the minority, were religious fanatics, disciples of Sheikh Qāsim—roughly divided the country among them. As time went on, each became overlord of an area, from which he recruited his men, drew his provisions, collected taxes by threats, and in which he established courts dispensing summary justice to "traitors"—i.e., those who refused to pay taxes, or were suspected of collaboration with the enemy.

Unlike in 1936, when Kaukji had been appointed Supreme Commander, no unified command was established, in spite of attempts to appoint one gang-leader, Abdel Rahim el-Hajj Muhammad, overlord of Samaria, as Supreme Commander. Various attempts were made to induce Kaukji to return to the scene. All of these endeavors failed, primarily because of distrust of the Mufti by various Arab governments outside Palestine, as well as by groups within the country. Each gang was linked in some way with the political committee based in Damascus and, to the extent that funds, arms and ammunition reached it from there, obeyed its orders.

The Haganah had taken advantage of the truce to strengthen and broaden its ranks. In 1938 it numbered some 21,000 members in

about 250 settlements. It was able to reunite with the bulk of a group—
the Irgun Zeva'i Le'ummi, the National Military Organization—
which had broken away in 1931. (The minority, however, retaining
the name and some of the stores, remained outside; they were mainly
members of the Revisionist Party.) Since the rebellion this time
was aimed directly at the British Government there was an obvious
common interest between the British and the Jews, and the years
1938–39 mark the peak of their collaboration. It was then that the
Jewish Settlement Police was legally established, to protect the
settlements and communications with them. It was then also that
the legendary Orde Wingate, with the reluctant acquiescence of his
superiors, established the S.N.S.—Special Night Squads—consisting
of a select group of youngsters who, in protecting the oil pipeline
in the north, undertook daring raids into terrorist home country,
aiming at bases and supply lines. Some of the outstanding commanders
of Israel's army were to come from the ranks of the S.N.S. At the
same time, British Armed Forces in Palestine were once more reinforced—to a peak of two divisions, in 1938.

The signal for the uprising having been given by the murder of
Andrews, two Jewish buses were attacked in Jerusalem a few days
later, on 14 October 1937, and during the night all outlying Jewish
quarters in the city were showered with fire. Lydda airport, at the
time under construction, was attacked and burned. Telephone lines
in Hebron were sabotaged, and a passenger train was derailed and
attacked near Lydda. The pipeline was sabotaged and the petroleum
set on fire.

This set the pattern. Soon telephone communications were interrupted throughout most of the country, powerlines were cut,
and railway service became unreliable. Police stations in Arab parts
of the country were captured, with feeble or no opposition from
the predominantly Arab police. Except for Gaza and Beersheba,
where police had been reinforced by military units, no police station
remained functioning in any Arab locality. If during the day some
semblance of British authority was maintained, the night belonged
exclusively to the gang leaders, who terrorized the people in their
areas and controlled them completely.

Attacks against Jews, Jewish traffic, and settlements also abounded,
but they were marginal to the main thrust: the undermining of British
authority. The only attack designed to conquer a Jewish settlement—
directed against the newly-established Tirat Zevi in the Beisan Valley
on 28 February 1938—was repulsed by its defenders. (The settlement

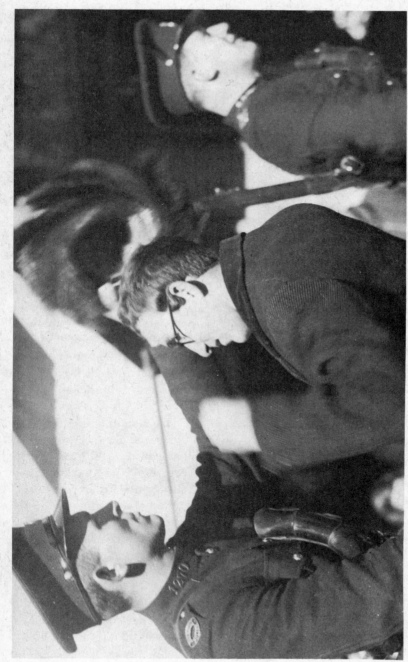

British police searching Jew for arms, 1938.

Arab bus searched for arms in Jerusalem, 1938.

was to repel a similar attack ten years later.) No Jewish settlement was evacuated. On the contrary, new settlements were established, mostly on land previously acquired, to consolidate Jewish positions in the area presumably alloted to the Jewish state. Settlements were established, with preliminary housing and defenses all constructed within a single day, along the Lebanese border, in the Beisan Valley, and further south.

On 2 October 1938 the *Yishuv* and the Haganah suffered one of the worst setbacks in their history, when an armed gang, estimated at 300 members, attacked Tiberias simultaneously from three sides after having blocked all means of approach. After capturing and burning Government House, they entered the modern Jewish quarter of Kiryat Shemuel, halfway up the mountain, which was indifferently guarded and devoid of any fortifications from the direction of attack, namely, up the slope. They entered one house after another, in one massacring a mother with her five sons, in another a family of four, in the pogrom style of Hebron 1929. For about 40 minutes the gang controlled Kiryat Shemuel, leaving 19 killed, including 11 children, before they withdrew with hardly any casualties. The same month witnessed another Arab success, when the rebel commander of Jerusalem was able to gain virtual control of the Old City for 48 hours, with British army and administration helplessly looking on. The Arab flag was hoisted on Damascus Gate. Now military government was decreed for Jerusalem, and within a few hours the army recaptured Old Jerusalem with only minimal opposition from the Mujahedeen, the Holy Warriors. Military government was soon extended throughout the country.

From October 1938 the rebellion petered out, for a combination of reasons: drastic punitive and offensive action by the British army and police; protective measures mostly planned and designed by Sir Charles Tegart—the building of a fence along the Lebanese border (an operation to be repeated after the Yom Kippur War of 1973) to isolate Arab fighters from their sources of supply, and the establishment of defensible police fortresses in key points (these were to play a major role in the War of 1948); the greater efficiency of the Haganah and, last but not least, among the Arabs themselves there was a growing disillusion with gang rule, which claimed many Arab lives and completely disrupted Arab society and economy. Internecine strife among Arab leaders and difficulties with supplies were additional reasons for the rebellion's loss of momentum. The military stick wielded by the British, with active help from the Jews and at least passive assistance from moderate Arab elements, had together paid their dividend.

It was not therefore military necessity that caused the British to proffer, simultaneously, a political carrot. And yet this was precisely what happened. The Partition Commission was the first step. It arrived in April 1938, and soon concluded that partition was unworkable. Two of its members proposed a partition scheme of their own—a Jewish state from Rehovot to Zikhron Ya'akov (about 1,000 sq. km.); an Arab state of about 8000 sq. km.; the rest of the country to remain under British Mandate. Simultaneously with the publication of their conclusions (the Woodhead Report) on 9 November 1938, the British Government published a declaration which declared partition to be dead and buried, and called for a Round Table Conference in London with the participation of Arabs from Palestine and from neighboring countries, and representatives of the Jewish Agency for Palestine. This was some weeks after Munich, and the spirit of appeasement, of "peace in our time," can readily be detected in its deliberations. It is a tragic irony that the date coincided with Crystal Night, the mass anti-Jewish pogrom in Nazi Germany. Only a few days later, 10,000 Jewish children from Germany were refused entry visas to Palestine.

The Round Table Conference—in fact there were two separate conferences since the Arabs refused to share a table with Jewish representatives—took place in February 1939. It did not result in any agreement. The Jewish side was willing to make farreaching concessions as long as the principles of immigration in accordance with absorptive capacity, of economic development and of non-subordination of one community to the other were maintained. The Palestinian Arab representatives, however, led by Jamāl al-Husseini, the Mufti's cousin recently released from the Seychelles, and those of five independent Arab states—Egypt, Iraq, Saudi Arabia, Yemen, and Transjordan—refused to recognize any special link between the Jews and Palestine, which they considered an Arab country like any other. The only "concession" they were willing to make was to enable those Jews already in the country to stay there.

The Conference having failed, the British government saw its way clear to publish, on 17 May 1939, the MacDonald White Paper which in effect annulled the Balfour Declaration and the obligations contracted under the Mandate *vis-à-vis* the Jewish National Home. It decreed drastic limitations on land sales in Palestine, and the restriction of Jewish immigration to 15,000 per annum for the following five years, at the end of which period Palestine would become an independent state, with its permanent Arab majority reflected in its governmental institutions. The White Paper marked the end

Jewish protest against White Paper outside the Jeshurun Synagogue, Jerusalem, 18 May 1939.

of a 20-year-old partnership between the Zionist Movement and Great Britain. Tragically, it came at a time when the need for Jews to emigrate from Europe was greatest. It represented a striking Arab victory, gained by the use of violence, although by no means predicated on military success. On the contrary, as has been seen, the military uprising had been broken some time before. In the years 1937–39, a total of 415 Jews had lost their lives to Arab terror; the peak month was June 1938, when 60 people were killed; the area that suffered most was Haifa and its vicinity, which paid with 87 lives. Together with those killed in 1936–37, the total number was 520 Jews killed, more than one in a thousand of the Jewish population of the country. No figures are available of the number of Arabs killed—in fighting with British, Jew and Arab; no doubt the figure was many times greater.

World War II, which started a few months later, and saw six violent years in Europe, Asia and Africa, was a period of uneasy truce between Jew and Arab in Palestine. Axis forces reached as far as El Alamein, west of Alexandria, maintaining contact with Egyptian nationalists in Cairo; at the same time Vichy France controlled Syria; Rashid Ali el Kilani staged an uprising in Iraq with Nazi support. Yet Palestine, aside from some Italian air raids, remained almost miraculously unscathed, as if it were the eye of the tornado.

The Arabs were politically appeased, confident that the White Paper policy enunciated by the British Government would continue to be its policy during and particularly after the War, when long-term arrangements would be made. The Jewish Agency on the other hand, was bitterly disappointed by the White Paper, although its head, Ben-Gurion, had declared: "We shall fight against Hitler as if there were no White Paper, and we shall fight against the White Paper as if there were no war against Hitler." It realized, though that the successful outcome of the War against Hitler deserved absolute priority, as it was a necessary prerequisite not only for the waging of a struggle against the White Paper, but for the physical survival of the *Yishuv* in Palestine. To the extent that violence was applied in the Palestinian context during these years, it was directed by dissident Jewish groups— the Irgun and the Stern group—against British officials. The assassination of Lord Moyne, British Resident Minister for the Middle East (and his chauffer) in Cairo was the most widely publicized of such acts of violence.

Some 32,000 young Jewish men and women from Palestine volunteered for service in the British Armed Forces. Although—through no fault of theirs, but owing to a British political decision—only a fraction of these served in fighting units, they gained valuable experience in many facets of the organization, logistics and services of a modern army. Some, primarily soldiers of the Jewish Brigade Group which was finally established in 1944, gained some battle experience toward the end of the War, in the north of Italy; others flew with the R.A.F. or served with the Royal Navy.

In Palestine itself, before El Alamein in 1941 when the possibility of Palestine being overrun by Axis forces from North Africa and from the Caucasus had to be faced, the Haganah High Command—had to plan for the eventuality of British evacuation from the country, with the *Yishuv* left alone to meet its fate. The decision was taken to defend the *Yishuv* at all costs; if necessary to fall back on Fortress Carmel, an enclave based on Haifa, whose proximity to the seashore gave hope for eventual support from the Royal Navy and Air Force. The Haganah was looking into an abyss, said Yizhak Sadeh many years later, and it did not blink. Fortunately, the danger receded. It was at that time that the Palmah—commando troops of the Haganah—was created with help from the British army, for the defense of the *Yishuv*. Some of its members served as guides for the Australian troops who took over Syria from Vichy France in 1942. (It was on such a mission that Moshe Dayan lost his eye.)

At the same time, few Arabs joined the Allied forces. The Mufti not only discouraged his followers from doing so, but was active in recruiting Moslems, primarily in occupied Yugoslavia, to serve with Axis forces.

The end of the War revealed, for the first time, the full extent of the Holocaust that had overcome European Jewry; the unspeakable horror which had resulted in the death of six million Jews. The realization that some of it might have been avoided had Palestine been available as a haven; the accession to power in Britain of the Labor Party which, in opposition, had repeatedly stated its sympathy for Zionist aspirations and its rejection of the White Paper; the Jewish and Palestinian contribution to the war effort—all these gave good grounds for hope that the White Paper would be reversed, and that the wretched remnants of the Holocaust would be enabled to come to Palestine. These hopes were soon to be dashed. With Ernest Bevin in charge of the Foreign Office, the British Government pursued the White Paper policy, and with a vengeance. The *Yishuv*, in its totality, saw no choice but the waging of a bitter struggle against this policy—indeed, against British rule itself. "Illegal" immigration, "illegal" establishment of new settlements, and forays against installations designed to obstruct these aims—wherever possible without the loss of British lives—these were the main thrust of the activity of the Haganah during this period. The Irgun and Stern groups—which for a time operated in co-ordination with the Haganah, but split following the blowing up of British Military H.Q. in Jerusalem's King David Hotel—concentrated on raids against military installations, or attacks against personalities. While divided on tactics, and for some time bitterly and violently opposed to each other, all three organizations considered British rule or British policy as the objective. During those years Palestinian Arabs were onlookers, not participants.

2

The War of Independence

In February 1947, after futile attempts to reach a joint U.S.-British policy on Palestine, the British Government decided that the Mandate for Palestine was unworkable, and transferred the problem to the UN, successor to the League of Nations. This body dispatched UNSCOP—the United Nations Special Committee on Palestine—which, after lengthy deliberations and extensive visits (including one to D.P. Camps in Germany where survivors of the Holocaust were interviewed) recommended the partition of Palestine into three units: a Jewish State, an Arab State, and an international enclave around Jerusalem. It was the Peel Commission's recommendation revived, with some notable differences, particularly the inclusion of the Negev in the Jewish State, as a vast empty land reserve which only Jewish capital and technology were in a position to develop. The three units were to be united economically. It was envisaged that with the authority of the UN, the plan would be implemented without bloodshed, and thus the boundaries were drawn up without reference to military considerations.

A Resolution on the Partition of Palestine based on these recommendations was adopted by the UN General Assembly, against virulent Arab opposition, on 29 November 1947, by a vote of 33 to 13, with 10 abstentions. The following day marked the beginning of Israel's War of Independence, the war waged by the Jews of Palestine for survival, freedom and political independence, against the Arabs, mainly from neighboring countries, between the end of November 1947 and July 1949.

The war was to be divided into two distinct phases. The first began on 30 November 1947, the day after the UN General Assembly had adopted its resolution on the partition of Palestine, and ended on 14 May 1948, when the British forces and administration were withdrawn from the country. The second started on the day after the

British evacuation, and came to an end on 20 July 1949, when the last of the armistice agreements (with Syria) was signed. In the first phase, the *Yishuv* and its defense forces, organized in the Haganah, were under attack by Palestinian Arabs, aided principally by irregular volunteers from Arab countries. In the second phase, the army of newly independent Israel—officially established on 30 May as the Israel Defense Forces—fought primarily against regular troops from Egypt, Iraq, Transjordan, Syria, and Lebanon, who were supported by volunteer detachments from Saudi Arabia, Libya and the Yemen. In the first phase, the avowed purpose of the Arabs was to frustrate the UN partition resolution and prevent the establishment and consolidation of the Jewish State; in the second phase, it was the destruction of the State and, when that proved impossible, its truncation.

The First Phase: 30 November 1947–14 May 1948

Jewish Forces

At the beginning of the first phase, Arab attacks were carried out by loosely organized bands led by representatives of the Palestine Arab political organizations. As early as October 1947, however, the Arab League had instructed its member states to train volunteers and collect money and arms for the Palestine Arabs. The first Arab onslaughts were resisted by the mobilized units and active reserves of the Haganah, which consisted—in addition to headquarters, service units, and a small ordnance industry—of four battalions of Palmaḥ, who numbered (in October) 2,100 men and women and 1,000 reserves; Ḥish (Ḥeil Sadeh—field force, or infantry), with 1,800 on active service and 10,000 reserves; and Ḥim (Ḥeil Mishmar—guard or garrison force), with 32,000 registered members, responsible for static defense. The Ḥish was organized mainly in area commands, named after the region (e.g., Givati, Golani, Carmeli), which later developed into brigades. There was also the Gadna, battalions of teenagers trained in auxiliary functions, who would later fill the ranks of the Palmaḥ and the Ḥish. On the eve of the war, the Haganah had in its secret arsenals over 15,000 rifles of various makes, a small quantity of light machine guns, and a few dozen medium machine guns and 3-inch mortars, as well as hand grenades, explosives, and Sten submachine guns manufactured in its clandestine workshops.

As to the two other armed underground organizations that operated independently during the first phase, the I.Z.L. (Irgun Zeva'i Le'ummi) numbered about 5,000 members at the beginning of the war, and Lehi (Lohamei Herut Israel) about 1,000 members.

Arab Forces

On the Arab side there were two paramilitary organizations, the Futuwa, sponsored by the Husseinis, and the Najada, by their opponents, composed mainly of urban youth. In addition to these, there were the veterans of the riots of 1936–39, ready—some eager—for fight and spoil. The age-old institution of the Faza'a was still in existence: an alarm system through which a sheikh could mobilize the males of his tribe, and a mukhtar could summon those of his village, for a number of days for a specific operation, such as the defense of a village or an attack on a convoy, each man bringing his rifle, his symbol of male strength. In addition, some thousands of Arabs were serving in the Palestine Police and the Transjordan Frontier Force, and these could be relied upon to aid and abet violence against Jews, even if for the time being their potential for direct participation was circumscribed. The same was true of the five companies of the Arab Legion, who served in Palestine as part of the British Army.

British Forces

By far the most powerful military factor in Palestine at the beginning of the war was the British military: some 100,000 soldiers, with armor, artillery, and air and naval support. Their disposition, and their political and strategic objectives, even the individual sympathies or otherwise of local commanders, were to be of decisive importance in the early stages of the war.

Repelling the Arab Offensive: 27 November 1947–March 1948

From the start, the nature of the Arab offensives was determined by a number of factors: the existence of a considerable number of Jewish settlements in predominantly Arab areas, the mixed Arab-Jewish populations of several cities, and Arab control of most of the hill region and of the major road arteries. The first attack took place on 30 November 1947, when a Jewish bus was ambushed near Lydda.

Commercial center in Jerusalem burns, 2 December 1947.

The next day the Arab Higher Committee declared a general strike, and on 2 December an Arab mob attacked and destroyed the commercial center in Jerusalem. There was also Arab firing in Haifa and on the border between Tel Aviv and Jaffa. After Arab attacks, on 10 December, on Jewish vehicles in the Negev and on the Jerusalem-Kfar Ezyon road, Haganah and I.Z.L. forces started to hit back at concentrations of Arab bands. During December, areas controlled by Arabs and Jews were gradually demarcated; in the mixed cities, areas between Jewish and Arab residential quarters were evacuated and contested. In the battle for the roads, which was gaining in intensity, the Arabs had the upper hand, largely as a result of the attitude of the British forces, which were neutral in theory and generally pro-Arab in fact. Certain Jewish settlements, 33 in number, which according to the partition resolution were to be excluded from the Jewish State, were not evacuated, for reasons of both politics and morale. Their defense, and the maintenance of communications with them, constituted a considerable strain on the meager resources of the Haganah.

On 10 January a 900-man force of the Arab Liberation Army, a motley body of volunteers from various Arab countries commanded by the Syrian Fawzi el-Kaukji and trained on the other side of the border, attacked Kfar Szold and was repulsed. The following days were marked by attacks on isolated Jewish settlements in the Jerusalem and Hebron hills, Upper Galilee, and the Negev. A platoon of 35 men, on its way to reinforce the isolated Ezyon bloc of settlements (Kfar Ezyon, Massu'ot Yizhak, Ein Zurim and Revadim) was wiped out in a fierce engagement near Beit Natif. There were continual attacks against Jewish population centers and against Jewish workers in enterprises employing both Arab and Jewish labor. Explosive charges were set off in Jewish areas of Haifa and Jerusalem; in the capital, the targets were first the offices of *The Palestine Post* (1 February), then Ben-Yehuda Street, one of the principal shopping thoroughfares (22 February), and later the Jewish Agency headquarters (11 March). The outlying Jewish quarters in the southeastern part of Jerusalem were cut off from the center. On most of the roads, Jewish communications were maintained by means of armored vehicles and convoys, which left at odd hours, usually at night, and used circuitous routes.

On 16 February the Arab Liberation Army attacked Tirat Zevi and was forced to withdraw with heavy losses. In March, having failed to capture any Jewish settlement, the Arab forces concentrated on the battle for the roads, while continuing their attacks on outlying districts in mixed towns and on settlements in the north, the Jerusalem mountains, and the Negev. Nevertheless, a convoy of armored trucks succeeded in making its way from Negba to Gat, which had been cut off for a long period, and an Arab arms convoy was ambushed and destroyed near Kiryat Motzkin. In general, the Arabs scored considerable success in the battle for the roads: on 26 March, Jewish traffic on the coastal road leading to the Negev came to a complete stop; a convoy on its way back to Jerusalem from the Ezyon bloc was trapped near al-Nabi Daniel. Its survivors were released through the good offices of the International Red Cross, but its armored cars and weapons were taken over by Arabs. Thus, most of the armored vehicles which had been operating on the road to Jerusalem were lost, and Jerusalem was effectively cut off from Jewish centers in the coastal strip. Another convoy which tried to reach Yehi'am was ambushed and wiped out, leaving Western Galilee isolated from Haifa.

These military attacks had immediate political repercussions. The United States, formerly a supporter of partition, now faced with the risk of direct military involvement, began to waver, and its representative at the UN proposed a trusteeship plan, which in effect implied postponing the establishment of a Jewish state *sine die*. Arab violence—a demonstration of force designed to erode support for partition—seemed about to achieve its aim.

Throughout this period, however, the Jewish defense forces made substantial progress in organization and training. By the end of March, some 21,000 men aged 17–25 were under arms. The manufacture of anti-tank projectors, submachine guns and explosives was greatly stepped up, and large quantities of light arms, purchased in Czecho-

slovakia, were expected to arrive. The *Yishuv*'s air force consisted
of 30 light planes for reconnaissance, transportation and supply to
isolated areas. Arab forces—both the locally organized National
Guard and the volunteers from the Arab states—were also growing
in number.

Jewish Forces Take the Initiative:
April 1948–15 May 1948

The hour of military decision was fast approaching. The impending
British evacuation made action imperative in order to gain effective
control of the territory allotted to the Jewish State and to improve
the Jewish position in the face of an invasion by Arab regular armies
expected at the termination of the British Mandate, on 15 May. The
growing strength of the Haganah now enabled it to take the initiative.
A comprehensive operational plan ("Plan D") had been adopted for
execution in stages, depending upon the rate of British withdrawal
and developments on the various fronts. "Plan D" marked a distinct
departure in the Haganah's strategic thought. Whereas in the past
Arabs had frequently captured and destroyed Jewish villages, and
much more frequently attempted to do so without success, the Haganah
for over 25 years had scrupulously refrained from capturing Arab localities. The sacred principle of Purity of Weapons, a basic tenet of the
Haganah, demanded that these be employed in self-defense only.
Jewish settlements were to be established alongside Arab ones, not
replacing them. Now, for the first time, Haganah units were ordered to
capture Arab localities, with the strict proviso that Arabs willing to
stay on under Jewish rule be allowed to do so.

The first objective of Jewish military initiative was to reopen the
road to Jerusalem. Its 100,000 Jewish inhabitants had been increasingly
isolated ever since the beginning of the war; after the fate of the
al-Nabi Daniel convoy referred to above they were completely cut
off. Supplies were running low, and a strict system of rationing had
been introduced. No less worrying was the desperate shortage of
arms and ammunition for the city's defenders. The convoy system
was found to be no longer adequate; Arabs captured Jewish homemade armored vehicles at a rate far greater than that of their production.
It was now decided to capture and secure a corridor on both sides of the
road, varying in width from six miles in the plains of the Shefelah,
to two in the mountainous region. For this purpose Operation Naḥshon
was planned. A force of 1,500 men was mobilized and equipped, in

part with Czech arms which had been secretly landed on 1 April.
Two preparatory actions were carried out: the blowing up of the
headquarters of Hassan Salameh, the Arab area commander, near
Sarafand, and the capture of Castel, an Arab village dominating
the approaches to Jerusalem. Operation Nahshon began on 6 April,
Haganah forces taking the Arab village of Huldah, the Wadi al-Ṣarar
camp, and Deir Muhaysin (Beko'a). They encountered fierce opposition, especially on the Castel hill, which changed hands several
times until 10 April, when the Arabs finally withdrew; on the previous
day, the commander of the Arab forces in the Jerusalem area, Abd-el
Kader Husseini, was killed in battle. By 15 April, when Nahshon
came to an end, three large convoys carrying food and arms reached
Jerusalem.

Meanwhile, further north, the Arab Liberation Army, still under
Kaukji's command, had made another attempt to capture a Jewish
settlement. On 4 April it had shelled a settlement named Mishmar
ha-Emek—the "Guardian of the Valley [of Jezreel]"—following
up with an infantry attack, which was beaten back. A second attack,
on the next day, was halted by the intervention of British troops
and a cease-fire was proclaimed, during which the women and children
were evacuated from the kibbutz. At the end of the cease-fire, Haganah
forces under Yizhak Sadeh counterattacked, capturing several strongholds southeast of the village on 12 April and routing an Arab force
which was trying to renew the attack. Kaukji appealed for help to the
commander of a battalion of Druze mercenaries encamped at Shefaram.
This force attacked two strongholds east of Ramat Yohanan between
12 and 14 April, but was repulsed with heavy losses. The unexpected
ferocity of Jewish resistance persuaded it to take no further part in the
war. Kaukji was now in danger of being cut off from his base, and he
decided to withdraw to Jenin in the Samaria region. The artillery
at his disposal was transferred to Jerusalem and in early May the
shelling of the Jewish quarters of the city began.

The success of Nahshon and the defeats inflicted on the Arabs
at Mishmar ha-Emek and Ramat Yohanan encouraged the Haganah to
continue the implementation of "Plan D". On 18 April, troops of
the Golani area command (later the Golani Brigade) and the Palmah
cut in two the Arab part of Tiberias, where the Jewish quarter was
under heavy attack. In spite of earnest appeals from Jewish leaders,
the Arabs decided to leave the town and were evacuated with British
aid. On 21 April, when the British started to concentrate their remaining forces in the Haifa port area, the battle for Haifa began.

The Jewish forces captured it within 24 hours and most of the Arab inhabitants left, despite Jewish assurances that no harm would befall them if they stayed. Haifa had for decades been a city of exemplary co-existence between Jew and Arab; the Mufti, however, who had by then established his headquarters in Beirut, telephoned orders to the Arabs of Haifa to abandon the city, promising them that they would soon be back in the wake of victorious Arab armies.

The capture of Tiberias and the opening of roads leading to Eastern Galilee made it possible to reinforce Haganah troops in the "finger of Galilee," at the northern tip of the country. On 14 April, a Palmaḥ unit infiltrated into Safed, bolstering the defenses of the besieged Jewish quarter. As part of Operation Yiftaḥ—designed to win Upper Galilee and gain control of its major arteries—Haganah forces occupied the Rosh Pinnah police fortress and a neighboring army camp as soon as these were evacuated by the British, on 28 April. Two attempts were made to capture Nebi Yusha, the fort on a ridge dominating the Huleh Valley which had been handed over to the Arabs by withdrawing British forces. These failed, with the loss of 28 Haganah men. On 1 May the Arabs launched an attack on the beleaguered village of Ramat Naftali, with the support of Lebanese army artillery and armored cars. With the help of a few Piper Cub aeroplanes, the settlers managed to hold out, and Operation Yiftaḥ could proceed according to plan. On 3 May, a Palmaḥ battalion entered Safed with orders to gain control of the town, but its first attack, on 6 May, ended in failure; the Arabs brought in reinforcements and began using artillery. A new attack, on 10 May, resulted in the capture of the key positions in the town. The Safed Arabs, numbering some 10,000, fled en masse, followed by the Arab villagers of the Huleh Valley. On the eve of the invasion by the Arab states in mid-May the Jewish forces were thus in control of a continuous area in eastern and Upper Galilee.

Further south, Golani troops occupied the Arab town of Samakh (Zemaḥ) and the police fortresses at Samakh and Gesher as soon as the British had withdrawn from them, on 29 April. Arab Legion troops, supported by artillery and armored cars, attacked Gesher, but were beaten back. Beisan (Beth-Shean) fell to the Haganah on 12 May, as did a number of villages in the Mount Tabor area—Arab Shajara, Bethlehem (in Galilee), the erstwhile German colony of Waldheim, and Umm el-Zinat in the southern Carmel. In Operation Ben-Ami, troops of the Carmeli area command captured the strongholds dominating Acre, Akhziv and Bezet, and re-established overland connection with Nahariyyah, which for some weeks had been reached only by sea, neighboring Yeḥi'am, and the Ḥanitah group of settlements, in Western Galilee. Acre itself was taken on 17 May.

In the Tel Aviv area, the Alexandroni, Kiryati and Givati brigades (commanded respectively by Dan Even, Michael Bengal and Shimon Avidan) launched Operation Ḥametz ("unleavened bread") on the eve of Passover and occupied several Arab villages adjacent to the city, including Hiriya, Sakiya, Salame and Yazur, and encircled Jaffa. They refrained, however, from attacking Jaffa itself, which had been included in the area of the Arab State envisaged in the partition resolution. Meanwhile, I.Ẓ.L. forces, whose commanders did not recognize partition boundaries as binding, attacked Manshiye and other northern quarters of Jaffa. They met with heavy resistance and British forces, hurriedly brought back from Egypt, intervened. The attack was renewed on 26 April and Manshiye was cut off. The encirclement of Jaffa was completed on 29 April, and most of its 70,000 Arab inhabitants fled. Its final surrender, however, came only on 13 May, when British troops had left.

On 9 April, a combined I.Ẓ.L. and Leḥi force attacked Deir Yasin, an Arab village on the outskirts of Jerusalem. 200 Arabs, including women and children caught up in the fighting, were killed. The Jewish Agency immediately expressed its condemnation of the killing of civilians. Nonetheless, the heavy casualties were given wide publicity in the Arab world as "proof" of a policy of deliberate massacre. The distortion and exaggeration of events in Deir Yasin by Arab propagandists keen on stirring up hostility toward the Jews intensified panic among the Arab population, and became one of the principal causes of their flight. On 13 April, a convoy to the Hebrew University and the Hadassah Hospital on Mount Scopus was attacked by Arabs, and 77 people—mainly University teachers, doctors and other medical personnel—were massacred. British troops stationed nearby made no attempt to interfere with the slaughter.

In view of rumors that the British intended to advance the date of their evacuation of Jerusalem, the Harel Brigade of the Palmaḥ, hitherto responsible for the Corridor to the city, was transferred to the capital. As soon as the brigade convoy had passed through, the Arab Liberation Army seized the strongpoints dominating the road to Jerusalem, and once again the city was cut off. Although the rumors of an earlier British withdrawal proved false, it was decided to launch Operation Yevusi to re-establish the links with the isolated quarters and nearby settlements: Neveh Ya'akov, Atarot, and Mount Scopus in the north, and Mekor Ḥayyim, Ramat Raḥel and Talpiyyot in the south. An attack on Nebi Samuel, a dominant hill north of Jerusalem, on 22 April, resulted in 33 Palmaḥ soldiers killed and ended in failure. While Harel troops succeeded in taking the Sheikh Jarrah quarter of Jerusalem, on 26 April, British troops forced their withdrawal. The British High Commissioner was scheduled to pass that way en route to the Kalandia landingstrip, on the last day of the Mandate. Evidently the British High Command had decided to take no chances, and in order to make sure that his entire route would be under continuous Arab control, it had decided to exclude the possibility of any interference with the smoothness of His Excellency's trip.

Two days later, an attempt was made to capture the Augusta Victoria buildings on the Mount of Olives and thereby gain control of the road to Jericho, but this, too, was unsuccessful. A successful attack was launched on 29 April on the St. Simon Convent in the Katamon quarter, which was held by Arab volunteers commanded by Iraqi officers. Both sides had reached the point of exhaustion when Haganah reinforcements were sent in and decided the issue. The resulting capture of Katamon made it possible to reinforce the long-isolated Mekor Ḥayyim quarter. In another attempt to open the road to Jerusalem—Operation Maccabi—although the Harel Brigade took the village of Beit Mahsir and the Givati Brigade captured the Latrun detention camp, only a few dozen trucks got through to Jerusalem before the road was once more blocked.

On 4 May the Arabs attacked the Eẓyon Bloc, four lone Jewish settlements not far from the Hebron road, with the support of an Arab Legion armored unit and four British tanks. The attack was beaten off, but the defenders suffered heavy losses, which were irreplaceable in view of the utter isolation of the four villages. On the eve of 12 May the Arabs succeeded in cutting the bloc in two; on the following day they captured a strongpoint dominating the area between Kfar Eẓyon and Massu'ot Yiẓḥak, and Arab Legion armored cars penetrated into Kfar Eẓyon. After the defenders had surrendered, many were massacred by Arab villagers from the Hebron area, and on 14 May the survivors were taken captive by the Arab Legion.

On the same day, 14 May, when the last British troops left Jerusalem, forces of Eẓyoni, the capital's infantry brigade, launched Operation Kilshon ("Pitchfork"). Its northern prong seized "Bevingrad", the security zones in the heart of the city evacuated by the British, to prevent their being taken over by the Arabs. The Davidka, a primitive homemade type of mortar with limited range and questionable precision, but with an impressive capacity for making noise, had a decisive influence on the outcome of the southern prong of the operation—the capture of Allenby Barracks, on the road to Talpiyyot and Bethlehem.

In the six weeks preceding the establishment of the State of Israel and the invasion by regular Arab armies, the Jewish forces had taken over Haifa, Jaffa, Safed, and Tiberias, encircled Acre, and captured about 100 Arab villages. Apart from the Latrun sector of the Jerusalem road, Jewish armed forces could move freely on most of the major arteries of communication. The Palestine Arab forces had been routed, and the Arab Liberation Army had suffered heavy defeats in the north and in the Jerusalem Corridor. The Jews had lost several hundred men, but they now had 30,000 young men under arms, ready to meet the invaders. The arrival of the first boatload of Czech arms and the acquisition of anti-tank and anti-aircraft guns had considerably improved the quantity and quality of the arms at their disposal, but they still totally lacked field artillery, armor, and fighter planes.

The Second Phase: 15 May 1948–20 July 1949

The Arab Armies Invade

On 12 May Yigael Yadin, Chief Operations Officer of the Haganah, was invited to survey the military situation before the People's Administration:

> We will not discuss the problem whether or not there will be an invasion. We have been planning all this time on the assumption that an invasion will take place. Our information indicates that it is a certainty. Our plans for such an invasion are simple: all our forces and all our arms—all of them—will have to be concentrated in those places which are likely to be battlefields in the first phase of the battle . . . The regular forces of the neighboring countries— with their equipment and their armaments—enjoy superiority at this time. However, evaluation of the possibilities cannot be merely a military consideration of arms and units versus units, since we do not have those arms or that armored force. The problem is to what extent our men will be able to overcome enemy forces by virtue of their fighting spirit, of our planning and our tactics. It

From the invasion to the first truce of the War of Independence, May 15–
June 11, 1948.

has been found in certain cases that it is not the numbers and the formations which determine the outcome of battle, but something else. However, objectively speaking, there is no doubt that the enemy enjoys a great superiority at this time.

Our Air Force cannot even compare with theirs. We have no Air Force. The planes have not arrived yet. It is possible that they may yet come on the decisive day, but I cannot rely on that. Even then, if the neighboring Arab countries activate their air forces, a comparison will be invidious. Their air force is a hundred to a hundred and fifty times the size of ours. At this moment, our planes operate contrary to all the rules of aerial tactics.

No other pilots would dare to take off in planes like ours. The planes are antiquated and obsolete, some of them are patrol planes or trainers; even with these planes we have had grievous losses and are now in a poor state, so it would be best not to take them into account as a military factor.

To sum up, I would say that the outlook at this time seems delicately balanced. Or—to be more honest—I would say that their superiority is considerable, if indeed their entire forces enter battle against us.

The Chairman of the People's Administration, David Ben-Gurion, summing up the discussion, posed the question: "Do we foresee any real chance of withstanding and repelling invasion?" Yadin's reply was: "If we are able to increase our armed forces, by mobilization in the country and immigration from abroad, if we are able to intensify our training and add to our equipment, partly through our own manufacture in the country, but mainly by transferring to the country what we have purchased abroad, we will be able to repel, indeed, to win; not, however, without grievous casualties and shocks, and the *Yishuv* must be prepared for that."

Two days later the leaders of the *Yishuv* assembled in the City Museum of Tel Aviv, to proclaim the establishment of a Jewish State in Palestine. That night the armies of five Arab states began to invade the country. The invasion, heralded by an Egyptian air attack on Tel Aviv, was vigorously resisted. From the north, east and south came the armies of Lebanon, Syria, Iraq, Transjordan and Egypt. Saudi Arabia sent a formation that fought under Egyptian command, and Yemen considered itself at war with Israel. It sent no contingent.

The Jews found themselves in a precarious situation. The invading forces were fully equipped with the standard weapons of a regular army of the time—artillery, tanks, armored cars and personnel carriers, in addition to machine guns, mortars and the usual small arms in great quantities, and full supplies of ammunition, oil, and gasoline. Egypt, Iraq and Syria had air forces. As sovereign states, they had no difficulty (as had the pre-state Jewish defense force) in securing whatever armaments they needed through normal channels from Britain and other friendly powers.

In the first days of the war the Jews had no matching artillery, no tanks, and no warplanes. Some supplies of these weapons arrived in the days that followed, however, and helped to turn the tide. Little more than small arms—and not enough of those to go around—a few homemade, primitive armored cars, and some light training planes were all that had been available to the Haganah, the underground defense force controlled by the responsible Jewish authorities during the British Mandate. It could now emerge aboveground as the army of the sovereign State of Israel, though the constitutional formalities establishing the army were completed only on 28 May with the publication by the Provisional Government of the Israel Defense Forces (I.D.F.) Establishment Order. Haganah's general staff and commanders continued their functions in the I.D.F., with the difference that their identities were now no longer secret. Many of the senior Haganah commanders now adopted as their Hebraicized family names the codenames under which they had gone in the underground. Thus, for the first time, the citizens of Israel became acquainted with the names and faces of their senior military commanders, headed by Ya'akov Dori, Chief of the General Staff.

The two dissident military organizations, Irgun Zeva'i Le'ummi (I.Z.L.) and Lohamei Herut Israel (Lehi), agreed to discontinue their independent activities and to the absorption of their members into the I.D.F., except in Jerusalem, which came under Israel military government, though not yet incorporated in the State. Their Jerusalem units were finally disbanded in September, following an ultimatum by the I.D.F.

Invaded from all directions, Israel had suddenly to cope, as it were, with the outbreak of a thousand fires, and to do so with limited means. Numerous settlement outposts in Galilee and the Negev were isolated, open on all sides to Arab attack, and had to rely on their own tenacity and meager armories to stave off defeat. The hastily mobilized army had to engage in offensive action to dislodge the enemy from key positions, block the advance of their columns, and rush to seal gaps in the country's defenses.

Until the First Truce: 15 May–11 June 1948:
The Egyptian Advance

In the south, Egyptian forces jumped off from their advance bases in Sinai and crossed the frontier. Passing through Arab-populated territory, one formation moved up the coastal road to Gaza, another was landed by ship at Majdal further north, while a third drove up from Abu Aweigila northeast to Beersheba, some of its units pressing on to the Arab towns of Hebron and Bethlehem, where they linked up with Transjordan's Arab Legion and took up positions just south of Jerusalem. The major enemy forces were those at Gaza and Majdal, and their main thrust was aimed at Tel Aviv, though they could also penetrate from Majdal to other vital sectors in the interior of the country. To stop them Israel deployed the Negev Brigade, under Nachum Sarig, operating south of the Majdal-Beit Guvrin line, while part of the Givati Brigade, under Shimon Avidan, was deployed north of it. There were also some 27 settlements scattered in the area, 22 of which had fewer than 30 defenders. Five of these kibbutzim lay along the coastal road, the ancient Via Maris. The Egyptians decided to wipe them out before proceeding to Tel Aviv, in order to protect their rear and flanks.

Their first target was Kfar Darom, a religious kibbutz 7 miles (11 km.) south of Gaza, which had already withstood attacks by units of the extremist Egyptian movement, the Muslim Brothers, in the pre-state fighting. In an assault only a few days earlier, the Orthodox Jewish defenders had filled the small bags that held their *tefillin* with TNT and flung them at their assailants, after they had exhausted their stock of hand grenades. On the morning of 15 May, eight Egyptian tanks approached the kibbutz, their guns blazing, followed by infantry. Having no artillery, the 30 defenders had no other course but to wait until the enemy came within range of their small arms, and then they opened fire. One Piat anti-tank weapon that had been rushed to the kibbutz during the night was quickly put into action, and direct hits were scored on the enemy's lead tanks. The remaining tanks thereupon turned around in retreat, exposing the infantry to fire from the kibbutz. Enemy armored vehicles returned later, but only to cover the retreat of the infantry. As a parting gesture they mortared and shelled the kibbutz, but made no further attempt to take it, contenting themselves with occupying positions covering its perimeter.

While Kfar Darom was under attack another formidable Egyptian column attacked kibbutz Nirim, with its 40 defenders, further to the south. Nirim lost more than half its men in killed and wounded, but repulsed the enemy. Next day the Egyptians resumed their attack, this time accompanied by air bombardment. They were again driven back. Thereafter they did not attempt a ground assault, but kept the settlement isolated, and subjected to periodic shelling and air bombardment. The pattern at Kfar Darom and Nirim was to be typical of all but a few encounters between the enemy and kibbutzim on all fronts throughout the country.

There was, however, one kibbutz which the Egyptians considered vital to liquidate if they were to proceed with their drive on Tel Aviv. This was Yad Mordekhai, close to the coastal highway between Gaza and Majdal, and blocking the linkup of these two Egyptian bases. After their bitter experience, the Egyptians prepared the attack more carefully and assigned larger forces—two infantry battalions, one armored battalion, and one artillery regiment. Nevertheless, it took them five days of hard fighting to overcome the defenders, who numbered, together with reinforcements from the Negev Brigade, no more than about one hundred men, comprising one infantry company. Shortly before dawn on 24 May, their plight desperate, with many killed and wounded, amunition spent, and their last machine gun out of action, the defenders abandoned the settlement, creeping through enemy lines under cover of darkness and carrying their wounded with them. Although Yad Mordekhai fell, the five days of resistance proved crucial. It held up the main Egyptian advance, and in that time the I.D.F. was able to strengthen the defenses nearer to Tel Aviv, dispatch reinforcements to the south, and bring into the country heavier weapons and some fighter planes, acquired before 14 May, which were to play a key role in the major confrontation.

The major phase of this confrontation began on 29 May, when the Egyptian forces had regrouped after the Yad Mordekhai battle and a column of brigade strength, numbering some 500 vehicles, moved north from Majdal, passed Ashdod, and halted at the Ashdod bridge 2 miles (3 km.) to the north. The I.D.F. units in this area were from the Givati Brigade, and their sappers had blown up the bridge the night before. With the column held up, the G.H.Q. of the I.D.F. sent the first four Messerschmidt fighter planes, which had just arrived and been hastily made ready for action, to attack it. It was the first time the Egyptians had seen Israel fighter planes, and this new factor made the column vulnerable. They accordingly proceeded to dig in. Now they were subjected to another weapon that they had not encountered from Israel before—some 65 mm. artillery which had just been landed and rushed into action. These guns shelled the column while other Givati units harassed it continuously. The destroyed Ashdod bridge, only some 20 miles (32 km.) from Tel Aviv, was to prove the northernmost limit of the Egyptian advance throughout the war. Though halted and harassed, the Egyptian brigade had not lost its fighting capacity, and during the next few days it sought out targets in the vicinity. Attacks on kibbutz Negba failed, but the attack on kibbutz Nitzanim, launched on 7 June, succeeded. Givati also had its gains and failures in attacks and counterattacks.

By now, after feverish efforts at the United Nations, it was evident that a truce would soon be called, and each side tried desperately to improve its positions before it came into effect. The most important Israel failure was the unsuccessful attempt to take the police fort in the village of Iraq Sueidan, and thus to breach the east-west line from Majdal through Sueidan to Faluja. This meant that the Negev was cut off from land communication with the north. On 11 June the first truce began: it was to last a month.

The Fight for Jerusalem

Jerusalem and its Corridor to the west had been the scenes of continuous bitter fighting throughout the four weeks that ended with the June truce. The Israelis suffered heavy losses and several serious setbacks, the most important of which were the loss of the Jewish Quarter of the Old City and the failure to take Latrun at the western end of the Corridor. But they emerged with West Jerusalem (the New City) intact, and in possession of a tenuous link with the coast. The Arabs had several military successes, but they failed in their major objective—the conquest of West Jerusalem, whose 100,000 Jewish citizens were holding out on starvation food rations, and whose troops were on comparable rations of ammunition.

The main problem was the shortage of water. The pipelines bringing water to the city from Ein Fara to the northeast, and from Rosh ha-Ayin in the west, had been ruptured. Jerusalem had to survive on the water stored in its reservoir, and in the thousands of cisterns found under many private homes, which had been filled, registered and sealed at the end of the previous winter. The People's Guard, *Mishmar ha-Am*, consisting of elderly men, undertook the distribution of the water rations, which toward the end of the siege were reduced to one-and-a-half gallons per person per day. At first they drove about the streets of the city with tankertrucks. When fuel ran out, they switched to donkey-drawn carts, continuing distribution in spite of constant shelling by Arab Legion pounders and Egyptian heavy artillery from positions near Bethlehem, which caused hundreds of civilian casualties. Instructions were issued to the population concerning the best ways of economizing water, including the recurrent use of water for washing, laundry and sanitary purposes. Food and cigarettes were strictly rationed; toward the end of the siege the daily ration of calories was reduced to 900 calories per day—well below starvation diet. Jerusalemites complemented their diet with khuseiba, the fruit of a common shrub which was discovered to be edible. The shortage of fuel was equally critical. All motorized traffic was paralyzed, gasoline being reserved for military operations and ambulances, while electric current was supplied only to hospitals, bakeries, some vital industries, and military headquarters. Fuel for domestic purposes had run out early in the siege, and cooking was done on woodfires. All trees in Jerusalem had been trimmed for the purpose, and a quantity of wood was brought from nearby Kiryat Anavim.

As the British departed and the Arab Legion came in, the Eẓyoni Brigade, commanded by David Shaltiel, had succeeded in the above-mentioned Operation Pitchfork in consolidating all the Jewish areas in the New City and beating off all the enemy's attempts at penetration. But the perimeter of these areas was now the frontline. The main Jewish outpost in the south, the Eẓyon Bloc, had fallen to the Arab Legion on 14 May. Most of the surviving settlers of one of its settlements—Kfar Eẓyon—were massacred. The settlers and defenders of the remaining three were taken into captivity to Mafraq, in Transjordan. On that night and the next, the two northern settlements in the heart of the Arab hills, Atarot and Neveh Ya'akov, were evacuated. On 21 May, there was a powerful attack by units of the Arab Legion and the Egyptian Muslim Brothers on Ramat Raḥel at the southern edge of Jerusalem, which changed hands three times in the next four days, being repeatedly captured during the day and recaptured at night. On the 25th, the defenders, assisted by a unit from the Harel Brigade under the command of Yiẓhak Rabin, routed their assailants in a day-long battle. Successive attempts by the Arab Legion to break into the New City were all repelled, often in hand-to-hand fighting, while armored cars were knocked out at close range with Molotov cocktails—bottles containing a homemade explosive brew of prodigious potency. The next determined attempt to penetrate took place near the Monastery of Nôtre Dame, on 24 May. When that failed, the Arab Legion command desisted, and decided to reduce the city to surrender by siege and starvation.

In the most desperate position was the Jewish Quarter of the Old City, close to the Western Wall, whose strategic vulnerability was far outweighed by its deep meaning for world Jewry. The Jews living there, mostly elderly folk engaged in religious study, with their families, were completely surrounded by Old City Arabs and Arab Legion forces. The local Jews had been reinforced during the previous months by some 80 members of the Haganah, some of whom had been there throughout that period, and others who had fought their way through the walled city to help organize its defenses. There were also some I.Z.L. personnel. On 16 May the Arab Legion attacked from all directions, and although the Jews resisted with home made incendiary bombs, hand grenades, submachine guns, and a meager quantity of explosives, they were steadily pressed back from house to house as each was destroyed by the powerfully armed Legion. On 19 May, whilst an Ezyoni company tried, unsuccessfully, to penetrate near Jaffa Gate, a Harel unit managed to blast the Zion Gate and reach the Jewish Quarter; but it withdrew the following day.

Defenders of the Jewish Quarter of the Old City of Jersalem surrender to Arab Legion, 28 May 1948.

Legion pressure mounted, but renewed attempts to reinforce the beleaguered defenders failed. On 28 May the Jewish Quarter surrendered, whilst Israel soldiers looked on, helplessly, from neighboring Mount Zion.

To break the siege of Jerusalem, it was essential to capture Latrun, astride the highway from the coast. For this task Israel's G.H.Q. set up a special brigade, the 7th, under Shlomo Shamir. It was composed of one hastily-assembled armored battalion, with half-tracks that had just reached Israel's shores; one infantry battalion with men drawn from existing formations; and one battalion made up of new immigrants who had also just arrived in the country and who had undergone a certain amount of training with dummy weapons in the displaced persons' camps in Europe and in the detention camps for Israel's deported "illegal" immigrants in Cyprus.

The 7th Brigade was thrown into action immediately, without time to organize and train together. At the last minute, a veteran battalion of the Alexandroni Brigade was included. A two-battalion attack was launched on 25 May, Alexandroni making a frontal assault on the Latrun police fort and village, with the battalion of new immigrants assigned to secure its right flank. The assault should have started in darkness, but there was a delay, and it was past dawn when they approached the fortified Arab Legion positions. The element of surprise was lost, and the assault came under such fierce fire that they were forced to retire with heavy casualties. The brigade tried again on 30 May, the Alexandroni battalion being replaced by a battalion from Givati. The armored battalion made the main assault this time, fighting its way right up to the police fort, and even succeeding in breaking into the courtyard. But the battalion sappers, who were to breach the wall of the fort, were hit by Legion shells, and the untrained infantry units failed to reach them. The battalion retired. The third attempt to capture Latrun was made on the nights of 9 and 10 June, the Yiftaḥ Brigade of the Palmaḥ, which had been operating in Galilee, replacing the 7th Brigade, and a Harel battalion taking part as well. This attack also failed, and it was about to be resumed, when the cease-fire took effect on 11 June.

In the meantime, however, an alternative link between Jerusalem and the coast had been discovered and rendered serviceable. This was a rough dirt track, broken by a steep wadi, on which hundreds of elderly men worked night after night to make it fit for vehicles. They dubbed it the "Burma Road". Already before it was completed, with 5 kms. of the most difficult terrain still separating the sappers

Supply trucks wait for the clearing of the Burma Road, 1948.

working up from Tel Aviv from those working down from Jerusalem, this route was used for the resupply of Jerusalem, elderly men carrying sacks of flour on their backs to waiting vehicles.

The opening of the Burma Road came in the nick of time. Unbeknown to the Arabs—and to the Jewish population of Jerusalem itself—the city was down to two days' rations of bread, to its last emergency ration of flour. When the truce came into effect, the Road was passable, and soon afterwards the piping of water to Jerusalem was resumed. Jerusalem was now linked to the coastal plain, its siege days over.

In the Coastal Strip

In the central sector, the narrow coastal strip in the Sharon was gravely threatened during the same weeks by the tough fighting Palestinian Arabs in the Samarian bulge, stiffened by the surviving irregulars of the Arab Liberation Army under Fawzi al-Kaukji. Their chief centers were the towns of Nablus, Jenin and Tulkarm, the point of a dagger thrusting at nearby Netanyah on the coast. On 24 May one Iraqi armored brigade and two infantry brigades occupied this "triangle" and prepared for offensive operations. The Iraqi forces had started crossing the Jordan River on 15 May and were active in the southern part of the Jordan Valley, south of the Syrian invaders. But they had suffered two severe setbacks, being repulsed at kibbutz Gesher and by a Haganah unit at the Crusader castle of Belvoir, overlooking the Jordan Valley. When the Arab Legion moved its main forces in the "triangle" to the Latrun and Jerusalem sectors, the Iraqis moved in. The defense of the Sharon was in the hands of the Alexandroni Brigade.

On 25 May the Iraqis tried to cut through to Netanyah, capturing one kibbutz and attacking three others near Tulkarm. The captured kibbutz was retaken by the Alexandroni Brigade, commanded by Dan Even and the Iraqi drive was temporarily stopped. But it was evident that the only way for the Israel forces to prevent an all-out assault toward the coast by so powerful an enemy force was to keep it on the defensive. Accordingly, on 29 May, the Golani Brigade, commanded by Nachum Golan, penetrated the "triangle" from the north, taking several villages as well as the strongholds of Megiddo and al-Lajjun, which offered a good base for an attack on Jenin. This was undertaken on the nights of 31 May and 1 June by one battalion from Golani and two battalions of the Carmeli Brigade, under the command of Moshe Carmel, which had been operating in western Galilee. Golani captured all enemy positions in the valley leading to Jenin, and on the following night the Carmeli formations seized the two key hills southeast and southwest of the town, holding them against fierce counterattacks throughout the next day. The men of Golani then entered and took the town. The Iraqis rushed up more reinforcements, and the fighting was heavy. Israel troops, on one of the hills overlooking the city, were compelled to withdraw, a direct hit on the command post having killed or wounded many of the key commanders. Since, in any case, the I.D.F. could spare no forces for an operation to take the whole of the Arab bulge, it decided on an orderly withdrawal from Jenin. This was carried out on 4 June, with the Israel units taking up defensive positions on the southern slopes of Mt. Gilboa. Shortly thereafter, an Alexandroni unit captured the key village of Qaqun just north of Tulkarm. The only Iraqi gain before the truce was the seizure of the headwaters of the Yarkon River and the pumping station at Rosh ha-Ayin (Ras al-Ayn).

The Syrian Attack Repulsed

In the north, the Syrians crossed into Israel just south of Lake Kinneret and spearheaded their invasion on the night of 15 May with a crack infantry brigade, a battalion of armored cars, one of artillery, and a company of tanks. Facing them in the Jordan Valley was a cluster of kibbutzim whose members were a kind of Haganah garrison force and a Haganah battalion for offensive action drawn from the Golani Brigade. The Syrian aim was to rout the kibbutzim, cross the Jordan, and then make a lightning dash westward through the mostly Arab-held territory of Lower Galilee to Haifa. The first Syrian targets were

Zemaḥ (at the southern tip of Lake Kinneret), and Sha'ar ha-Golan
and Massadah (not to be confused with Masada on the Dead Sea),
the two easternmost kibbutzim in the area. Though they suffered
heavy losses, the Jewish defenders held all three positions. On the
18th the enemy again assaulted Zemaḥ in full force. It fell after stubborn
fighting; Sha'ar ha-Golan and Massadah had been evacuated shortly
before. The front line now shifted to Deganyah, the very first kibbutz
to have been established (in 1909).

The attack on Deganyah was launched early on 20 May by a Syrian
infantry company, five tanks and numerous armored cars, after the
kibbutz had been heavily shelled. They managed to reach the outer
perimeter and came steadily on. Then one tank was knocked out.
A second, which had made its way right through to the kibbutz,
was halted by a Molotov cocktail (the remains of the tank are still
there), and a third was disabled by a three-inch mortar. Armored
cars that reached the trenches were put out of action by Piats and
Molotov cocktails. The infantry was held back by small-arms fire.
At noon two old pieces of artillery, which had just arrived in the
country, were rushed to Deganyah and put into action against Syrian
concentrations of armor and support units. Although they had arrived
without sights, and their fire was therefore inaccurate, their unexpected
arrival on the scene probably tipped the balance, for the Syrians then
retired, evacuating Zemaḥ as well, and taking up positions in the
hills to the east. Apart from minor clashes, the Syrians made no further
attacks in this sector, and their aim of a lightning drive to Haifa was
abandoned.

Instead, they sought to make local territorial gains and use their
powerful force to nip off the northeastern tip of Upper Galilee. While
they were regrouping, a huge supply base was blown up by a Haganah
sabotage squad, and the Syrian assault was postponed. It came however
on 6 June, directed against Mishmar ha-Yarden, north of Lake Kinneret,
near the Bridge of the Daughters of Jacob, astride the classical highway
from Damascus. It was accompanied by heavy shelling and air bombardment of the kibbutzim in the area. The attack was repelled with
heavy losses on both sides, but a renewed attack on 10 June was successful, so that the truce found the Syrians with a foothold on the Israel
side of the Jordan. On the same day Ein Gev, then the only Jewish
kibbutz on the eastern shore of Lake Kinneret, fought off a heavy
enemy attack, and did so again when it was attacked the next day
despite the truce. The cease-fire thus became effective in this sector
only on 12 June.

The Lebanese Assault

The invasion route chosen by the Lebanese army was through Malkiyah, just west of the powerful Arab-held police fort of Nebi Yusha, on the ridge dominating the Huleh Valley. Jewish defense in this sector was the responsibility of the Yiftaḥ Brigade of the Palmaḥ, under Yigal Allon, the Palmaḥ commander, which had effected the remarkable capture of the Arab parts of Safed a few days earlier. On the night of 14/15 May, a Yiftaḥ battalion cut across the mountains on foot toward the Lebanese border, skirted the Nebi Yusha fort, and without resting went straight in to storm Malkiyah and nearby Kadesh, the eastern gateway from Lebanon into Israel. Both fell after heavy fighting. But the next day the Lebanese put in a determined counter-attack, and the Palmaḥ men were forced to retire, taking up positions between the border and Nebi Yusha. That night, a unit of the battalion infiltrated deep into Lebanon and cut an important supply route. This action, together with the casualties suffered in retaking Malkiyah and Kadesh, stopped the Lebanese from pursuing the Yiftaḥ battalion, who accordingly attacked Nebi Yusha the next night, successfully.

On the 18th the Palmaḥ launched another attack on Malkiyah, taking the enemy by surprise by approaching from the rear—from inside Lebanese territory. Malkiyah fell. With the Lebanese advance halted, the Yiftaḥ Brigade was rushed south to take part in the urgent actions in Jerusalem and the Corridor. Replacing Yiftaḥ was the newly formed Oded Brigade, led by Uri Joffe, consisting of men from local settlements, a Haifa Haganah battalion, and new recruits.

In western Galilee the Carmeli Brigade, ready to meet a possible Lebanese invasion through Rosh ha-Nikrah on the coast, cleared the stretch from Haifa to the border, taking Acre on 17 May. Carmeli later operated in the Jordan Valley, and in the Jezreel Valley just north of Jenin.

On 6 June, simultaneously with the Syrian attack on Mishmar ha-Yarden, a combined two-brigade force of Syrians, Lebanese, and Kaukji's reorganized Arab Liberation Army attacked Malkiyah and overran the small Israel garrison that had been left there. Through this gap poured units of the Liberation Army that proceeded to consolidate themselves in heavily Arab-populated central Galilee, remaining there when the truce went into effect.

The First Truce: 11 June–9 July

The truce was supervised by Count Folke Bernadotte, the mediator for Palestine who had been appointed by the UN General Assembly on 21 May, together with teams of UN observers made up of army officers from Belgium, France, Sweden and the United States. It was to last 28 days (the UN hoped it would be extended), and the observers were to ensure that neither side gained any "military advantage" during the truce by the acquisition of additional arms or "fighting personnel."

On the tenth day of the truce, a grave inter-Jewish incident occurred when an I.Z.L. arms vessel, the *Altalena*, which had left a French port early in June, attempted to land its weapons on the shores of Israel. The I.Z.L. refused to hand it over to the Israel government. When I.Z.L. persisted in its refusal to agree to the government's conditions, the landing was resisted by force. The ship was set on fire just off the Tel Aviv beach by I.D.F. troops, who then waded into the water to rescue I.Z.L. personnel. There were casualties on both sides.

In the meanwhile, both the Arab and Israel armies used the truce to improve their positions. The I.D.F. engaged in more rigorous training of its men—including established settlers, new immigrants (Gaḥal) and volunteers from overseas (Maḥal) with World War II battle experience; it regrouped its forces, and readied for action more of the newly-arrived heavy weapons and planes, which were flown by local pilots as well as overseas volunteers. Toward the end of the truce period it became clear that the truce would not be prolonged. The one agreement Bernadotte was able to arrange between the two sides saw the demilitarization of the Mount Scopus area in Jerusalem. The truce ended at 6 a.m. on 9 July and hostilities were resumed. They lasted ten days and were followed by the second truce.

The "Ten Days": 9–18 July:
On the Egyptian Front

In the south, the Egyptians had taken advantage of the truce to bolster their Majdal-Bet Guvrin line, cutting northern Israel off from the Negev. Their strength was now four brigades. Just 24 hours before the truce ended, on the morning of 8 July, they launched a series of attacks on both sides of the line, displacing an I.D.F. unit from Kaukaba to the south, but suffering heavy losses when they tried to take Beit

Daras to the north. That night, Givati units attacked the lines from the north, capturing the villages of Iraq Sueidan, Beit Affa and Ibdis, the last in a tough battle in which they routed two Egyptian companies and captured a large quantity of weapons and ammunition. A Negev Brigade unit, attacking the line from the south, was less successful; it seized several positions but failed in its assault on the Iraq Sueidan police fort. (Sueidan village and later Beit Affa had accordingly to be abandoned.) For the next eight days, the two I.D.F. brigades fought continuously to contain the more powerful Egyptians, break their line, and join the defense of local kibbutzim, notably Negbah and Be'erot Yizḥak, which held out miraculously against overwhelming enemy forces.

On the night of 17 July, with another truce about to be called, the I.D.F. launched a determined attack on two positions astride the Egyptian line, Hatta and Karatiyya, located between Iraq Sueidan and Faluja. Taking a key role in the combined action of the Givati and Negev Brigades was a commando battalion from a newly-created armored brigade that had made a spectacular dash through the town of Lydda a few days earlier and had been rushed down to reinforce Givati. Hatta and Karatiyya fell, thereby breaching the Majdal-Faluja line, and opening a dirt track to the isolated and besieged Negev settlements. The Egyptians, however, improvised a detour further south, so that when the truce came into effect on the evening of 18 July, Egyptian east-west communications were tenuous, as were the Israelis' land connections with the Negev.

On the Central Front

The I.D.F.'s greatest offensive effort during the ten days of fighting was directed against the Arab Legion on the central front, the area between Tel Aviv and Jerusalem. With the major objective of taking the two towns of Lydda and Ramleh, clearing the central area, and then, if there was still time, attempting the capture of Ramallah and Latrun, the I.D.F. organized a strong force, headed by Yigal Allon, the commander of the Palmaḥ. It consisted of the Yiftaḥ Brigade, the new 8th Armored Brigade—comprising a tank battalion, and a commando battalion of jeeps and half-tracks—and two battalions from the Kiryati and Alexandroni Brigades, as well as additional artillery and engineering units. The action was called Operation Dani. Two forces struck in a pincer movement, one moving on Lydda and Ramleh from the northwest, the other from the southwest. Yiftaḥ, the southern

War of Independence, the "Ten Days," July 9–18, 1948.

force, captured Inaba and Jimzu and by the afternoon of the 10th
fought its way through to Ben-Shemen, to the rear of Lydda, which
for weeks had been cut off. One unit turned westward to Kfar Daniel,
which cut off Ramleh from the east. The armored brigade moved off
along the northern arc on the morning of the 10th and captured
Wilhelma, Tira, and other villages en route and then swung south
to Deir Tarif, ready to meet the southern pincer forces at Ben-Shemen.
In the course of this advance, a small force darted off to capture al-
Safiriyya and then pushed on to capture the Lydda airport.

Thus, within a day-and-a-half of the resumption of hostilities,
the largest airport in the Middle East and a dozen key villages had
fallen to the I.D.F. in the first engagements in which Israel units
had used armor. At Deir Tarif the tank battalion was held up by
strong Arab Legion forces based on Beit Nabala across the road,
on the western slopes of the hills. Fighting there was heavy, and Deir
Tarif fell only on the following day. The commando battalion did
get through to Ben-Shemen, however, on the afternoon of the 10th,
having bypassed Deir Tarif. Then, without pausing to rest or wait
for the required artillery support, it made a surprise dash to Lydda,
breaking into the city past Arab positions, driving right through it
and shooting it up, and repeating the same maneuver on its way back.
This was one of the most daring actions of the war and caused utter
confusion in the enemy ranks. They were still dazed when Yiftah
troops moved in to capture the city. The Arab Legion counterattacked
the next day, though without success. On 12 July, Kiryati units took
Ramleh, which by now was surrounded. It surrendered after a brief
engagement and, north of this sector, the vital springs of Rosh ha-Ayin,
which had been seized by the Iraqis in June, were recaptured.

The Arab Legion now regrouped its forces to strengthen the defenses
of Ramallah and Latrun. With reinforcements brought from Jerusalem,
the Legion held the Latrun enclave with a full brigade and considerable
armor. For the next few days it fought stubbornly—and effectively—
being saved by the truce from the attacks of the Yiftah and Harel
units. But north of Latrun, Israel units pressing eastwards from Lydda
and Ramleh captured Shilta, Barfilyya, Burj, Bir Ma'in and Salbit.
This brought them to positions from which they dominated the
Ramallah–Beit-Nubba–Latrun road. Southeast of Latrun, Harel,
again responsible for the Jerusalem Corridor, widened it by capturing
important positions on its southern edge, including Hartuv.

In and around Jerusalem, Ein Kerem and Malha were captured
by local Jerusalem units, who had been engaged in heavy fighting

throughout the ten days in various quarters of the city. But an attempt to capture the Old City by way of a breach at the New Gate failed, and the truce found the Old City still held by the Arab Legion. The one Legion gain was the capture of a building belonging to a certain Mr. Mandelbaum. This later became the celebrated Mandelbaum Gate, the crossing-point between Jordan and Israel during the period from the armistice to the Six-Day War.

Operations in the North

The most spectacular operation in the north during these ten days of fighting was Operation Dekel, which culminated in the capture of Nazareth. It was carried out by a group consisting of the 7th Brigade, under Ḥayyim Laskov, and a battalion from Carmeli, with some support from Golani. After capturing several Arab positions between the coast and the foothills southeast of Acre, the force successfully attacked Shefaram (Shefa Amr) on 14 July and pressed on southeast to take Zippori the following day, after stubborn fighting. The opposing Arab force in this region was Kaukji's Arab Liberation Army, which at that moment was applying very heavy pressure on the Jewish settlement of Sejera, to the east. With the fall of Zippori and with Kaukji's main force still being resisted by Sejera, the people of Nazareth began to panic as the main brigade column advanced on the city. At the same time, a small unit from Golani moved toward Nazareth from the Jezreel Valley, suggesting to Kaukji that he was also threatened by a strong force from the south. When the brigade was less than a mile from the town, however, the commander of Nazareth sent out an armored car unit to block its advance. The brigade column went straight on without pausing, firing as it moved.

After desultory fighting, the city surrendered on the evening of 16 July. Orders were issued that all holy places be respected, and that the normal life of the Arab population be not interefered with. The Arab residents of the city, aware of the fate of their neighbors in Haifa who had credulously believed the Mufti's call to abandon, stayed put. Kaukji himself, together with the bulk of his forces, succeeded in escaping into the mountains to the north through a loophole that the I.D.F. troops had not yet had a chance to seal. The result of Operation Dekel was to free the entire belt of Lower Galilee from Haifa Bay to Lake Kinneret.

Further to the north, the Carmeli brigade, now headed by Mordekhai Maklef, undertook operations whose major aim was the elimination of the Syrian salient at Mishmar ha-Yarden and whose ancillary purpose was the containment of the enemy within the area of the bridgehead. They coincided with a major Syrian effort to break out of the salient in order to cut off and subsequently to capture the Finger of Galilee. Fighting was intense throughout the entire ten days, with positions like Dardara and Hill 223 changing hands as many as three times. The battles ended in a stalemate, with the Syrians still in Mishmar ha-Yarden; but the Syrians were stopped from advancing even the short distance westward to cut the Rosh-Pinnah–Metulla road, the main artery of the Finger of Upper Galilee.

Air and Naval Operations

The Israel air force, commanded by Aharon Remez, with its newly acquired warplanes, though inferior in number and type to those of the enemy, was very active during these ten days, carrying out support, pursuit, and bombing missions. Three World War II Flying Fortresses carried out air attacks on Egypt en route to Israel on 14 July, one bombing Cairo and another attacking Rafa and El Arish. Damascus was also bombed. The Israel navy, having feverishly reconditioned the hulks of "illegal" immigrant boats, bombarded Arab centers along the Carmel coast, sabotaged ships near Gaza, and shelled the Lebanese port of Tyre. Most of the navy's casualties, however, were suffered on land when an amphibious company was rushed to the southern front to reinforce Givati during the critical operation to break the Egyptian Majdal-Faluja line.

The Second Truce

Breaches of the second truce, which went into effect at 7 p.m. on 18 July, began almost from the first day. In the Jerusalem area the Arab Legion intensified its bombardment of the New City, and during the remainder of July, August, September and October, Jerusalem was shelled, mortared, and machine-gunned almost every night. (The attacks stopped only on 30 November, when both sides agreed to a "sincere cease-fire.") On 12 August the Legion destroyed the Latrun pumping station, even though it was under UN control, but Israel quickly laid a pipeline along the "Burma Road" and kept Jerusalem supplied with water. In the north, Kaukji's Arab Liberation Army kept up sporadic harassment of Jewish positions.

Clearing the Road to the Negev: 15–22 October

In the south, the Egyptians soon ignored the truce provisions and denied Jewish convoys passage through the Hatta-Karatiyya gap in their line. They seized positions outside the truce boundaries and then extended their attacks to several I.D.F. posts that covered the gap. On 15 October the Israel army and air force turned to the offensive after the Egyptians had attacked a convoy proceeding south and raided inter-kibbutz communications. In a brisk seven days' campaign, the road to the Negev was opened and the Negev was cleared of Egyptian troops.

During this period, Operation Yo'av (also still known by its provisional name, Operation Ten Plagues) was carried out. In the reorganization that the army had carried out during the preceding truce months (when, incidentally, officers had been given ranks for the first time), the country had been divided into four military commands. The southern front command, headed by the Palmaḥ commander, Yigal Allon, was responsible for Operation Yo'av. The force consisted of three infantry brigades—Negev, Givati and Yiftaḥ—plus an

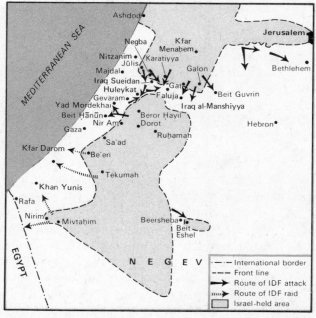

Operation Yo'av of the War of Independence, Oct. 15–22, 1948.

armored battalion from the 8th Armored Brigade, and the largest artillery formation that had ever been available to the I.D.F. (The Oded Brigade joined the command on 18 October.) During the truce months, Yiftaḥ was flown south in an extraordinary airlift—since the Egyptians had blocked the road—to relieve the Negev Brigade, which was lifted north to rest, reorganize, and prepare for resumed action.

On the night of 15 October the Israel air force bombed bases from which Egyptian assaults had been launched and also attacked Egypt's advanced airfield at Rafa. This action kept most of the Egyptian frontline fighters out of the skies and gave the I.D.F. air superiority for the first time. The Israel navy also took part in these southern engagements, shelling enemy coastal installations, preventing supplies from reaching Gaza and Majdal by sea, and scoring a spectacular triumph on the very eve of the truce when its special unit sank the *Emir Farouk*, flagship of the Egyptian navy, off the shores of Gaza.

On the ground, in order to pin down Egyptian forces in the coastal

I.D.F. Artillery in action in the Negev, October 1948.

strip and lead them to believe that it was there that the major blow would fall, Yiftah troops led off by carrying out a series of raids and sabotage actions against Egyptian concentrations and communications (in the strip north and south of Gaza) between Rafa and Gaza and between Gaza and Majdal. Soon afterwards, the Givati and the armored battalion went into action to break the Majdal-Bet Guvrin line. In heavy fighting, the tank unit failed to take Iraq al-Manshiyya, just east of Faluja. Next night, since the element of surprise had been forfeited, it was decided to shift the main thrust to the most important axis—the crossroads of the Majdal-Faluja road and the interior road, which was the major artery to the Negev. Givati units made a breakthrough west of Faluja, fighting their key battles at Hill 113 and nearby Egyptian strongholds dominating the crossroads. After stiff hand-to-hand engagements, the positions were captured and held against heavy Egyptian counterattacks. On the night of the 16th, Givati advanced southwards and took the Height of Kawkaba, commanding the road running north-south. But Yiftah failed to take the heights of al-Huleykat further south, which also commanded the road. Huleykat fell only on 20 October, after other Yiftah units had succeeded in capturing several nearby positions. The road to the Negev was now clear, in spite of the fact that the Iraq Sueidan police fort had successfully resisted a further Israel attack to capture it.

By this time Great Britain was concerned for the fate of its protegé, the Arab Legion (the military force of Transjordan), which was still commanded by British officers, and received its maintenance and logistical support from the British forces still stationed in the Canal Zone. Accordingly, it was Great Britain who prodded the Security Council into its anxious endeavors to effect a cease-fire, while the I.D.F. recognized that it had little time to exploit the successful opening of the Negev road. At 4 o'clock on the morning of 21 October, the I.D.F. moved to capture Beersheba. Taking part were the bulk of the 8th Brigade, a Negev Brigade battallion which had dashed south along the newly opened road within hours of the capture of Huleykat, and the Negev Brigade's commando battalion, which had already been operating in the south harassing the enemy in the Gaza-Rafa region. While some units took up blocking positions north and south of the town to hold up Egyptian reinforcements, and another carried out a diversionary action in the direction of Hebron, the main I.D.F. force advanced on the city from the west. Although the Egyptian commander of the garrison, unaware of the opening of the road further south, was completely taken by surprise, there was stiff fighting inside the city, but at 8 a.m. a white flag went up on the police fort, and by 9:15 the capture of Beersheba was complete.

During Operation Yo'av, the Harel Brigade was active in the mountainous area between the Jerusalem Corridor and Bet Guvrin, greatly widening the approaches to Jerusalem and cutting the Egyptian artery from Beit Guvrin to Bethlehem. Detachments from the Ezyoni and Givati Brigades took part in some of these actions. During one crucial night Ezyoni now commanded by Moshe Dayan tried unsuccessfully to capture the Heights of Beit Jallah, to prevent forces there from coming to the rescue of the Egyptians further south. A truce was ordered for 3 p.m. on 22 October, but there was some action in the days immediately following. The police fort of Bet Guvrin fell on 27 October, and after the Egyptians had retreated southward from Ashdod (28 October) and Majdal (6 November) to Gaza, I.D.F. troops occupied the coastal strip down to Yad Mordekhai. Trapped in a pocket, which was centered around Faluja, and included Iraq Sueidan on the west and Iraq el-Manshiyya on the east, was an entire Egyptian brigade, consisting of some 4,000 troops headed by a brave Sudanese commanding officer who refused to surrender. On 9 November the area of the Faluja Pocket, as it came to be called, was reduced by I.D.F.'s capture of the village and police fort of Iraq Sueidan, in one of the numerous actions in which both sides engaged to improve their positions despite the truce.

The Arab Liberation Army Driven Off: 29–31 October

In the north Kaukji's Arab Liberation Army, which did not consider itself bound by the United Nations truce, carried out local attacks during the cease-fire months. On 22 October, thinking that the I.D.F. would be too preoccupied with actions in the Negev, Kaukji launched a strong attack on the outpost of kibbutz Manarah, which was situated on the ridge near the Lebanese border above the Huleh Valley. They captured the strongpoint of Sheikh Abbad, repelled a counterattack by the local I.D.F. unit, and ambushed the reinforcements who were rushed in to relieve Manarah, inflicting heavy casualties on them as they tried to negotiate the steep heights. Israel's protests to the UN were unavailing. The Arabs continued to hold Sheikh Abbad and captured further hill positions, cutting the Manarah-Nebi Yusha track and dominating the Rosh Pinnah-Metullah road.

I.D.F. unit in Galilee fighting, October 1948.

On the night of 28 October the I.D.F. initiated Operation Hiram, striking not at the point of attack selected by Kaukji, but at his main bases, in an effort to rout his army. The forces available to the northern front commander, Moshe Carmel, comprised four brigades: the 7th (together with the armored battalion that had fought with it in Operation Dekel), Oded, Golani and Carmeli. The air force was active in bombing and ground-support missions. The main action fell to the 7th Brigade, which pushed off from Safed in a western and north-western drive on Sasa, in the heart of Upper Galilee. In less than 24 hours of hard fighting they made a lightning advance through the rugged hills and captured Meron (succeeding in the second attack), took Safsaf, sped on to the powerful stronghold of Jish, which had been reinforced by a Syrian battalion and which they overcame in stiff combat, and by nightfall on the 29th were in Sasa. In a coordinated action Oded started eastward at zero hour from bases near Nahariyyah, also aiming for Sasa, so that the Arab Liberation Army would be encircled and squeezed by Oded thrusting from one direction and the 7th Brigade from the other. Oded's first objective was Tarshiha. Several outposts near the approaches to the town were captured, but Tarshiha itself held firm. It surrendered only on the morning of the 30th, after Golani had undertaken a series of diversionary actions in the south that sent the Liberation Army northward.

In a quick change of plan, Golani was ordered to exploit its success and push on to Aylabun, which it captured, while the 7th Brigade, further north, also exploited its success by advancing northeastward on Malkiyah. Oded detachments, which by now were driving eastward beyond Tarshiha, engaged Arab forces retreating from the south and then, after reaching the frontier road with Lebanon, changed direction and pushed due west, clearing the entire road up to the Mediterranean coast. The 7th Brigade took Malkiyah by surprise, approaching it from the south. and captured it. This relieved the pressure on Manarah, and the Carmeli Brigade, covering the eastern sector to prevent a Syrian breakthrough from Mishmar ha-Yarden, now moved to the offensive. It crossed into Lebanon and captured a number of villages lying near the Manarah road. Some of its detachments reached the Litani River. (The Lebanese villages were relinquished by Israel in the armistice agreement signed in March 1949.) When the survivors among Kaukji's forces realized that they were being squeezed from the east, south, and west, and particularly after the fall of their key centers at Jish, Sasa, and Tarshiha, they started evacuating the pocket, using little-known tracks to make their way northward into Lebanon. When the cease-fire was ordered on 31 October, 60 hours after the start of the action, the entire Galilee was clear of the Arab Liberation Army.

Expelling the Egyptians: 22 December– 7 January

In the south there were infractions of the truce by both sides throughout November and December; those of the Egyptians were more serious, as they had more to gain, having lost so much. They attacked Jewish settlement communications, sabotaged the inter-settlement water pipeline, and attempted to seize Negev outposts in order to improve their military positions. They also refused to implement a Security Council order (which Israel accepted) to start armistice talks, unless Israel first allowed the release of the trapped Faluja brigade. Israel said it would release the force as soon as talks got under way. Egypt remained adamant, and its forces continued their harassing activities in the Negev. Israel thereupon decided to launch Operation Horev, aimed at expelling the Egyptians from the borders of the country. The forces taking part, under the commander of the southern front, were the 8th Armored and the Negev Brigades, which had participated in Operation Yo'av; the Alexandroni and Golani Brigades, which replaced Givati and Yiftah; and two battalions and an additional unit from the Harel Brigade. The Egyptians were entrenched along two main wings. The western and the stronger of the two forked north from Auja al-Ḥafir along the Sinai border into the coastal strip through Rafa to Gaza, while the eastern one curved in an arc northeast from Auja through al-Mushrifa and Bir Asluj to 15 miles (24 km.) south of Beersheba. The main effort called for in the first phase of I.D.F.'s operation was the destruction of the eastern arm, with its heavily defended strongpoints ranged all along the main, hard-topped Beersheba-Auja highway.

To effect surprise, the I.D.F. decided to use a little-known Roman road cutting directly across the desert through Wadi al-Abyad from Beersheba to Auja, which would bring its forces in the rear of Auja and of the Mushrifa and Bir Asluj bases. This ancient track had to be repaired by the engineers to take vehicles, however, and such work could not be started without losing the element of surprise until the campaign was under way. It was accordingly decided to start operations with feinting and diversionary attacks on the western Egyptian wing, which would also promote the impression that this was the main objective, and then deliver the principal punch to the east wing.

On the afternoon of 22 December the coastal strip was heavily shelled, and that night Golani units went into actions aimed at cutting enemy communications between Rafa and Gaza and trying to seize key hills. For the next 48 hours I.D.F. fought bitter battles and suffered many casualties in strong Egyptian counterattacks, displaying particular heroism in the battle for Hill 86 (from which they eventually had to retreat). But they fulfilled their task of diverting the enemy's attention from the eastern wing and misled them as to I.D.F.'s actual intentions.

On the morning of 25 December (storm and flood having forced the postponement of zero hour by a day) the 8th Armored and Negev brigades set forth from al-Khalasa, south of Beersheba, on their appointed tasks. The Negev Brigade cut southward, aiming for Mushrifa, and had to fight a series of stiff battles for the well-defended group of hills round Bir al-Thamila, near the Auja-Bir Asluj road. The Egyptians counterattacked heavily, and one Negev unit lost half its men trying to hold one key height. But it was soon regained, and by the morning of 26 December the key middle bastions of the Egyptians between Auja and Bir Asluj were in Israel hands, with Bir Asluj, the northeastern terminal of the Egyptian line, cut off and the rear of Auja undefended.

The Armored Brigade had meanwhile had a very difficult drive southwest across the Roman road to the south, and despite the brilliant

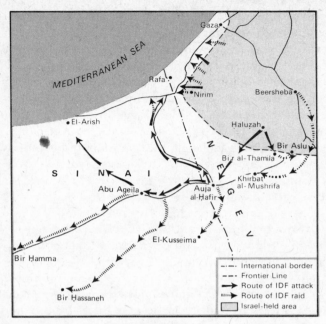

Operation Horev of the War of Independence, Dec. 22, 1948–Jan. 7, 1949.

work of the engineers in making the track passable there were delays. The main force, which was to have reached the Auja area by dawn on the 26th, did not get there until the late afternoon, when it engaged Auja's outpost but was not in a position to launch its main attack. The offensive was carried out on the morning of the 27th, after road-blocks had been set up north and west of Auja. The attack, in which the commando battalion of the Armored Brigade played a key part, was heavily resisted; Egyptian ground forces were aided by their air force, which bombed and strafed the Israel units. But by 8:00 a.m. Auja fell, and thereafter Egyptian troops began evacuating their strongholds in the rear of Auja, with Israel units in pursuit. The Negev Brigade completed its task of clearing the entire line up to and including Bir Asluj which it occupied just after midday, and then raced westward along the paved road, joining up with the Armored Brigade at Auja in the afternoon. The Beersheba-Auja highway was now open, and no Egyptian troops were left on Israel soil.

   I.D.F. then continued westward and northwestward from Auja into Sinai in pursuit of the Egyptian forces. On the night of the 28th, the Negev Brigade together with the Armored Brigade's tank battalion carried out an attack on Abu Ageila, some 30 miles (48 km.) west of the international border, commanding the important junction of the road west to Ismailia and the road northwest to El-Arish. Golani units assisted by carrying out operations to halt enemy reinforcements. Captured enemy transport was used for the fast move, which led to a mishap soon after they crossed the border when, with enemy markings still on them, they were attacked by Israel planes.

The column advanced, battling against defensive strongpoints en route, until they reached the outposts of Abu Ageila itself. There was stubborn fighting through the night, but the outposts were finally captured, and by dawn Negev units entered Abu Ageila. Almost without pause, part of the force pressed forward to raiding operations, though subjected to Egyptian air bombing. The tanks and commando units advancing northwest reached the El-Arish airfield, destroying installations and capturing one Spitfire intact, and went on to fight a brisk battle with the battalion-held outpost of Bir Lahfan, which they captured. But with no supporting troops, and the tanks badly in need of maintenance, the units returned to Abu Ageila on 30 December. On the previous day as well, a light mobile unit sped westward to raid the air base at Bir al-Hamma more than 50 miles (80 km.) west of Abu Ageila, and returned. The 30th was spent in capturing Egyptian defense positions between Abu Ageila and El-Arish, between Auja and Rafa, and el-Kusseima, some 20 miles (32 km.) south of Auja.

By this time, however, with I.D.F. formations inside Sinai in pursuit of the enemy, strong diplomatic pressure was being exerted on the government of Israel. Britain even threatened military intervention under the Anglo-Egyptian Treaty of 1936 unless the I.D.F. withdrew to the international boundary. The front command was accordingly given orders to evacuate Sinai by 2 January 1949 but to continue operations within the boundaries of Mandatory Palestine. The last Israel actions inside Sinai were a Harel raid in Bir Hassneh and the destruction of a large brigade spanning the Ismailia-Abu Ageila road. The next few days were spent in bitter fighting, hampered by severe sandstorms, in the Rafa area, mostly by the Golani and Harel Brigades, supported by the Armored and Negev Brigades. Several outposts of Rafa, stubbornly contested by both sides, kept changing hands. With the enemy squeezed back toward the coast, the I.D.F. prepared to attack Rafa itself, but was prevented from doing so by the cease-fire, which became effective on the afternoon of 7 January. On that day, five British fighters zoomed low over Israel battle positions and were shot down by Israel planes. It transpired later that they were on armed reconaissance flights, but they had been taken for Egyptian warplanes which had been strafing Israel units daily. This action caused a furor in the British Parliament where the government was strongly criticized—particularly by Winston Churchill, then Leader of the Opposition—for sending planes over the battle area in what seemed an open act of British intervention.

The Alexandroni Brigade had been assigned to contain and then subdue the Egyptian brigade trapped in the Faluja Pocket. It attacked Iraq al-Manshiya on the night of 27 December and fought a hard battle. But the defenders under their Sudanese commander put up very stout resistance, battling with bravery and skill and effecting determined counterattacks when any position fell. The Israelis withdrew. The Faluja brigade was released only with the signature of the Israel-Egypt armistice agreement at Rhodes on 24 February and was saluted for its bravery by its Israel adversaries as it left.

Negotiations for that armistice began on the Island of Rhodes on 13 January 1949, under the auspices of Ralph Bunche. At first the mediator met the representatives of each side separately; when there were signs of progress, the parties held informal meetings; and when agreement was reached, the representatives met under his chairmanship to affix their signatures.

The Armistice Agreement with Egypt signed on 24 February gave Israel the entire Negev down to the border with Sinai, but left the Gaza Strip under Egyptian occupation. A demilitarized zone was established around Auja al-Hafir (Nizanah). To ensure *de facto* control over the Negev, two infantry columns were sent out at the beginning of March 1949 in Operation Uvdah ("Fact"). On 10 March the advance party reached the abandoned police post at Umm Rash Rash on the Gulf of Akaba, ensuring Israel's outlet to the Red Sea and restoring the biblical name Eilat.

Under the agreement with Lebanon, signed on 23 March at Ras al-Nakura (Rosh ha-Nikrah), the former international frontier was specified as the demarcation line, Israel forces withdrawing from the Lebanese villages they had occupied.

The agreement with Jordan, signed on 4 March after a month's negotiations, established a winding border 330 miles long. It left under Jordanian occupation the thickly populated hill country of Judea and Samaria (called the "West Bank" after its annexation by Transjordan), including East Jerusalem, and ran through the Dead Sea down the Mandatory border of western Palestine to the tip of the Red Sea (the Gulf of Akaba), about three miles west of Akaba Port.

It was agreed that the Arab Legion should replace the Iraqis in the "Triangle" area.

Under the agreement with Syria, which was not signed until 20 July, the Syrians withdrew from the areas they had occupied west of the international frontier and Israel agreed, in return, that the areas should be demilitarized and the Arabs who had abandoned them during the fighting be permitted to return. Thus Israeli control over Lake Kinneret and Lake Huleh was assured, but the demilitarized zones were a frequent focus of friction during the following years. Iraq did not conclude an armistice agreement with Israel.

Although the agreements specifically reserved to the parties the right to make territorial claims in the future, the preamble stated in each case that the agreement was concluded "in order to facilitate the transition from the present truce to permanent peace in Palestine." Article 1 went on to state that "No aggressive actions by the armed forces—land, sea, or air—of either Party shall be undertaken, planned or threatened against the people or the armed forces of the other," and Article 2 stated that "No warlike act or act of hostility shall be conducted from territory controlled by one of the Parties . . . against the other Party." The demarcation lines thus constituted *de facto* boundaries as long as they were respected by both sides and, despite repeated violations, they served as such until the Six-Day War of 1967. A United Nations Truce Supervision Organization (UNTSO) composed of soldiers from various countries under the command of a chief of staff, and four Mixed Armistice Commissions (MACs), each with Israel and Arab representatives under an UNTSO officer as chairman, were set up to supervise the execution of the agreements and consider complaints. In default of unanimity, the UN chairman acted as arbiter.

The armistice agreement concluded with Syria on 20 July 1949, at the Customs Building just east of the Jordan River, formally concluded Israel's War of Independence. It had lasted 20 months; it had cost 6,000 killed, almost one percent of the entire population of the State when it was born. But it had established the Jewish State firmly as a fact on the map of the Middle East.

After the War

Mandatory Palestine was a thing of the past. It had been partitioned into three units, but neither in the manner nor with the results envisaged by the UN Resolution of 29 November 1947. Most of its territory was now included in the State of Israel, which had been established out of the chaos left behind by the British Government.

To the east, the mountains of Ephraim (Samaria) and Judea had been annexed by Transjordan, which now came to be called the Hashemite Kingdom of Jordan. In the southwest a narrow coastal strip, the Gaza strip, nominally under the "All Palestine Government" sponsored by the Mufti of Jerusalem, was in fact under the rule of Egypt, which treated the strip as territory under military government. The military forces of the Palestinian Arabs had been totally defeated, the Liberation Army smashed and dispersed. The regular Egyptian army had been beaten and put *hors de combat*, at least for a considerable period. Other regular Arab armies had suffered severe casualties. They had not been completely destroyed, but their objective—a military victory over the fledgling Jewish State—had not been achieved.

A large number of Palestinian Arabs had become refugees as a result of the war. Count Bernadotte, in his last report, mentioned the figure of 360,000; in later reports the figure was doubled; Arab propagandists refer to a million. Even today it is difficult to establish the precise figure of those who fled in 1948, and more so, of their descendants.

Why did they flee? Whoever considers the demographic mosaic that was Palestine at the end of the war—Jewish and Arab villages side by side; mixed cities, quarters, even individual houses—will readily understand that war, under such circumstances, would result in a flow of refugees: Arab, should Israel win; Jewish refugees, had it lost. Whoever decided on war must squarely face the responsibility for its consequences—the dead, the wounded and the refugees. Arab leaders had foreseen an exodus of Jewish refugees, and it is known that the British Government had made certain preparations for the temporary accommodation of Jewish refugees from Palestine in other countries. In fact, there were Jewish refugees. Not one Jew was left in areas overrun by Arab armies—the Jewish Quarter in the Old City of Jerusalem, the Ezyon Bloc, Neve Ya'akov and Atarot, Mishmar ha-Yarden, Kfar Darom and others—whilst over 200,000 Arabs stayed behind in Israel territory. If the number of Jewish refugees in Palestine did not exceed 7,000, there is only one reason: the failure of Arab armies to achieve victory. And hundreds of thousands of Jews who had been living for centuries in neighboring Arab countries, far removed from the battle arena, became refugees in the wake of the war.

It was Haganah policy to permit Arabs to stay on under Israel rule, and continue their normal lives. In Haifa, for example, the Jewish mayor made an emotional appeal to Arab citizens to continue their lives, side by side with the Jews, as they had done for generations. However, as stated in a subsequent memorandum to the Heads of Arab States, the representatives of Haifa Arabs "proudly refused to sign the Armistice, and asked for facilities for evacuation . . . we are happy to state that the Arabs kept their honor and their tradition." British eyewitnesses testify that "from the Jewish side everything possible was done to persuade the Arab population to stay on . . ."

There is no doubt that the Mufti, in an attempt to instigate Arab governments to join the war, was actively encouraging the exodus, promising the refugees a speedy return in the footsteps of the victorious Arab armies. True, there was the tragedy of Deir Yasin, and other isolated instances of maltreatment of Arab populations. The *Yishuv*, the Haganah, and subsequently the Government of Israel, condemned such acts. But, as an Arab journalist born in Deir Yasin put it, "the reason [for the flight from other Arab villages] was the error of our leaders, who broadcast and exaggerated Jewish crimes in order to incite the Arabs and the strong Arab armies to fight the Jews . . .thus they sowed fear and panic amongst the Palestinians, and we watched them deserting their homes and their properties to the enemy." It was only towards the end of the war that Palestinian Arabs came to doubt the irresponsible promises made by their leaders, and decided to stay on when the I.D.F. gained control.

3
The Armistice Years

Following the signature of the first armistice agreement with Egypt, Israel's Foreign Minister Moshe Sharett issued a somewhat euphoric statement, in the course of which he said: "This is the first agreement, ever since the historic treaty of Weizmann and Feisal, which has been signed jointly by official representatives of Jews and Arabs; it is the first agreement achieved between the State of Israel and a neighboring Arab state . . . In the course of the long and difficult years preceding the renaissance of Israel, we have always declared that only equality of political status will cause the Arab world to recognize us and to accept us as a fact. That assumption has today been proved. The General Armistice Agreement between Israel and Egypt is the first of its kind; under no circumstances will it be the last. It is but a link from which a new chain of developments will start. It will be recorded as a farreaching turning point in the history of Israel's foreign relations and as an epoch-making event in the life of the Middle East" (*Ha-aretz*, 25 November 1949). Replying to a question, he said that "the friendly, one might even say intimate, talks in Rhodes have created an opening [toward permanent peace] and there is no doubt that peace negotiations will follow as a result."

Indeed, as mentioned above, the preamble to each of the General Armistice Agreements stated that they were to be considered as a transition to permanent peace, and that they could not be altered except by mutual consent. Dr. Ralph Bunche, who presided over the negotiations and patiently mediated between the parties, was awarded the Nobel Prize for Peace in recognition of his services. However, by the summer of 1949, the Lausanne Conference convened by the Conciliation Commission for Palestine in order to promote an agreement by negotiation, conducted with the P.C.C. or directly, in order to achieve a final settlement of the questions still pending, had been deadlocked. All the same, the Secretary-General of the UN, Trygve

Lie, adopted a moderately optimistic tone at a press conference on 21 July 1949, the morrow of the signature of the last General Armistice Agreement: "Conciliation, mediation and compromise," he stated, "are slow work, but they are, in the long run, the only firm foundation of a peaceful world . . . lasting peace cannot be founded upon force. It has to be founded upon consent freely given and agreement voluntarily arrived at. I think all who believe in working for a peaceful settlement . . . should take heart from what has been accomplished by mediation and conciliation on the island of Rhodes . . . "

As late as 1953, when all hope for a definitive peace settlement in the foreseeable future had vanished, Trygve Lie stated that "complaints are bound to recur so long as an armistice régime that was designed to be a short-term transition to peace continues to be maintained as though it were permanent. Yet unless Arabs and Israelis reach a peace settlement on a basis of mutual give and take, there is no alternative to continuing the armistice régime unimpaired."

The Government of Israel, however, had realized much earlier that indeed they were faced with an alternative—a second round. In his speech to the Knesset on 15 June 1949, following Israel's acceptance as a member of the United Nations, Moshe Sharett stated: "The storm which has been raging around us will not soon be stilled. Nor do we hold the certainty in our hearts that it will not break out anew, with greater violence. Our vital interest is in a comprehensive peace soon, and we are duty bound to lend our best efforts to its achievement. But with all our striving for peace, we must not lose patience if it tarries in coming. If destiny has so decreed it—we are strong enough to wait with composure."

At the beginning of 1950 intensive secret negotiations took place with King Abdullah of Jordan. They terminated in the initialling of a non-aggression pact, the most farreaching document negotiated between Israel and any of its neighbors. But before the agreement was signed, Abdullah broke off negotiations as a result of violent opposition from Arab governments and the threat of expulsion from the Arab League. In return for breaking off these talks, the Arab states acquiesced to the annexation of the West Bank by Jordan, which heretofore they had determinedly opposed. The annexation was formalized in April 1950. A year later, Abdullah was assassinated by a member of the Husseini family, a relative of the ex-Mufti of Jerusalem, Hajj Amin al-Husseini, as he left the al-Aksa Mosque in Jerusalem after Friday prayers.

On 25 May 1950 the United States, Britain and France had stated

THE ARMISTICE YEARS   83

in a tripartite declaration on the Middle East, that they would take action if necessary to prevent any violation of frontiers or armistice lines by any state in the area. Arms supplies to Middle East countries, the declaration said, would be governed by their needs for internal security, legitimate self-defense, and their role in the defense of the area. For several years, however, it was chiefly the Arabs who received Western arms, while Israel had to rely mainly on semi-obsolete equipment from various sources.

There was no progress toward the "permanent peace" envisaged by the armistice agreements. In June 1950 the members of the Arab League concluded a collective security agreement against "the Zionist danger" and "Jewish expansionist aspirations." The Arab states continued to regard themselves as at war with Israel, refusing to recognize it or to negotiate a peaceful settlement of outstanding problems. They replied to Israel's calls for direct negotiations with, on the one hand, a refusal to recognize its right to exist and, on the other, demands for "the implementation of UN resolutions," which they interpreted as meaning the unconditional repatriation of all Arab refugees and the restriction of Israel to the boundaries drawn in the 1947 partition plan. The very existence of Israel was regarded as "aggression", and its destruction became a fundamental aim of Arab national policy. Sometimes indirect terms were used, such as "the restoration of the stolen rights of the Palestinian people," "the liberation of Palestine," the reconquest of the "stolen territory," or "the liquidation of Zionist aggression," but it was frequently stated in the plainest terms that the aim was a "second round" in which Israel would be destroyed and its people "pushed into the sea." The Arab League established a ramified boycott organization to dissuade businessmen in other countries, by economic pressure, from trading with Israel or investing in her economy. Egypt denied passage through the Suez Canal and the Straits of Tiran to shipping and cargoes belonging to, or bound for, Israel.

It was impossible to protect every kilometer of the long and winding borders by sentries or patrols. Border violations by Arab infiltrators bent on plunder, shooting by trigger-happy Arab soldiers, mine-laying on Israel roads and tracks, and, later, armed incursions by trained and organized bands, were almost daily occurrences. In the period 1951–56 over 400 Israelis were killed and 900 injured as a result; there were 3,000 armed clashes with Arab regular or irregular forces inside Israel territory, and some 6,000 acts of sabotage, theft, and attempted theft were committed by infiltrators. UNTSO was powerless; the Mixed Armistice Commissions could do no more than register complaints, appeal for restraint or, at best, pass resolutions of censure. The Security Council took no action to rectify the situation, and Israel had to look to its own defenses. The Defense Service Law, passed in September 1949, provided for two years' compulsory service in the armed forces for men and women, with reserve training up to the age of 49. In an emergency the reserves could be summoned to their units in a matter of hours. Reprisals against Arab attacks were carried out from time to time but, although they may have discouraged even graver violations of the Armistice Agreements and at certain periods induced the governments concerned to restrain infiltration for a while, they did not put an end to the chain of violence. As each reprisal was a reaction to a series of attacks, it was generally on a larger scale, and since these operations were carried out by I.D.F. units, they were immediately censured by the Mixed Armistice Commissions and often by the Security Council.

The troubles with the Syrians mainly concerned the demilitarized zones, for they objected to Israel's development works there on the ground that these would give Israel military advantages. At the beginning of 1951, when Israel started work on the Huleh drainage scheme near Mishmar ha-Yarden, there were several exchanges of fire. In March, seven Israelis were killed in the el-Hamma area and the Israel air force bombarded two Arab villages in reprisal. On 19 May, after General Riley, chief of UNTSO, had failed to obtain agreement, the Security Council ordered Israel to stop the works on Arab-owned land in the zones. A new dispute broke out at the beginning of September 1953, when the Israelis started work in the demilitarized zone, south of the Huleh, on the first stage of a major project to channel part of the Jordan waters to the Negev. The Syrians protested, and General Bennike, the new UNTSO chief, ordered Israel to suspend the work until agreement was reached with Syria. Under international pressure, Israel ultimately complied, "pending urgent consideration of the matter by the Security Council." In January 1954 a proposal calling for a compromise between Israel and Syrian interests was blocked by the Soviet veto in the Security Council, and Israel revised its plans in order to keep the works out of the demilitarized zone.

Meanwhile, in October 1953, U.S. President Eisenhower sent a special envoy, Eric Johnston, to the Middle East to present proposals for a constructive solution of the water problem to the governments of Israel, Syria, Lebanon, and Jordan. Johnston submitted a plan prepared by Gordon Clapp, chairman of the Tennessee Valley Author-

ity, for the utilization of the Jordan and Yarmuk waters by the four
countries for agricultural development and refugee resettlement
on the basis of mutually agreed quotas. In 1955, a Unified Water
Plan, which assured each country of the quantities of water claimed
by its experts, was accepted by the parties on the technical level, but the
Arab League, meeting in October, refused to give political approval.
Israel stated, however, that it would not use more than the quantities
of water allotted in the plan. Repeated Syrian attacks on Israel fishing
on Lake Kinneret led to further Israel reprisals in December 1955,
in which the Syrians suffered about 100 casualties.

A serious dispute with Jordan over the blocking of the road to
Eilat by Legion forces in November 1950, followed by three murders
by infiltrators in and around Jerusalem and an Israel reprisal, was
settled in February 1951, the Jordanians agreeing to co-operate to
stop infiltration. But the position deteriorated. The Jordanians refused
to carry out their undertaking in Article 8 of the Armistice Agreement
to negotiate arrangements for Israel's use of the Latrun road to the
capital and access to Jewish holy places in Jerusalem and the Jewish
institutions on Mount Scopus. In January 1953 the Jordanian prime
minister announced the annullment of the agreement to prevent
infiltration and there were numerous attacks by infiltrators and
Jordanian troops on Israel civilians and soldiers. In June 1953 the
Jordan government renewed the agreement for the prevention of
infiltration, but the attacks continued.

At first Israel reprisals were carried out by ordinary army units,
but it soon became clear that these troops, consisting mainly of in-
experienced draftees—many of whom were newcomers to the country—were unsuitable for such commando-type raids. A special
body of volunteers called Unit 101 (later merged with the paratroops)
was therefore formed for the purpose. One of its raids, on the village
of Qibya, in which 45 houses were blown up and heavy casualties
were caused to civilians hiding in them, was severely censured by the
Security Council (15 October 1953).

Israel initiated an attempt to obtain agreement on a *modus vivendi*
by invoking Article 12 of the Armistice Agreement, under which
either party could summon a conference to consider the working
of the agreement. At the end of the year, the UN Secretary-General
issued invitations for such a conference at Israel's request, but Jordan
refused to attend. The vicious circle of repeated Arab attacks, reprisals
by Israel, and international condemnations of Israel continued throughout 1954; outstanding examples were the killing of passengers in an

Terrorist ambush of bus to Eilat at Ma'aleh Akrabim, 17 March 1954.

Israel bus at Ma'aleh Akrabim ("Scorpions' Ascent") on 17 March; the killing of three Jews in the Jerusalem Corridor on 9 May and of three more in the same area on 19 June; and a three-day outbreak of shooting by the Legionaires from the Old City wall later in the month. In the following year much of the infiltration was carried out by bands organized by the Egyptians in the Gaza Strip and sent into Jordan to operate from there.

Egypt took the lead in the Arab boycott by banning Israel shipping and the passage of "contraband goods" or "strategic goods" (later extended to include foodstuffs) through the Suez Canal. This practice was defined by General Riley, the chief of UNTSO, in a report to the Security Council as "an aggressive action," and the Council called on Egypt on 1 September 1951, to terminate the restrictions. The resolution stated that "since the armistice régime . . . is of a permanent character, neither party can reasonably assert that it is a belligerent" (Paragraph 9). Egypt ignored the resolution, and cargoes destined for Israel were confiscated from Norwegian, Greek, and Italian ships trying to pass through the canal. In September 1954 an Israel vessel, the *Bat Galim*, and its cargo were confiscated at the entrance to the Canal and the crew was imprisoned for three months. In 1949 Egypt occupied the uninhabited islands of Tiran and Sanafir in the Red Sea, at the entrance to the Gulf of Akaba; later it established a garrison at Sharm el-Sheikh, interfered with Israel and international shipping to and from Eilat, and banned Israel planes from the airspace over the Gulf.

On 18 August 1952, Ben-Gurion welcomed the Egyptian officers' revolution, led by General Naguib, and declared that there was no reason for any antagonism between the two countries. But there was no improvement in relations under Naguib or his successor, Gamal Abdel Nasser. Sporadic incidents on the Gaza Strip and Sinai borders, which claimed a score or more casualties—seven or eight fatal—in each of the years 1951–53, became more serious and frequent in the last quarter of 1954. Tension was increased by the trial in Cairo of 11 Jews charged with belonging to a "Zionist espionage and sabotage group." Two were executed in January 1955 and the rest were sentenced to long periods of imprisonment. On 2 February Israel's minister of defense resigned due to disagreements with the Prime Minister arising from a dispute over the responsibility for an ill-advised security operation, of a nature undisclosed to the Israel public at the time. Ben-Gurion returned from retirement at Sdeh Boker to take up the post of defense minister under Sharett's premiership.

Toward the end of February Egyptian saboteurs, known as *fedayeen* ("suicide fighters"), penetrated deep into Israel territory, and on the 28th a clash with an Egyptian force on Israel territory opposite Gaza developed into the fiercest battle since the War of Independence. The fight was carried over into the Strip. In an Israel attack on an army camp near Gaza, 38 Egyptians were killed and 44 wounded. The ill-fated Baghdad Pact, concluded in 1955 on U.S. initiative and designed to bring together the countries of the "Northern Tier" in an alliance which would stop the gap between NATO and SEATO, thus completing the encirclement of the U.S.S.R., had just aroused Nasser's anger against the West. He accordingly turned to the Soviet Bloc for weapons to strengthen his forces. At the end of August came the first reports of an Egyptian deal with the Soviet Union for the supply, through Czechoslovakia, of large quantities of modern heavy arms. Meanwhile the Arab attacks were stepped up; many of them were carried out by *fedayeen* recruited and trained by the Egyptians but operating mainly from the Gaza Strip and Jordan, as well as from Syria and Lebanon. Israel's proposals for a high-level meeting with Egyptian representatives, as well as for the erection of a security fence along the border and other methods of reducing tension, were rejected.

On 27 September 1955 Nasser broadcast an announcement of the Czechoslovakian arms deal; two days later it was reported that large quantities of tanks, artillery, jet planes, and submarines were already on their way to Egypt and that Syria was also receiving generous supplies of weapons from the East. Although the Western powers expressed grave concern at the development, they gave no clear reply to Israel's appeals for arms to redress the balance, and the United States warned against any "hasty action." A wave of anxiety swept the country. Israelis from all walks of life came forward spontaneously with donations of cash and jewelry for the purchase of arms.

On 17 October Egypt and Syria signed a military pact. The Syrians renewed their attacks on Israel fishing boats on Lake Kinneret, and an Israel reprisal was followed by Egyptian attacks in the south. Foreign Minister Sharett went to Paris and Geneva, where the Big Four foreign ministers were meeting, but his interview with Molotov of the U.S.S.R. was fruitless, and only France responded sympathetically to Israel's request for arms. The Egyptians had encroached on the demilitarized zone at Niẓanah and attacked an Israel police post, and their planes had repeatedly violated Israel airspace. In retaliation, the Israel army attacked an Egyptian military camp at Kuntilla in Sinai. Presenting his new cabinet to the Knesset on 2 November, Ben-Gurion announced his readiness to meet Egyptian and other Arab leaders at any time to discuss a settlement, but warned that "if the armistice lines are opened for the passage of saboteurs and murderers, they shall not be closed again to the defenders." The same night Israel forces ejected the Egyptians from Niẓanah, inflicting heavy casualties. Egyptian attacks multiplied all along the front; there were four or five incidents a day, and the activities of the *fedayeen* from the Gaza Strip and Jordan were stepped up. Typical *fedayeen* tactics were also used in attacks from Lebanese territory.

On 26 August U.S. Secretary of State John Foster Dulles had suggested territorial changes as part of a possible Arab-Israel settlement. The idea was echoed in a speech at London's Guildhall on 9 November by the British foreign minister, Sir Anthony Eden, who suggested a compromise between the Arab demand for a return to the partition plan boundaries and Israel's insistence on the borders demarcated by the Armistice Agreements. On 15 November Ben-Gurion categorically rejected any idea of truncating Israel's territory; Eden's approach was likewise rejected by Egypt. France agreed to supply Israel with a number of Ouragan planes, but continued to sell arms to Egypt, while the U.S. and Britain went on sending armaments to Lebanon, Iraq, and Jordan.

As 1956 opened, the war clouds were visibly gathering. On 2 January Ben-Gurion warned the Knesset of "the danger of the approaching attack from Egypt, and perhaps not only by it." While the U.S.S.R. virulently denounced Israel, the Western powers spon-

THE ARMISTICE YEARS 89

sored a Security Council resolution censuring her for a reprisal operation against Syrian posts that had fired on fishermen on Lake Kinneret.
The U.S. still refused to sell arms to Israel, but consented to France
supplying her with advanced Mystère aircraft. On 13 February the
Soviet foreign minister declared that the U.S.S.R. could not remain
indifferent to developments in the Middle East and warned the Western
powers against unilateral action in the area. UN Secretary-General
Dag Hammarskjöld paid several visits to the Middle East in unsuccessful
attempts to achieve a settlement. The dismissal of General Glubb, the
British commander of the Jordanian Arab Legion, was followed by
an increase in Egyptian influence in Jordan. Israel speeded up the
building of shelters, the training of civil defense personnel, and the
fortification of border villages. At the end of April, after artillery
duels on the Gaza Strip border and widespread *fedayeen* attacks,
Hammarskjöld announced agreement on a general, unconditional
cease-fire between Israel and its neighbors, but the arms race continued.
Jordan agreed to facilitate the operation of *fedayeen* from its territory
and the Arab countries competed in threats against Israel.

For some time there had been differences between Sharett, who
favored greater trust in the UN and international opinion, and Ben-
Gurion, who emphasized the need for Israel to rely first of all on its
own strength. In June, feeling that complete harmony between prime
minister and foreign minister was essential in view of the coming
dangers, Ben-Gurion replaced Sharett by Golda Meir. Attacks from
Jordan continued throughout July; at the end of the month, after
Egypt nationalized the Suez Canal, there were a number of incidents
on the southern border as well. The clashes continued in the following
months and rose to a peak in October, while international tension
grew over the future of the Canal.

On 13 October the Security Council called for "free and open
transit through the Canal without discrimination" and declared that its
operation "should be insulated from the politics of any country,"
but Nasser announced that no Israel ships would be allowed to pass.
Two days later Ben-Gurion told the Knesset that Israel was being
subjected to a guerilla war conducted by bands of *fedayeen* organized,
equipped, and trained mainly in Egypt and recalled the right to self-
defense guaranteed by Article 51 of the UN Charter. He also said
that Israel reserved freedom of action if the *status quo* was violated
by the entry of troops from Iraq (which had not signed an Armistice
Agreement with Israel) into Jordan. On 25 October, after an election
victory for pro-Nasserist elements in Jordan, that country joined the

Egyptian-Syrian military pact against Israel. Abu-Nawar, commander of the Arab Legion, declared: "We and not Israel will fix the time and place of the battle."

The growing attacks on Israel and the threat of a concerted offensive from the north, east, and southwest coincided with growing apprehension in Britain and France over the threat posed by unfettered Egyptian control of the Suez Canal to their communications and interests. Thus, Israel's danger was matched by the opportunity. According to subsequent statements by Christian Pineau, the French foreign minister, and others, Ben-Gurion paid a secret visit to France in October to ask Prime Minister Guy Mollet for help. Large quantities of French heavy armaments were sent to Israel and unloaded in secret. On 27 October Ben-Gurion submitted to the cabinet a proposal for a large-scale operation to demolish the bases of the *fedayeen* and the Egyptian army in the Sinai Peninsula and the Gaza Strip, and to occupy the shore of the Gulf of Akaba in order to safeguard navigation—even if, as he expected, Israel would be compelled by international pressure to evacuate the territory occupied.

4

The Sinai Campaign
and After

The reasons for the Anglo-French attack on Egypt, and its objectives, were quite different from those of Israel. Nevertheless, the previously co-ordinated timing of both campaigns, which was termed by many outside observers as a "collusion" between Israel and the West European powers, had a direct tactical impact on Operation Kadesh, as the Sinai Campaign was officially termed. The objectives of Israel's operations, as defined in the order given to the I.D.F., were: destruction of the *fedayeen* bases in the Gaza Strip and on the Sinai border; prevention, for however short a time, of an Egyptian attack on Israel by destroying Egypt's logistic establishment and the airfields in Sinai; and opening the Gulf of Eilat to undisturbed Israel shipping. These objectives were all achieved.

The I.D.F. had undergone many changes since the War of Independence: methods had been introduced for the rapid mobilization of reserve units, civilian vehicles, and heavy mechanical equipment; weapons had been standardized and the forces trained in their use, especially in the air force and the armored corps; and a new system of tactics had been formulated and inculcated.

The Campaign

The Sinai Campaign lasted less than eight days—from 29 October to 5 November 1956. It may be divided into three phases: the opening phase on 29—30 October; decision, 31 October to 1 November; exploitation, 2–5 November.

In view of a number of uncertainties—concerning the reaction of Egypt itself; that of its allies, Syria and Jordan, with whom it had

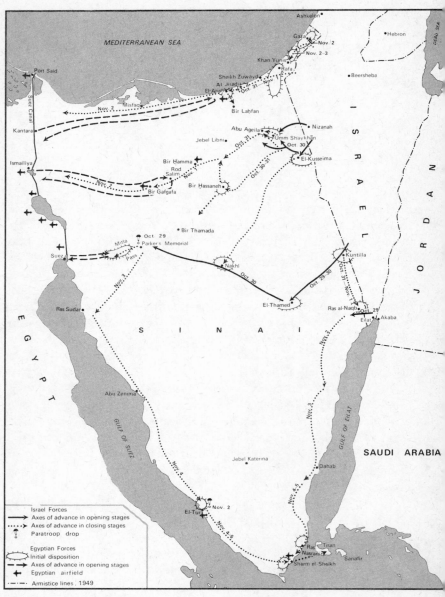

The Sinai Campaign, Oct. 29–Nov. 5, 1956.

established a unified command; that of Great Britain and France, who were locked in a conflict with Egypt over the Suez Canal; and (last but not least) that of the Superpowers—the objectives of the operation were initially left flexible and vague. The maximum objective would be a total defeat of the Egyptian forces in Sinai; the minimum, a large-scale impulsive reprisal raid. On 28 October the cabinet decided to "review the scope of operations" within a day or two, by which time it was expected that at least some of these uncertainties would be cleared up.

Egypt had about 45,000 soldiers in Sinai at the time, mainly in the Rafa–El-Arish–Abu Ageila triangle in the northeastern corner of Sinai, where the 3rd Division was concentrated, and the adjoining Gaza Strip, occupied by the 8th Division including a Palestinian brigade, one of whose tasks was to assure the *fedayeen* of a firm base for their incursions across the armistice lines. Further important concentrations were situated along the central road from El-Kusseima to Ismailia; along the southern route—Kuntilla, Suez; and at the extreme southern tip of the Sinai Peninsula, Sharm el-Sheikh. It should be pointed out, however, that Egypt's deployment was offensive rather than defensive—the main concentration being in the triangle, close to Israel's frontiers. Israel had mobilized a force approximately similar in size for the operation. In terms of armament, the Egyptians enjoyed an edge, provided they knew how to employ the arms they had obtained in large quantities, particularly from the Soviet Union. The Russian T-34 medium tank outgunned and outran the Sherman; the Russian tank destroyer compared favorably with the French AMX. Egypt enjoyed superiority in numbers of jet aircraft, although the Russian MIG-15 did not equal Israel's fighter plane, the French Mystère. Of particular concern to Israeli planners was the fact that Egypt had about 50 Ilyushin bombers which could penetrate deep into Israel, whereas Israel had no bombers at all. On the other hand, Egypt was suffering from a shortage of pilots.

The operations were planned in four phases to employ anything up to five independent forces.

Phase 1: a parachute battalion would be dropped in the Mitla area at sunset on D-day, 29 October. At the same time, the remainder of that airborne brigade would cross the frontier to Kuntilla and advance with all possible speed to reinforce its parachute battalion. It would have to travel about 130 miles (208 km.) and, on the way, would have to take three strongly-fortified positions at Kuntilla, El-Thamed, and Nakhl, respectively. In case it was held up, a central task force was to cross the frontier at Sabha, 60 miles (96 km.) to the north, and capture the road junction at El-Kusseima. From El-Kusseima this force could go to the help of the parachute battalion by way of Nakhl or, alternatively, by way of Bir Hassneh.

Phase 2: this was to be a 24-hour pause. At the end of it, the decision would be taken what to do next. If it was decided to embark upon a full-scale campaign, the next phase would follow.

Phase 3: an independent force, the 9th Infantry Brigade, would make its way down the western shore of the Gulf of Akaba to take Ras Nasrani and Sharm el-Sheikh. If necessary, it would be assisted by forces from the Mitla area coming down the road along the Gulf of Suez and attacking Sharm el-Sheikh in the rear. At the same time, the central task force, part of which would already have taken El-Kusseima, would attack the triangle at its Abu Ageila apex; and the northern task force would attack another apex of the triangle at Rafa.

Phase 4: the central task force, after taking Abu Ageila, would exploit success by moving westward to the Canal opposite Ismailia. The northern task force, after taking Rafa, would take El-Arish and exploit to the Canal at Kantara. Once El-Arish had fallen, the Gaza Strip would be sealed off and would inevitably fall. To help it to do so, a fifth force which would be kept in reserve during the first three phases, would attack Gaza from the east.

Phase 1: 29 October–30 October

In the late afternoon of 29 October the parachute battalion was dropped, as planned, near Col. Parker's Memorial in the west-central area of the Sinai Peninsula, just east of the Mitla Pass, the main gateway to the Suez Canal in the central sector. The move came as a complete surprise to friend and foe alike. Although the U.S. government had been aware of the large-scale mobilization of reserves during the preceding days, the assumption—not discouraged by Israel—was that the I.D.F. would move against Jordan, which had recently joined the Egyptian-Syrian defense pact. At approximately the same time, 4 p.m. on 29 October, the leading elements of the remaining two battalions of the same airborne brigade crossed the frontier near Kuntilla. Only part of their vehicles had arriv.d, and some of these had already been disabled travelling overland from Ein Hussub, on the Jordanian border, where they had concentrated in order to enhance the likelihood of surprise. Over 24 hours later, at 10 p.m. on 30 October, they linked up with the parachute battalion near the Mitla Pass.

En route they had captured, almost without casualties, the strongly fortified positions at El Kuntilla, Thamed and Nakhl. Their capture was facilitated by the element of surprise, sheer audacity and the utilization of sunlight, attacking Kuntilla from the west at dusk, and Thamed from the east at dawn.

The parachute battalion had meanwhile been exposed to Egyptian counterattacks. As expected, the Egyptians felt compelled to react to a parachute drop only 37 miles (60 km.) from the Suez Canal. Egyptian positions in the Mitla Pass, to the immediate west of the battalion, had been reinforced during the night by two battalions from across the Suez Canal. Egyptian planes also joined in the fray; however, that was the pre-arranged signal which permitted Israel's air force to enter the battle in support of ground forces. The Israel air force soon gained air superiority over the battle arena, long before Anglo-French air forces attacked airfields in Egypt.

In the early hours of 30 October, the vital road junction of El-Kusseima was captured, affording an additional gateway into Sinai from the east. This directly exposed the southern flank of the 3rd Egyptian division in the northeast corner of Sinai. The seizure of the road junction further enabled Israel forces to outflank the 3rd Division and, at the same time, provided a second link with the paratroopers near Parker's Memorial.

The same evening the British Government sent an ultimatum to both Israel and Egypt, demanding that the troops of both should keep clear of the Suez Canal, and that an area extending to 10 miles (16 km.) on each side should, in effect, be demilitarized. At a midnight session the Israel Government decided to accept. At the same time it was decided to continue the operation. No other Arab country had shown any inclination to come to the help of Egypt; the attention of the U.S.S.R. was engaged in Hungary. The U.S. government was still bewildered but an adverse reaction was to be expected. UN Security Council intervention was considered imminent, and therefore speed was of the essence.

Phase 2: 30 October–1 November

On the afternoon of 30 October, a reconnaissance company ascertained that the Dayqa Pass was free of enemy forces. This enabled the armored brigade of the central task force to avoid a frontal clash with Egyptian forces, to get to the rear of the Abu Ageila positions and, in the most spectacular armored battles of the campaign, it seized the Abu Ageila

road junction and the enemy positions at the Rawafa Dam. These
feats blocked the escape route of the Egyptian brigade at Umm Kataf
and Umm Shaykhan, between the frontier and Abu Ageila. On the
same afternoon, Israel forces captured the enemy positions at Auja
Masri near the frontier, along the Nizanah-Ismailia road. By early
evening the positions at Tarat Umm Basis, four-odd miles (7 km.)
from the border, had been occupied.

During the night an infantry force, supported by artillery, took up
positions on both sides of the road at Umm Turfa, half way between
Umm Basis and Umm Kataf, encircling the positions at Umm Kataf
and Umm Shaykhan. In spite of transport difficulties caused by an
Egyptian attempt to block the road through Umm Shaykhan, fuel
and ammunition reached the Israel armored brigade in the rear of
enemy positions. Head-on I.D.F. attacks on these positions had failed,
because they had been based on incorrect information and errors
of judgment, but during the night of 1–2 November, Egyptian troops
withdrew from their positions, leaving their heavy equipment. During
the next few days these soldiers roamed aimlessly in the area between
El-Arish, Abu Ageila and the Canal, until they were rounded up and
taken prisoner.

At the same time, one armored force advanced westward. It had
been reported that an Egyptian armored force was moving from the
Canal Zone eastward, and the Israel force laid an ambush at the Jebel
Libni road junction. However, the Egyptian armored force never
reached this point, for on the morning of 31 October pilots of the
Israel air force sighted it on the road between Bir Gafgafa and Bir
Hamma and proceeded to immobilize 90 of the vehicles. The remaining
vehicles withdrew, and the Israel armored force continued its advance
westward, meeting stiff resistance from armor and artillery intended
to delay the Israel advance and allow the main body of Egyptian
troops to withdraw across the Suez Canal. Orderly and organized
retreat, however, had already become impossible.

During the night of 31 October–1 November the I.D.F. northern
task force attacked in the northern sector and the fortified positions
at Rafa were stormed, thus opening the way to the Suez Canal for an
armored brigade. By the evening of 1 November, armored forces had
reached El-Arish, fighting all the way. At the same time there was a
bloody clash in the southern sector, where the airborne brigade
advancing westward from Parker's Memorial ran into an enemy
ambush positioned in the caves of the Mitla Pass. Only after fierce
fighting were the paratroopers able to overpower the enemy. The

general retreat from Sinai, ordered by the Egyptian high command on 1 November, soon turned into a rout, with attacks by the Israel air force increasing the turmoil. Many Egyptian officers abandoned their men in order to save their own lives. It was during this phase that the Egyptian destroyer *Ibrahim al-Auwal* was captured off Haifa by a combined operation of the Israel navy and air force.

Phase 3: 2–5 November

In compliance with the Anglo-French ultimatum the armored spear-heads of the I.D.F. halted at points ten miles from the Canal on 2 November, near Ismailiya on the central axis, and on 3 November in the vicinity of Kantara on the northern axis. There still remained two objectives: the capture of the Gaza Strip, and the seizure of the

Israel armor during the battle of Rafa, 31 October 1956.

The frigate Miznak passing through the Straits of Tiran, December 1956.

Egyptian strongpoints at Ras Nasrani and Sharm el-Sheikh on the Straits of Tiran. After the capture of Rafa, the Gaza Strip was cut off, and there remained only the troublesome task of mopping up scores of fortified positions and taking over the townships of Gaza, Khan Yunis, and Beit Hanun. This action began on 2 November and was completed the following day.

The capture of Ras Nasrani and Sharm el-Sheikh was allotted to a reserve infantry brigade moving as a mobile column down the western shores of the Gulf of Eilat. On 31 October this column reached Kuntilla and on the following day Ras al-Naqb, which had been seized two days earlier by other I.D.F. troops. Since the Israel air force was fully occupied in the central axis, the mobile column waited until 2 November before continuing its advance. As poor road conditions and sporadic clashes with the enemy caused further delay, the general staff ordered the parachute brigade to move from Parker's Memorial toward the southern tip of the Sinai peninsula along the eastern shore of the Red Sea as far as the oil fields of Ras Sudar. Simultaneously paratroopers were dropped on the airfield at el-Tur. A pincer movement now threatened the last remaining Egyptian positions in Sinai. Ras Nasrani was evacuated by its garrison and, as the final act of the Sinai Campaign, Sharm el-Sheikh was stormed by the reservists on 5 November.

I.D.F. losses in the campaign were 171 dead, several hundred wounded, and four Israelis taken prisoner. Egyptian loses were estimated at over one thousand dead, and many more wounded, while 6,000 prisoners were taken. Immense quantities of armored vehicles, trucks, guns, and other military equipment were seized.

Operation Musketeer

Twelve hours after the expiration of the British ultimatum of 30 October, which had been accepted by Israel—as mentioned above—but rejected by Egypt, British and French planes from Cyprus, Malta, and aircraft carriers in the Mediterranean, began to bombard Egyptian airfields in the Delta and Canal areas. An Egyptian frigate was sunk in the Bay of Suez. President Nasser of Egypt ordered the blocking of the Canal by scuttling 47 ships loaded with cement. However, it was not until 5 November—with the fighting in Sinai practically over, and a few hours before the Israeli operation had achieved its final objective, the capture of Sharm el-Sheikh—that Anglo-French paratroopers landed at Port Said at the northern end of the Suez

Canal. The French and British flotillas arrived at Port Said at dawn on 6 November. After a battle which lasted for a few hours the Egyptian garrison in that city surrendered. Light patrols started moving south along the Canal.

Throughout the week that had passed since 29 October, the Security Council had been paralyzed since two Big Powers, Great Britain and France, each carrying the right of veto, had been directly interested and subsequently involved in the issue. The General Assembly, which was in session at the time, took over on 2 November and again on 7 November. With rare harmony between the U.S. and the U.S.S.R., it called for an immediate cease-fire and the withdrawal of all Israeli and Anglo-French troops from Egypt. The U.S.S.R. presented Israel, as well as Great Britain and France, with a thinly-veiled threat of direct intervention in case of a refusal to comply. On 4 November the General Assembly decided on the establishment of a UN Emergency Force to take the place of the withdrawing troops. Israel, which had secured its major objectives, agreed to the cease-fire on condition of reciprocity. The British Government, under vigorous attack at home and pressure from abroad, particularly the U.S., decided that the operation in which its own troops were participating, which had lost its momentum and had become bogged down, would also stop. Although the French attitude was more determined, they saw no way to continue alone. Thus the cease-fire took effect at midnight, between 6 and 7 November. The UN Emergency Force took over the positions captured by the Anglo-French expeditionary force, only to hand them back to Egypt a few days later. By December, Port Said and the entire Canal were once more under exclusive Egyptian control. Great Britain and France had gained none of their objectives; on the contrary, by demonstrating their complete economic and strategic dependence on the U.S., they had lost the last trappings—or pretense—of Big Power status.

From 7 November onwards Israel stood alone in its struggle to salvage whatever was possible politically from its military success. Its government was receiving letters of violent intimidation from Soviet Premier Bulganin. In Washington it was exposed to American threats to acquiesce in Israel's expulsion from the UN and the imposition of economic sanction, in case of refusal to withdraw, offset only slightly by vague promises of greater American concern for Israel's security after withdrawal. As late as 5 November Prime Minister Ben-Gurion had stated that Israel would not allow foreign forces to set foot in any of the conquered territories; on 7 November he had to retreat. Israel's acceptance of withdrawal was, however, made conditional on the conclusion of satisfactory arrangements for the deployment of the UN Emergency Force. This formula was designed to enable Israel to insist on a system of free navigation in the Straits of Tiran, and on guarantees that the Gaza Strip be kept free of Egyptian troops and *fedayeen* bases. Documents captured in the Strip provided conclusive proof of direct Egyptian responsibility for the *fedayeen* raids of the previous years.

Israel now embarked on a policy of phased withdrawal coupled with an energetic effort to gain understanding and support for its position on Gaza and Sharm el-Sheikh. It was soon found that, standing alone and apart from Great Britain and France, Israel could muster much greater support. By 22 January 1957, Israel forces had withdrawn from all the conquered territories except for the Gaza Strip and the coast of the Gulf of Eilat. During February discussions took place in Washington as a result of which the U.S. and France stated that they would give support to Israel if she exercised her right of self-defense against any renewal of the blockade in the Straits of Tiran or any resumption of *fedayeen* raids from Gaza.

The "hopes and expectations" expressed by Foreign Minister Golda Meir in her speech to the General Assembly on 1 March 1957 had been drafted in consultation with the United States and endorsed by all the major maritime powers; they included the prevention of the return of Egyptian forces to the Gaza Strip; sole responsibility of the UN for administration of the Strip, to be maintained until there was a peace settlement or a definitive agreement on the future of the Strip. Withdrawal from Sharm el-Sheikh was premised on the confidence that there would be continued freedom of navigation for international and Israeli shipping in the Gulf and through the Straits of Tiran. Soon afterwards Israel completed its withdrawal. The "understanding" on Gaza broke down a few days later when the Egyptians sent their administration back into the Strip. The Straits of Tiran were kept open, however, and the assumptions and "understandings" on that point were submitted to an acid test only ten years later, in 1967. Throughout the intervening years no violent clashes took place between Egyptian and Israeli forces along the Gaza Strip.

Although compelled to give up all of the territory captured in the course of the campaign, Israel's Armed Forces had proved their worth in the field of battle, and had established Israel as a military factor to be reckoned with in the Middle East, not least by Egypt, its most powerful neighbor.

5

The Years of "Understanding"

President Nasser had been able to present his military defeat as a political victory, largely owing to the half-hearted involvement of Great Britain and France and the determined opposition of the Superpowers. However, he was aware of Egypt's military inferiority. He had been particularly disappointed by his Arab allies, none of whom had come to the rescue in the hour of need.

He kept up a verbal barrage against Israel, whose establishment he described as "the greatest crime in history," and whose existence he denoted variously as "a stain," "a shame," "a disgrace," "a bleeding wound" or a "cancer." The climax came in 1958, when he officially endorsed the *Protocols of the Learned Elders of Zion*, the infamous anti-Semitic forgery. At the same time he was careful, for the time being, not to provoke Israel to large-scale military activity. He never forewent the ultimate aim of the "liberation" of Palestine, but he now coined the slogan that Arab unity was the way to achieve it. Arab unity, which in Nasser's idiom meant Egyptian hegemony, was the immediate aim; liberation of Palestine, the ultimate result. It was in tune with this doctrine that the United Arab Republic (U.A.R.) was established in 1958, combining Egypt and Syria; systematic subversion was meanwhile instigated by Egypt against "reactionary" Arab regimes—in Saudi Arabia, Lebanon and Jordan. Subversion in Lebanon caused the U.S. to land Marines in that country in 1958, to save a moderately pro-Western government from being overthrown by Nasser's "radical" supporters, in line with the Eisenhower doctrine, approved by the U.S. Congress in the previous year, which authorized the President of the U.S. to "extend assistance against armed aggression from any country controlled by international communism."

King Hussein of Jordan, Nasser's future ally—who at the time was being characterized by Egyptian propaganda as "the Hashemite harlot," "the imperialist lackey" and "the treacherous dwarf"—was being pressured so much by the U.A.R. that Great Britain found it necessary to rush troops to his assistance, and the U.S. provided supplies by air, utilizing Israel's air space.

In 1961 the U.A.R. broke up, striking a blow to Nasser's slogan of unity as the road to liberation. This was particularly disappointing to those Palestinians who had put their faith in Nasser and his road to salvation. An additional blow came the following year, when Nasser's Egypt became bogged down in a long and inconclusive war in the Yemen, where he supported the Republican rebels against the ruling Imam. It became increasingly obvious that nothing divided the Arabs more than the attempt to unite them; the liberation of Palestine was being relegated to the distant future.

Disappointment in Nasser was exploited and fanned by his rivals among the Arab rulers, particularly those in Iraq and in Syria who, while accepting his philosophy, rejected his hegemony. From 1962 Algeria was added to these, not only as a new center of Arab nationalism, but as a mentor and model of the Palestine Liberation Movement (which is discussed below). If Algeria had been able to prevail alone against the powerful French military establishment by using guerilla tactics, why should the same not be possible in Palestine?

Whilst all this was happening beyond Israel's borders, those borders themselves were comparatively quiet. For ten years after 1957 there were no major violent clashes along the Egyptian frontier. Tension broke out from time to time with Jordan and, even more sharply, with Syria. Toward the end of 1957 Jordan tried to obstruct communications with the Israel enclave on Mt. Scopus, and in May 1958 an UNTSO officer and four Israel policemen were killed by Jordanian fire. UN Secretary-General Hammarskjöld discussed the problem with the Jordanian and Israel governments and three times sent special representatives to deal with it, as well as paying a personal visit to the area, but Jordan refused to fulfill its obligations under Article 8 of the Armistice Agreement. At the end of 1958 and the beginning of the following year there were a number of serious incidents in the north in which Israel settlements were machine-gunned and shelled by the Syrians. Israel appealed to the Security Council, but without result. In the spring of 1959 Egypt again interfered with ships carrying goods for Israel through the Suez Canal.

Israel made considerable efforts to keep the local balance of power in its favor, which could only be done by obtaining more arms from the West. Relations with France in this sphere became even closer; the United Kingdom sold Israel submarines; and the United States also began to be co-operative. Despite the opposition of the left-wing members of the coalition, which led to two cabinet crises in 1958–59, military supplies were also brought from West Germany.

By 1963 Nasser realized that his policy of verbal violence combined with military restraint did not intimidate Israel; moreover, it was likely to cost him his hegemony in the Arab world as well. His response was to call a Summit Meeting in Cairo in January 1964. It was attended by the heads of 13 Arab states commanding an area of four million square miles and a population of 80 million. The motive of their disquiet was their failure to intimidate a country with one-fortieth their population and one-five-hundredth their area.

The alarm bell which shook the Arab leaders into a realization of their own impotence was Israel's completion of the National Water Carrier in 1964. This project was of high value to Israel's economy. In scale and technical imagination it would have done credit to a larger state; in human terms it carried a special appeal by making the wilderness bloom. But its implications went deeper. What was ostensibly an engineering enterprise had now become a decisive political issue, for the Arab governments had publicly sworn that the Galilee water would never flow southwards. Israel, for her part, had defined the free use of her share of the Jordan water as a vital national interest, which like the integrity of her territory and the freedom of passage in the Gulf of Akaba, would be defended at any cost. Thus the Arab states and Israel faced each other across the ancient river in a test of resolve and deterrent power. If this Arab threat proved hollow, why should any other Arab menace be believed?

The Arab governments could not have chosen any less favorable ground than the water project to call world opinion to their cause. The enterprise was patently innocent. It caused harm to no-one, and the threat to oppose it by force was generally regarded as senseless malice. In January 1964, while waiting for Pope Paul VI at Megiddo, where he was to begin his pilgrimage to the Holy Places, the Soviet Ambassador in Israel, of all people, informed Prime Minister Eshkol that "Israel had a right to its share of the Jordan waters."

The Upper Jordan, Lake Kinneret and the Yarmuk River were the primary sources of fresh water for irrigation projects in Israel and Jordan. There was, at most, a possibility of some marginal use of this water in southern Syria and Lebanon; it would have been legitimate for the riparian Arab states to press their claims for larger allocations. But it was quite irrational to affirm that Israel, through whose territory the Jordan flowed for 65 miles, had no right at all to divert a single cubic meter to its arid territory in the south. Moreover, an objective external adjudication had been made with the support of international public opinion. It has been noted that in 1958 Eric Johnston, as President Eisenhower's emissary, had presented a plan formulated by irrigation engineers and legal experts. This allotted each country enough water for its need according to normal international criteria. Even Arab engineers had admitted that this suggestion was objectively fair. But their governments had refused to ratify the agreement on avowedly political grounds. Yet the objective judgment stood on public record and had its effect. Israel, although not formally bound by a plan which her neighbors had refused to sign, decided voluntarily to accept the limitations which it imposed. It was disappointing that the plan gave Israel no more than 35% of the total resource. But in a bid for world support, Israelis preferred the political advantages of third party arbitration to the unilateral assertion of their own claims.

For several years Israeli engineers had been building a pumping station to raise the water 1,100 feet above Lake Kinneret and have it flow in a series of pipes and acqueducts towards the northern and central Negev. The U.S. was associated in every stage of the enterprise, to which Presidents Kennedy and Johnson committed their written support. Arab governments had failed to win approval anywhere for their desire to obstruct the project. It must have been plain to Nasser by early 1964 that Israel would not endure thirst and aridity merely to gratify his malice and that when the switch was thrown and the water gushed southwards, most of the world would applaud. Thus he could neither thwart the enterprise by military force nor impede it by international pressures. On 11 June 1964 the water began to flow in the National Carrier. The Arab threat had been quietly but firmly frustrated.

The Arab Summit Conference in 1964 was followed by another in 1965. It reacted to the Arab dilemma by a doctrine of delayed response. On 11 July 1965 Nasser said: "The final account with Israel will be made within five years if we are patient. The Moslems waited 70 years until they expelled the Crusaders from Palestine." Two years later Nasser was to take a more impatient view of his options; but for the time being he played a waiting game. In reply to Syrian pressure for immediate war, he said with complete veracity: "We cannot use force today because conditions are not ripe."

Evidently the will to make war was strong but the capacity was deficient. A Palestine Liberation Organization was therefore formed at the Summit Conference to fight Israel in the undefined future and destroy King Hussein's regime in the more immediate present. A Joint Arab Command was established under the command of the Egyptian General Abdul Hakim Amer to plan the eventual military assault. And instead of preventing the flow of water to the Negev by making war immediately, it was decided to choke off Israel's irrigation channels by a perverse and expensive diversion of the Upper Jordan streams into areas of Lebanon and Syria which had no need of them. The singularity of Arab policy was revealed here in typical form: the aim was not to advance Arab interests, but to harm those of Israel.

Thus the Arab Summit Conference of 1964 and 1965 sought to postpone the armed conflict in practice, to keep its prospect alive in policy and rhetoric and to stir enough irritation to prevent any long-term tranquillity. The plan sounded impressive, but its weaknesses were great. It reflected a tendency in Arab politics to prefer the form of things to their substance: the Palestine Liberation Organization was ferocious enough in pamphlets and broadcasts; its martial qualities were dubious. Indeed, the organization derived a comic-opera aspect from the spectacle of its leader. Mr. Ahmed Shukeiri's corpulent gait, pompous demeanor and blatant concern for his own vanity and comfort were reassuring to his prospective victims. Israelis reflected that if Shukeiri was their chief danger, they must be tolerably safe.

Similarly, the Joint High Command soon ran adrift. Its budget was in constant deficit, and other Arab states politely declined to have Egyptian troops on their soil. There remained the plan for diverting the Jordan at its source, but this depended on the unlikely premise of Israel's quiescence. Geographical conditions were such that the work of throttling Israel would have to be conducted within the range of Israel's tank fire, and ultimately the diversion could only be carried out by building a canal within a few hundred yards of Israel's border. In November 1964 Israel aircraft and tanks, responding to Syrian fire in a border clash, scored hits on Syrian machinery at work in the survey stage of the diversion. The Syrian project was again interrupted by Israel fire in March 1965. What grounds were there for believing that more substantial efforts to steal the water would pass unscathed?

As a design for keeping the fires of hostility aglow, the Summit decisions and all the associated apparatus were comprehensible;

as a program for Israel's liquidation, they were a failure. Within a few years, the Summit technique had played itself out; and with the Arab states polarized between the "conservatives" and the "revolutionaries", it became impossible for their leaders to meet at all.

Frustration resulting from the lack of effective action by Arab governments, headed by Nasser, and the inspiration which the Algerian example could bestow upon a Palestinian entity, led to the formation of dozens of fronts, organizations and associations of Palestinians in various countries. All of these were united by the realization that the Palestinians, who so far had been regarded as an inert mass of refugees, or—at best—puppets of various Arab governments, must play an independent role in the "liberation" of this country, not only politically, but also as a military vanguard. By terrorist activities they hoped not only to keep the conflict alive, but ultimately to engage the regular Arab armies in full-scale war against Israel.

Most of these groups, which sprouted like mushrooms, particularly in the refugee camps in Lebanon and on campuses in Western Europe, disappeared in the course of time. Some survived and continue to play a role. Thanks largely to the single-minded tenacity of its leader, one of them was destined in time to stand out among the others, in political and (to a lesser extent) in military terms. That organization, El-Fatah (reverse acronym of the Movement for the Liberation of Palestine) was founded by Yasser Arafat, a distant relative of the ex-Mufti of Jerusalem, Hajj Amin al-Husseini, in Kuwait in 1958. He was engaged as an engineer in that country, and was able to gather around him a group of like-minded Palestinian entrepreneurs and intellectuals.

Subsequently, he moved his headquarters to Lebanon, where—with some interruptions—it has been ever since. At one time he enjoyed wholehearted support from the newly established Algerian government. The Syrian Ba'ath (Socialist Renaissance) régime, counting on its ability to exploit Arafat's opposition to Nasser for its own ends, enabled him to establish training bases and secure havens for terrorist activities against Israel on its own territory. Subsequently, when the Ba'ath found that Arafat would not bend to its dictates, he and a number of his colleagues were jailed in Damascus; this in spite of the fact that in 1965—when, following another military coup a new group came to power in Syria, which had formed a renewed alliance between the Syrian government and El-Fatah—the Syrian premier warned: "We shall set the entire area afire and any Israel movement will result in a final resting place for Israel."

By 1964 the first group of terrorists organized by El-Fatah was ready to cross the border into Israel, but some of its members backed out at the last moment, and revealed the plan to Lebanese security officers supervising the camp in which they had been recruited. The members of the group were jailed, whilst El-Fatah boisterously published its Military Communiqué No. 1, relating an operation which had not in fact taken place. A few days later another group, infiltrating through Jordan, placed an explosive charge in the Israel Water Carrier in the Valley of Beit Nekofah. The small charge, which was discovered and dismantled before causing any damage, was hailed by El-Fatah as a major military achievement.

Arab governments were taken by complete surprise. An Egyptian propaganda organ in Lebanon went so far as to claim that SEATO agents connected with Israel had set up El-Fatah with the aim of offering Israel an excuse for attacking Arab states and preventing the diversion of the Jordan River's tributaries. President Nasser considered El-Fatah's operations as a direct challenge to his authority, and his attitude was echoed by Shukeiri, who claimed for the Palestine Liberation Army, which he controlled, the sole right of authorizing military operations and recruiting Palestinians. He denied Fatah's right to fix the time for the liberation. All the same, Fatah carried out ten sabotage raids during the first three months of 1965. The terrorists were mostly veterans, recruited for each operation and generously paid. Most of them came from the outer fringes of society.

By the end of 1965, Fatah raids had mounted to 35, 28 of which came from Jordan. By directing most of the effort to Jordanian territory, Fatah leaders, supported by Damascus, calculated on entangling King Hussein in border conflicts with Israel, and on relieving Syria from responsibility and consequent Israel retaliation. King Hussein, fully aware of the implications of Fatah operations for his own survival, ordered a determined campaign against the organization, particularly following Israeli warning operations against Kalkiliya, Jenin and Shuna (in May 1965) and once more in Kalkiliya, in September of the same year. So far the West Bank, the territory west of the River annexed by Jordan in 1948, had been Fatah's main recruiting and staging ground. On the local level, it had frequently been aided and abetted by Arab Legion commanders.

The stern measures taken by Lebanon and Jordan had their effect. In the first months of 1966, only nine raids were carried out, four of them from Syria. Although according to the doctrine of popular war the West Bank should have been the focal point, in practice it was effectively neutralized.

In July 1966, following careful consideration, President Nasser reversed his attitude to terrorist activities. Aware of the danger to his shaky hegemony, annoyed with Saudi Arabia because of its opposition to his operations in Yemen, he broke up the Summit of Heads of Arab States and gave the green light to Shukeiri to engage in guerilla warfare against Israel. The fact that so far Israel had refrained from reprisals against Syria, which had backed Fataḥ from the outset, encouraged Egyptian policy-makers to think that sabotage activities on a small scale would not risk all-out war or massive retaliation. *Fedayeen* operations were now undertaken by a variety of organizations, including one operated directly by the Syrians. Fataḥ could do nothing to stop the competition. The methods were always the same, directed against civilian targets. There was one exception—an ambush for military transport. In reply, Israel staged its largest raid against the village of Samoa, in the Hebron mountains, in November 1966. Forty houses of terrorist supporters were blown up; Arab Legion units dispatched as reinforcements suffered relatively heavy losses. Subsequently, the question was raised in Israel whether this raid had indeed contributed to the Jordanian government's will and ability to combat the terrorists.

In the first half of 1967, the rate of terrorism doubled—37 operations, as against 35 for all of 1965, and 41 throughout 1966. Infiltration spread along all armistice lines—13 instances from Syria, 13 from Jordan, 11 from Lebanon. Only the Egyptian frontier remained closed, even though Egypt was by now publicly supporting the terrorists and Cairo Radio was broadcasting some of their communiqués.

Sabotage operations had only a limited effect on Israel. The weight carried by the harassing tactics of the terrorists was political and psychological, rather than military and economic; their scope and seriousness fell far below those of 1954–56. From January 1965 to May 1967, 11 Israelis had been killed and 62 wounded, in 113 sabotage operations of which only 71 met with some success. On the other hand, the saboteurs had suffered no more than 7 killed and 2 captured. With time and experience, tactics had somewhat improved, but they had been more than matched by Israel preventive measures—lights, fences, guard duty and intelligence operations.

Subsequently, El-Fataḥ would boast that by its activities, and the rallying point it had provided for Palestinian Arab aspirations, it had

THE YEARS OF UNDERSTANDING 109

triggered off the Six-Day War of June 1967; this contention has been contested by Arabs themselves, and indeed, it contains at best only a few grains of truth.

To comprehend the origins of the Six-Day War one has to turn elsewhere—to the Damascus-Moscow axis. As has been stated, three of the four Arab "confrontation" countries—those with common frontiers with Israel—seemed, as late as 1967, reconciled to temporary stability. President Nasser was militarily engaged in the Yemen, and whilst never foregoing the destruction of Israel as an ultimate aim—considered "as immutable as a permanent interest," in the language of traditional Moslem diplomacy—for the time being he favored tactical restraint in relations with Israel. King Hussein of Jordan and the Lebanese government, for reasons of their own, fell in step with Nasser's policy.

The exception was Syria. In March 1963 the Ba'ath movement seized power in Damascus and in Baghdad. It had started out as a proponent of pan-Arab solidarity and opponent of separate nationhood, which it condemned as regionalism; in practice, rivalling Nasser for supremacy in the Arab world, it soon developed a separatist policy.

Since Nasser at that time was in favor of tactical restraint in relations with Israel, the Ba'ath sponsored revolutionary activism. At the Arab Summit Conferences of 1964 and 1965 and thereafter, Syria alone called for immediate confrontation. In February 1966 there was yet another revolution in Damascus, and the Syrian pendulum took an even more drastic swing to the left. The new leaders urged that war against Israel must not be a distant dream; something must be done every day to give it reality and substance. If the balance of arms made the clash of regular forces unrewarding, it could be evaded and transcended by guerrilla techniques.

In the last months of 1966, terrorist units of a few dozen men had achieved significant results: the railway between Jerusalem and Tel Aviv had been made unsafe for regular travel; residences had been blown up within a few hundred yards of the Knesset; several roads in the north could only be traversed after initial probing by mine-detecting vehicles; a youth was blown to pieces while playing football near the Lebanese frontier; four soldiers were blasted to death in Upper Galilee and six others killed or wounded in the area facing the Hebron hills. If such results could be achieved by a few dozen infiltrators, what would remain of tranquillity if the terrorist movement were allowed to expand and to deploy its activities over a broader field? The unpleasant fact was that the Syrian leaders and the terrorist groups had uncovered Israel's most vulnerable nerve. No country in the world was more exposed to a form of aggression so cheap in risk and requiring such small investment of military valor and skill.

Apart from the sabotage technique there was another area of confrontation in which Syria had a special advantage. The kibbutzim in Upper Galilee and the Jordan Valley lie in the well-watered lowlands. On the hills looking down upon them were the Syrian gun emplacements and fortified positions on the Golan Heights. Part of the area to the west of the Syrian frontier had been defined in the 1949 Armistice Agreement as a "demiltarized zone." In Israel's interpretation, demilitarization meant nothing except the absence of armed forces: it did not imply that development activity was prohibited. Syria, on the other hand, asserted that the area, being demilitarized, was of undefined sovereignty and might again come under Syrian rule in the "eventual peace settlement," which Damascus paradoxically asserted would never come. Meanwhile the Arab governments insisted that the area must be frozen in its current state. The UN resolved this obscurity with typical ambivalence. The problem of sovereignty was left in suspense so as to satisfy Syria's claim or, at least, not to refute it. On the other hand, the Security Council ruled to Israel's advantage in 1951, and again in 1953, that the demilitarized status of the zones could not be invoked to impede "normal economic development." There were two sides to the question, and this time the United Nations was on both of them.

Late in 1966 and throughout the first part of 1967, the prospect of a tranquil Arab-Israel frontier was shattered by terrorist raids and by Syrian gun bombardment of Israel's northern settlements. On 14 July 1966 a Syrian MIG-21 was shot down by an Israeli Mirage. On 15 August Syrian aircraft disabled an Israeli motor launch on the Sea of Galilee; a Syrian MIG-17 was brought down by anti-aircraft fire from the vessel, while a MIG-21 was destroyed by Mirage fighters. The Syrians were unvarying both in the constancy of their assaults and in their operational inefficiency. Yet their political logic was sound: the aim was to prevent any stabilization of the frontier, and this was without any doubt achieved.

It was clear that sooner or later Syrian pressure would either have to subside or be resisted. Because the contingencies were grave, Israel decided to exhaust other remedies. On 14 October the Security Council, on Israel's initiative, discussed the murderous Syrian attacks. After many laborious weeks, a resolution was drafted expressing criticism of Syria in terms so mild as to be almost deferential. It was sponsored by nations from five continents—Argentina, Japan, The Netherlands, New Zealand and Nigeria. It expressed "a regret at infiltration from Syria and loss of human life caused by the incidents in October and November 1966." But even this mild resolution was to be denied. The Soviet Union vetoed the resolution on the grounds that it dared to imply an absence of total justice on the side of the colonels in Damascus. A similar fate had befallen a December 1964 resolution expressing regret at the shelling of the settlements of Dan, Dafna and She'ar Yashuv by Syrian guns. As far as the Security Council was officially concerned, there was an open season for killing Israelis on their own territory, whether the killing was done by regular armies or "guerrilla" groups.

Syrian aggression and Soviet bias thus intersected at the signpost pointing to danger. Since 1953 the Soviet Union had blindly supported every Arab cause in the controversy with Israel. But from 1963 onwards Moscow added a new refinement. While all Arab nations would be aided in their conflict with Israel, special favor and protection would be offered to the "progressive" regimes in Damascus, Cairo, Republican Yemen, Algiers and Baghdad, which were aligned against the West in the Cold War. These would receive a more fervent Russian embrace than that offered to "reactionary" Arab states, such as Saudi Arabia, Jordan, Lebanon, Tunisia and Morocco. Apparently, in the Soviet vocabulary, a "progressive" Arab state should devote all its resources to arms, at the expense of social progress, and make war against Israel the central aim of its policy. An "independent" state was one whose policy was dependent on that of the Soviet Union. By these standards, Syria was the most "progressive" and "independent" of any state that had ever existed in the Middle East. It would be nurtured by the Soviet Union in all its ordeals and protected by Moscow from the results of its excesses.

The Moscow–Damascus equation was the heart of Israel's dilemma. The most violent and aggressive of Israel's adversaries operated against her from the vast shadow of Soviet protection. Syria could thus combine a heroic posture with an unheroic absence of risk.

But when the Syrian Prime Minister declared in October 1966, "we shall set the whole region on fire," events were to prove him right. The threat to Israel's security came not from single exploits but from their accumulation. Machine guns and artillery on the Golan Heights gave Syria a local advantage, while the El-Fataḥ groups, operating through Lebanon and Jordan, enabled Damascus to harass

Israel over a broader front. Israel could never predict at what part of her body the rash of violence would erupt. It could certainly expect no permanent relief from insecurity until Damascus underwent a change either of heart or ideology. Neither contingency seemed probable. On 13 March 1966 the Syrian newspaper *Al Ba'ath* had written: "The revolutionary forces of the Arab homeland, the Ba'ath at their head, preach a genuine Arab Palestine liberation on the soil of Palestine, and they have had enough of traditional methods. The Arab people demand armed struggle and incessant day-to-day confrontation through a total war of liberation in which all the Arabs will take part."

This became the central theme of Syrian policy in 1967, and no Arab government was prepared to speak or work against it.

The Six-Day War

The imminence of war was not realized as 1967 opened. Foreign Minister Abba Eban was not alone in predicting, on the eve of the New Year, that with all the uncertainties of the future, two things would not occur in that year: peace or war. Although Nasser continued the rhetoric of war, predicting that Israel would be eliminated in one stroke when the Arabs were ready, he obviously felt that the time was not yet ripe. A considerable part of Egypt's forces were still involved in the Yemen, which some called Egypt's Vietnam. Arab unity (under Egyptian domination), considered by Nasser as the *conditio sine qua non* for the definitive "War of Liberation," was as far removed as ever.

However, the Syrians supported by the Soviet Union forced Nasser's hand until he completely lost control of events. An attempt initiated by the United Nations early in 1967 to reactivate the dormant Syrian-Israeli Mixed Armistice Commission, failed dismally because of Syrian intransigence. The Syrian government did not conceal its support for the popular "War of Liberation," and the guerrilla warfare orginating from its territory. When reminded of its obligations under the Armistice Agreement to prevent hostile acts emanating from its territory, it retorted that it was not obliged to serve as the guardian of Israel's frontiers. In April 1967 Syrian interference with farming operations in the demilitarized zones bordering on Lake Kinneret was stepped up, with increased shelling of Israel border villages. On 7 April 1967, unusually heavy fire was directed by long-range guns against Israel villages, and Israel aircraft were sent into action against them. An air battle developed in which Syria lost six planes. Israel planes went on to fly over Damascus. Fearful of Israel reaction to their provocations, the Syrians tried to impress on the Egyptians their apprehension of an impending Israel attack.

The urgent Syrian request for assistance was strengthened by the appearance in Cairo on 13 May of a Soviet parliamentary delegation, which informed the Egyptians that Israel had massed some 11 brigades along the Syrian frontier. The Soviets, with an embassy in Tel Aviv, were obviously aware that this information was untrue. All the same, the Soviet ambassador in Israel presented a stern note to the government of Israel, protesting against supposed concentration of Israeli forces near the Syrian border, and a presumed Israeli plan to attack Syria in order to overthrow its government. The Soviet Ambassador refused an invitation by Prime Minister Eshkol to accompany him, there and then, to the border in order to see with his own eyes that there was no base of truth to the allegation. The ambassador stated that his mission was to protest, not to inspect. Evidently the Soviet Union was interested in pressing Syria's case for political reasons. Syria had afforded the Soviet Union her first major foothold in the Middle East and, by influencing Egypt to threaten Israel from the south, it gambled on strengthening Syria's security and hence the régime in Damascus.

Following Israel's Independence Day, which fell on 15 May, events moved swiftly. Egypt, nettled by the criticism of other Arab countries and egged on by the Soviets, was put on a war footing. In a well-publicized mass demonstration, Nasser proceeded to move large forces through Cairo en route to Sinai. Within a few days, by 20 May, some 100,000 troops, organized in seven divisions of which two were armored (with over 1,000 tanks) had been concentrated in Sinai along Israel's border. A mass hysteria enveloped the Arab world. Nasser was again at the peak of his popularity, as one Arab government after the other volunteered support and was caught up in the enthusiasm of the impending strike against Israel.

On 16 May the Government of the United Arab Republic asked for the withdrawal of the United Nations Emergency Force from its positions along the Israel-U.A.R. border, as soon as possible. Already that evening the Secretary-General of the UN, U Thant, assured the Egyptian representative that if his Government decided to withdraw the consent it had given in 1956 for the stationing of UN forces on its territory, it was "of course" entitled to do so. On 18 May, in what was to become his most bitterly discussed action, contrary to the advice of the representatives of Canada and Brazil to temporize, U Thant ordered the withdrawal of the force "without delay."

The prompt and total withdrawal of the UNEF came as a surprise, above all to Nasser himself. It deprived him of a pretext for further stalling; it also encouraged him to believe that Israel's vital interests could more easily be threatened than he had assumed. Above all, he basked in his newly-found glory of hero, savior, and leader of the Arab world. Whilst U Thant was en route to Cairo for talks with Nasser on ways of defusing the crisis, Nasser, in a speech on 22 May to officers of the Egyptian air base at Bir Gafgafa, 100 miles from Israel's border, announced his fatal decision to impose a blockade on the Straits of Tiran, closing them to all shipping to and from Eilat. "We are in confrontation with Israel. In contrast to what happened in 1956, when France and Britain were at her side, Israel is not supported today by any European Power. The world will not accept a repetition of 1956. We are face to face with Israel. Henceforward, the situation is in your hands. Our armed forces have occupied Sharm el-Sheikh. We shall on no account allow the Israeli flag to pass through the Gulf of Akaba. The Jews threatened to make war; I reply *Ahlan Wasahalan;* welcome, we are ready for war. The water is ours."

The United States and a number of other maritime nations reiterated their view that the Straits of Tiran were to be considered an international waterway through which free and innocent passage for ships of all nations must be secured. It soon became evident, however, that diplomatic action would be of no avail in an effort to make President Nasser change his decision. The proposal of establishing a naval convoy of major maritime powers to implement the assurances— given to Israel in 1957—of free and innocent passage, came to naught.

Nasser openly proclaimed that he would consider an attempt to break the blockade as an act of war, tauntingly invited Israel to try to do so, and predicted a war whose aim would be to wipe Israel off the map. His declaration was echoed in other Arab capitals, culminating in the boasts of Ahmed Shukeiri, leader of the P.L.O., that now the Arabs "would throw Israel into the sea." Nasser's self-proclaimed confidence was no doubt based on the huge amount of Soviet equipment which he had received during the preceding years, ranging from supersonic MIG–21 planes, through modern T–55 tanks with infra-red equipment, ultra-modern artillery, up to and including the most up-to-date type of ground-to-air missiles, used for the aerial defense of the Soviet Union itself. In addition, he had signed a mutual defense agreement with Syria and now, in short order, and in spite of the deep split which had been in evidence between Egypt and Jordan, a similar pact with Jordan was signed on 30 May as a result of which the Jordanian armed forces were to be put under Egyptian command. This pact was followed within three hours by another with Iraq. Contingents arrived from other Arab countries, such as Kuwait and Algeria. Thus, unlike in 1956, the principal Arab countries seemed to be politically and militarily united, and mainly supported by the Soviet Union, whereas Israel stood alone.

Israel was ringed by an Arab force of some 250,000 troops, over 2,000 tanks, and some 700 frontline fighter planes and bombers. The world looked on at what was believed by many to be the impending destruction of Israel, but no action was taken, and every effort was made by the Soviet and Arab delegates to the United Nations to minimize the seriousness of the situation and to permit developments to take their course.

Although Israel had repeatedly made it clear that the closure of the Straits would be considered a *casus belli*, entitling it to the use of force in self-defense under Article 51 of the UN Charter, the Israel government, headed by Levi Eshkol, made urgent efforts to solve the crisis by diplomatic means, dispatching Foreign Minister Abba Eban to the heads of government of the Western great powers. The mission was in vain. A sudden change in French policy emerged as the traditional sympathy of the French government for Israel disappeared against the background of a new French bid for Arab support. "*Surtout, ne faites pas la guerre,*" President de Gaulle told Abba Eban, implying that the use of force to break the blockade, not the blockade itself, constituted an act of war. His advice was to wait patiently for concerted action by the four Great Powers, action which was not forthcoming. Paradoxically, de Gaulle brought a decision to make war closer, by decreeing an arms embargo a few days later. President Johnson had condemned the blockade as an illicit and provocative act, but it soon became clear that it was not in his power to assert the claim to free passage.

Whilst the waiting period, decided upon by the Israel Government, had gained better understanding for its position and sympathy for its plight, it had by now become clear that in the last resort Israel must take action to ensure its vital interests, in fact its very survival.

On 31 May it was decided to broaden the Israel government by the co-option of representatives of the opposition party Gaḥal, Menaḥem Begin and Yosef Sapir, as Ministers without Portfolio, and of Moshe Dayan as Minister of Defense. Frenzy in Arab capitals had reached a peak. Vast crowds gathered in the streets of Cairo, shouting: "Nasser, Nasser, we are behind you. We will slaughter them; we will destroy them. Slaughter, slaughter, slaughter . . . " The official Egyptian radio took care to broadcast these bloodcurdling threats to Israel. The Egyptian General Moutaghi announced: "In five days we shall liquidate the little State of Israel. Even without a war, Israel will collapse because she will be unable to bear the load of mobilization." In Damascus a leading general cried: "If hostilities break out, Egypt and Syria will be able to destroy Israel in four days at the most."

Moshe Dayan, in his first news conference as Minister of Defense, made it clear, however, that there was no doubt about Israel's ability to win a war, if that would be inevitable.

Israel Strikes

In the early hours of 5 June, Israeli radar screens indicated the approaching flights of Egyptian planes, and armored units moving towards the Israeli border; the I.D.F. was ready. Under the command of Major-General Yizhak Rabin it had been mobilized since 20 May, facing the massed Arab armies around Israel's frontiers. Israel's citizen army had been quietly and efficiently mobilized to defend the country against the impending Arab attack, which every Arab medium of mass communication announced was imminent. That morning the Israel Air Force, commanded by Brigadier-General Mordekhai Hod, undertook a pre-emptive attack designed to destroy the Egyptian air force and its airfields. Flying in low, under Egyptian radar screens, Israeli planes effectively destroyed the Egyptian air force. Despite the high-level war alert, the Egyptians were taken completely by surprise. In less than three hours 391 planes were destroyed on the ground and an additional 60 Arab planes were destroyed in air combat, compared to

An Egyptian armored division moving into position on Israel's frontier, 17 May 1967.

Three Egyptian Mig 21s destroyed on ground in the first hours of the Six-Day War.

Israel's loss of 19 planes, some of whose pilots were taken prisoner. This brilliant air operation accorded Israel complete superiority in the air, and thereafter the Israel Air Force was free to give close combat support in the ground operations which ensued.

At 8:00 a.m. on 5 June, while the Israel Air Force was pounding Arab strength, Israel's Southern Command, under Brigadier-General Yeshayahu Gavish, moved its forces against the massed Egyptian armies in Sinai. The command, facing seven Egyptian divisions, including some 1,000 tanks, was composed of three divisional task forces, commanded by Brigadier-General Israel Tal on the northern sector of the front, Brigadier-General Abraham Yoffe in the central sector, and Brigadier-General Ariel Sharon in the southern sector.

The breakthrough was achieved in the general area of Khan Yunis-Rafa by Tal's forces. The brunt of the fighting was borne by S. Brigade, which exploited the breakthrough by overcoming very heavily defended positions at Sheikh Zuwayd and al-Jiradi and reaching El-Arish on the evening of 5 June. The other main breach of the Egyptian front was effected jointly by the divisional task forces of Yoffe and Sharon. Yoffe's group moved across a trackless desert area and introduced itself in depth into a position north of the line Nizanah Abu Ageila in the rear of the Egyptian defensive positions. The morning of 6 June found this force firmly positioned in the area of Bir Lahfan and straddling the Abu Ageila-Bir Lahfan road, in the rear of the main Egyptian positions. Meanwhile Sharon's division carried out a perfectly executed night attack on the main Egyptian positions at Umm Kataf covering the crossroads at Abu Ageila. An infantry brigade marched across the dunes and attacked the positions from the north, while at the same time a parachute brigade landed by helicopter in the gun lines of the Egyptian force concentrated at Umm Kataf and Abu Ageila, and destroyed them. By morning an armored brigade had passed through these positions, destroyed the armored elements in the area, and proceeded to break through in the direction of Jebel Libni. Meanwhile Israel forces, following through the breakthrough at Khan Yunis, fanned northward and were engaged in bitter fighting with the Egyptian and Palestinian forces in the Gaza Strip. Following the capture of Deir al-Balah, parachute and infantry forces, after a fierce struggle, finally captured the Ali Muntar Hill dominating the town of Gaza.

The First Day: Jerusalem and the Jordanian Front

On the morning of 5 June a message was sent by the government of Israel through General Odd Bull of the UN Truce Supervision Organization advising King Hussein that Israel had no design on Jordan and that, granted quiet on the Israel-Jordan border, no harm would befall his country. King Hussein, however, was unaware of the smashing defeat suffered by Egypt's air force on the same morning. From the Israel side a total news blackout was preserved, on the assumption that the Arabs, after all their boasting, would be reluctant to admit defeat, and that—in the absence of such admission—the Security Council was unlikely to intervene, thus enabling Israel to complete the task upon which it was now engaged. Egypt, seconded by Syria, was loudly proclaiming resounding (though fictitious) victories.

More directly, Hussein received similar information from General Amer, Commander-in-Chief of the Egyptian armed forces. Years later, King Hussein was to write: "We were the recipients of false information about what had happened in Egypt after the attacks by Israeli air forces on the air bases in the UAR. A new message from Field-Marshall Amer informed us that the Israeli air offensive was continuing; however, it went on to affirm that the Egyptians had destroyed 75% of the Israeli Air Force. The same communication

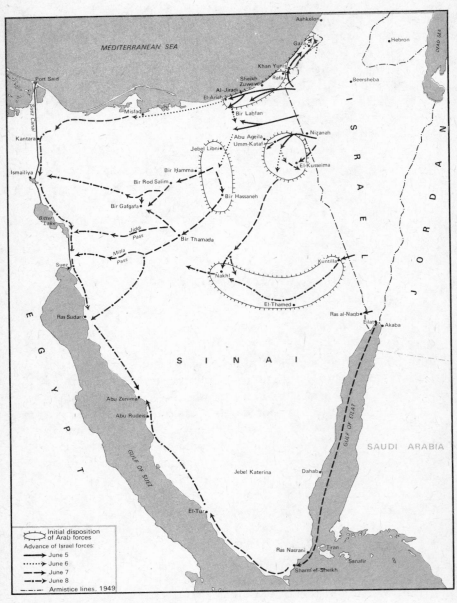

The Six-Day War, Egyptian front.

told us that the Egyptian bombers had counterattacked with a crushing assault on Israeli bases. Amer continued with the information that Egyptian ground forces had penetrated Israel through the Negev. These reports, which were fantastic, to say the least, contributed largely in sowing confusion and distorting our appreciation of the situation. At that point, when our radar signalled to us that machines coming from Egypt were flying towards Israel, no doubt crossed our minds; we were instantly persuaded that it was true. They were Israeli bombers returning after carrying out their mission against Egypt."

On the basis of this information, King Hussein decided that morning to honor his pact with Nasser, and his forces opened up a heavy barrage along the armistice lines, shelling Israeli villages and towns, including the outskirts of Tel Aviv, and sporadically bombing a number of inhabited areas.

The major brunt of the Jordanian shelling was felt in Jerusalem, where heavy indiscriminate shelling caused many casualties. At approximately 11 a.m. the Jordanian forces moved against Government House in a demilitarized area on the Hill of Evil Counsel in Jerusalem, used as UN Headquarters. Israel's Jerusalem Brigade counterattacked and drove the Arab Legion out of this position. The Israel forces maintained the impetus of their attack, taking a number of positions, including the village of Sur Bahir on the road to Bethlehem. In the meantime a reserve armored brigade broke into the Jordanian positions on the north of the Jerusalem Corridor, taking the heavily fortified "radar" positions near Ma'aleh ha-Hamishah and positions of Sheikh Abdal-Aziz. A further breakthrough was effected at Beit Iksa. These forces fanned out on the high ground north of the Jerusalem Corridor taking the Jordanian positions at Biddu and Nabi Samwil, and reaching the main road from the north to Jerusalem at Tell al-Ful south of Ramallah.

On the night of 5–6 June an infantry brigade attacked the Latrun enclave, captured the village and police post, and advanced into the Judean Hills westward along the Beit Horon road in order to join forces with the armored brigade at the gates of Ramallah. The Central Command, under Brigadier-General Uzi Narkiss, was thus committed in Jerusalem, and developing its counterattack toward the south of the city. Simultaneously, with an armored brigade followed by an infantry brigade from the coast, Central Command captured the dominant features to the north of the Corridor, and moved eastward to cut the link of the Jordanian forces based in Jerusalem with those based further north, in Samaria.

At this stage a reserve paratroop brigade under Colonel Mordekhai Gur, rushed to Central Command, was thrown into the battle on the night of 5–6 June without time for adequate preparation against the most heavily fortified Jordanian positions, which covered the northeast of Jerusalem and were manned by some two brigades. The fiercest fighting took place at the Police School and Ammunition Hill. The brigade suffered very heavy casualties before a breakthrough was achieved. It enabled the paratroopers to take the districts known as Sheikh Jarrah and the American Colony, and the Rockefeller Museum area, and to re-establish a direct link with the Israel enclave of Mount Scopus, which had been isolated from Israel by Jordanian forces for the past 20 years.

The fighting with Jordan was effectively over after less than 24 hours. At noon on 5 June Hussein had sent his reply to Israel's offer of mutual restraint, stating that since Israel had attacked the Egyptian Air Force, the Jordanian Air Force would attack Israel. At 12.30 p.m. that day, Israel planes, having returned from Egypt, attacked Jordan's two military airfields at Amman and at Mafraq. On the following day, 6 June at 12.15 p.m., the Egyptian General Riad, to whom Hussein had subordinated his forces, ordered the Jordanian forces on the West Bank actively to enter the war. The swiftness of the battle had two important results. It left the civilian population of the West Bank practically untouched by the fighting, quite unlike the situation in 1948, when Palestinian Arabs had been principal actors—and victims. Secondly, it enabled the I.D.F. subsequently to divert considerable forces to the north, to the Syrian front.

That, however, came only some days later. For the time being, Israel's Northern Command, under Brigadier-General David Elazar, participated in the battle against the Arab Legion by attacking from the north with an armored brigade supported by infantry. It broke into Jordanian-held territory on the West Bank along two axes of advance in the general area of Jenin. A heavy armored battle took place in this area, with the Jordanians reinforcing their armored forces from the Jordan Valley area. An Israel counterattack finally smashed the Jordanian opposition. After 24 hours of fighting, Israel's forces of the Northern and Central Command were converging from the south, the west and the north of the West Bank triangle in the face of very obstinate Jordanian opposition.

In the meantime, Israel's naval forces under the overall command of Rear Admiral Shlomo Erel were operating on the approaches to

Alexandria and a number of frogmen, who were later taken prisoner, succeeded in penetrating the defenses of that port and attacking a number of ships.

The Second Day: Simultaneous Fronts

The second day saw Tal's forces in the northern sector of the Sinai front fanning out from El-Arish, one force continuing along the coastal road westward toward the Suez Canal and another force, which moved southward after a tank battle to take the El-Arish air field, attacking the heavily fortified Egyptian positions at Bir Lahfan, already outflanked by Yoffe's intrusion across the desert. From this point the forces under Tal and Yoffe continued with a co-ordinated attack, Tal's task force advancing westward along the central road to the Suez and Yoffe's moving southward. Sharon's force continued to mop up in the general area of Umm-Kataf–Abu Ageila and southward toward El-Kusseima. At the same time a reserve infantry brigade, strengthened by armored forces and paratroopers, launched an attack on the city of Gaza, which was taken after very heavy fighting. The Gaza Strip was now in Israel's hands.

The battle for East Jerusalem was meanwhile being waged ferociously. To the north of Jerusalem the reserve armored brigade continued the battle to clear the area between Jerusalem and the town of Ramallah, a vital crossroads for the development of operations in the West Bank of the Jordan Kingdom. Tell-al-Ful was captured after an armored battle. Part of the brigade moved southward, taking Shua'fat to the north of Jerusalem and the general area of Givat Hamivtar, which fell after a second attack was launched against it. The hilly

Egyptian Migs attacking Israel Forces in Sinai, June 1967.

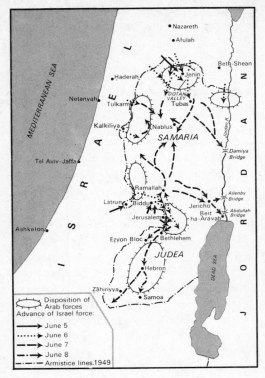

The Six-Day War, Jordani-
an front.

ground north of the Jerusalem Corridor was now safely in the hands
of the I.D.F., thus enabling it to develop its push northward. Ramallah
surrendered. Meanwhile the forces of the Northern Command
maintained their pressure southward toward the center of the West
Bank. An infantry force attacked from the west, taking Kalkiliya and
reaching al-Azzun. Jenin was finally taken by armored force at noon
on 6 June, and the armored brigade which captured the city proceeded
southward, engaging in a major armored battle at the Qabatiyya
crossroads.

An additional Israel armored force reached the Tubas-Nablus road
and was engaged by Jordan armor. At midnight the Israel forces
renewed their attack, taking Tubas and moving toward the Damiya
bridge on the Jordan River, thus sealing off the northern part of the
West Bank from possible reinforcements from eastern Jordan. The
Israel Air Force was by now free to give close ground support to the
forces on all fronts, which it proceeded to do with considerable effect.

The Third Day: The Capture of the Old City

Wednesday 7 June was to be one of the most memorable days in the history of Jewish arms. That morning Gur issued his orders for the capture of the Old City of Jerusalem, which had by now been completely surrounded by Israel forces occupying all the heights around the historic city. The Lion's Gate, otherwise known as St. Stephen's Gate, was chosen as the break-in point. A sharp battle took place there, the paratroopers, supported by a small armored force, breaking in at the Gate. Despite the fact that Israel forces had avoided attacking the Holy Places, the Arabs used the al-Aksa Mosque as a sniping post and the entire area at the Temple Mount as an ammunition dump, pleas to the contrary from the Jordanian governor of Jerusalem and the Moslem religious authorities notwithstanding. The area was rapidly cleared with a minimum of damage to the Holy Places; at 10:15 a.m. the Israel flag was raised over the Temple Mount, and the Western Wall was once again in Jewish hands. An awe-inspiring tremor passed through Israel and the entire Jewish world when, for the first time in almost 20 years, the *shofar* was sounded in front of the Wall, the most sacred place in the Jewish world.

Eastern Jerusalem would probably have fallen without battle, as a result of siege alone, but there was always the possibility of a Security Council resolution which might have frozen the military situation with the city still divided.

The armored forces which had taken Ramallah meanwhile continued toward Jericho, while the unit advancing from the direction of Nablus met with those coming from Ramallah and fanned down toward the Jordan River. At the same time the Jerusalem Brigade continued southward, taking Bethlehem and Hebron, which surrendered without a shot being fired, and also retaking the area of the Ezyon Bloc, the group of Jewish settlements which had fallen to the Arab Legion in 1948. The entire West Bank was in Israel hands.

In the south, naval forces sailing in the Gulf of Akaba took Sharm el-Sheikh and opened the Straits of Tiran. Once again shipping was free to move through the Straits to and from Israel; the belligerent Egyptian act which had precipitated the war had been set right. Meanwhile the race across the sands of Sinai was coming to its close as the three Israel divisional task forces pushed forward in an attempt to seal off Egyptian armored forces in the center of Sinai and prevent

their withdrawal to the Suez Canal. Tal's forces captured the Egyptian
military base of Bir Gafgafa and there withstood the last heavy armored
counterattack on the part of the Egyptians. Yoffe's forces captured
Bir Hassneh and rushed for the Mitla Pass in order to seal it off in
the face of the retreating Egyptian armored forces. A huge trap for
Egyptian armor was now being created. The Egyptian defenses in the
area of El-Kusseima, Abu Ageila and Kuntilla collapsed before the
advance toward Nakhl of Sharon's forces, which proceeded systematically to destroy the Egyptian forces attempting to withdraw.

The Fourth Day: Israel's Forces
Reach the Suez

On the fourth day of fighting, Tal's forces reached Kantara in the
north and Ismailia in the center and linked up along the bank of the
Suez Canal, part of Yoffe's forces advanced in a two-pronged attack
toward the city of Suez and in the direction of the Bitter Lake, while
another section of his forces moved south toward Ras Sudar on the
Gulf of Suez. Israel forces fanned southward along the Gulf of Suez
toward Abu Zenima where they linked up with the parachute forces
that had landed at Sharm el-Sheikh and were moving northward.
Desperate Egyptian attempts to break out were broken by the armored
forces and above all by the Israel Air Force, and the Mitla Pass was
converted into one huge Egyptian military graveyard. In this area
one of the largest battles in the history of armored warfare, with

Destroyed Egyptian armored vehicles near Mitla Pass, June 1967.

approximately 1,000 tanks participating, had resulted in a decisive Israel victory. The Israel flag was raised along the Suez Canal, the Straits of Tiran were open, and the Egyptian forces, which only four days before had been poised to destroy Israel, were in disarrayed retreat. They had lost about two-thirds of their 450 combat aircraft and had left behind vast quantities of equipment, including some 800 tanks.

Meanwhile in the north the Syrian forces had been continuously shelling the Israel villages along the border, and a number of infantry and armored attacks against Israel villages were beaten off.

When the Security Council, after days of wrangling, finally adopted a cease-fire resolution, Israel was first to accept it, on the basis of reciprocity. Jordan followed soon after, with Egypt, having rejected the call at first, acceding after 24 hours, on Thursday, 8 June, when the totality of its defeat had become clear to its leaders: Israel had complete control of the air, Egypt was on the verge of military collapse, and there seemed little if anything to prevent the I.D.F. from crossing the Suez Canal and advancing towards Cairo. Nasser later said: "We had no defenses on the west side of the Suez Canal. Not a single soldier stood between the enemy and the capital. The road to Cairo was open. The Egyptian plight was like that of the British at Dunkirk."

The Fifth and Sixth Days: The Golan Heights Taken

Lebanon, although joining in the clamor for war, had not taken any active steps during the preceding days. On the other hand, Syria, the most articulate advocate of war and its immediate instigator, had intensively shelled border villages, and had—unsuccessfully—attempted to capture one of them, kibbutz Dan. Except for attacks against its air force and airfields, Syria had so far gone unscathed. On 9 June there existed the possibility that the Arab country which had kindled the war would be the only one to emerge undefeated. This would have left Israel settlements in the valley below as vulnerable as before. When Syria refused to accept the cease-fire, the Israel government decided to seize the opportunity. The close link between Moscow and Damascus perforce conjured the risk of direct Soviet intervention; the majority, however, felt that if quick results could be achieved such intervention would be physically impossible, and after the event U.S. pressure would restrain the U.S.S.R.

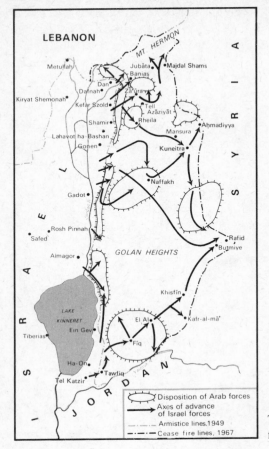

The Six-Day War, Syrian front.

Thus, on the morning of Friday, 9 June, the Israel Air Force, now freed from other fronts and having already destroyed the Syrian air force, brought Syrian gun positions under attack. At noon the I.D.F. attacked the Syrian army on the Golan Heights. All along the line the Syrians enjoyed tremendous tactical, topographical advantages, poised as they were atop a ridge whose scaling was a difficult enough undertaking under any circumstances. They had fortified their positions over the years, at tremendous cost. Clearly, after four days of fighting, no surprise was possible. Moreover, Israel forces were tired and worn after the fighting elsewhere, whereas Syrian forces were relatively fresh.

The main breaking point was chosen in the northern sector of the Syrian front in the area of Tel Azaziyat, the northernmost hinge of the

A Syrian tank in its dominating position at Tawfiq (Tel Katzir and settlements around the Sea of Galilee in background) June 1967.

Syrian system of fortifications. An infantry brigade and a reserve armored brigade bore the brunt of the attack against heavily fortified positions sited in tactically advantageous places, and the infantry forces dealt with one position after another in close hand-to-hand fighting, particularly fierce fighting taking place at Tel Fakhr. Losses were heavy on both sides. The armored force finally broke through the first line of defense, reaching the objective with two tanks in operation out of an entire battalion.

An additional armored force advanced and captured Banias, and while the breakthrough force now advanced rapidly toward Mansura and Kuneitra, a force under Brigadier-General Elad Peled, which had previously been in operation on the West Bank, attacked in the area of Tawfiq; paratroopers were landed from helicopters in depth behind the enemy lines; an additional armored force moved up through Darbashiyya; and at 2:30 p.m. on Saturday, 10 June, 24 hours after the commencement of the battle, the town of Kuneitra was in the hands of the I.D.F., which were now firmly established on the Golan Heights. The danger of Syrian shelling had been removed from the Israel villages. General Elazar's northern command forces ceased operation, following Syrian acceptance of the UN-sponsored cease-fire and established themselves along the lines reached by the advancing forces. The I.D.F. was now established on the main highway leading to Damascus.

Outcome of the War

In the course of less than six days—at the cost to Israel of 777 dead and 2,586 wounded, many of them officers, and 17 prisoners, mostly pilots, who were subsequently returned, as against 15,000 casualties and 6,000 prisoners and missing among the Arab armies—Israel, acting alone, had routed three of its neighbors who had been supported by a number of other Arab countries, in what will forever be remembered as one of the most swift and successful military campaigns ever. Well over 400 Arab planes had been destroyed, about 60 in the air; over 800 tanks had been destroyed or captured. The value of military equipment lost by the Arabs during the Six-Day War amounted to well over one billion dollars, constituting 70% of the heavy equipment of three Arab armies. The unity, cohesion, the calm discipline and determination of the people of Israel were matched by an unprecedented outburst of identification and sympathy from Jews everywhere, as well as the support of non-Jews in many countries.

Israel now held 26,476 square miles of territory previously in Arab hands: 444 square miles in the Golan Heights, 2,270 in Judea and Samaria, 140 in the Gaza Strip, and 23,622 square miles in Sinai.

A study made for the Institute for Strategic Studies in London by Michael Howard and Robert Hunter summarizes the campaign as follows: "The third Arab-Israel war is likely to be studied in Staff Colleges for many years to come. Like the campaigns of the young Napoleon, the performance of the I.D.F. provided a textbook illustration for all the classical principles of war: speed, surprise, concentration, security, information, the offensive, and above all, training and morale. Airmen will note with professional approval how the Israeli Air Force was employed first to gain command of the air by destruction of the enemy air forces, then to take part in the ground battle by interdiction of the enemy communications, direct support of ground attacks and, finally, pursuit. The flexibility of the administrative and staff system will be examined and the attention of young officers drawn to the part played by leadership at all levels. Military radicals will observe how the Israelis attained this peak of excellence without the aid of drill sergeants and the barrack square. Tacticians will stress the importance they attached in this, as in previous campaigns, to being able to move and fight by night as effectively as they did by day. Above all, it will be seen how Israel observed a principle which appears in few military textbooks, but which armed forces neglect at their peril: the Clausewitzian principle of political context which the British ignored so disastrously in 1956. The Israeli High Command knew that it was not operating in a political vacuum. It worked on the assumption that it would have three days to complete its task before outside pressures compelled a cease-fire."

7

The Years of 242

The Super-Powers

The effect of the Arab military defeat during the Six-Day War was traumatic. Just a few short days after having boasted that "this would be the final battle," President Nasser of Egypt faced the defeat of his military forces, the occupation of the whole of Sinai by Israel, with his two allies—Syria and Jordan—badly bruised, and their territory truncated. On 9 June Nasser abdicated but, following a carefully orchestrated mass demonstration, he acceded to the will of the people to carry on. His first concern was to find a scapegoat for the defeat during the war. The excuse invented was that it was not Israel, but the United States which had defeated Egypt. American and British planes—not Israeli planes—had brought about the debacle of the Egyptian air force during the first hours of the war. Outraged by this allegation, the U.S. and U.K. broke off relations with Egypt. The publication by Israel Intelligence of the tape recording of a telephone conversation conducted between President Nasser and King Hussein, in which that story had been concocted, ultimately gave it the lie.

Egypt's defeat was a major setback for the Soviet Union. In the first place it had backed the wrong horse—by instigating the war, through the misinformation of President Nasser (as Nasser himself was careful to point out in his speech of 9 June); and by promising that it would give Egypt "support in battle," and that it would not allow any power to intervene "until matters are restored to what they were in 1956," it had undertaken a special commitment to assist the Arab states, and primarily Syria and Egypt, at least in an effort to restore the situation to what it had been on 4 June 1967. Moreover, it had failed in the Security Council. Under pressure from its Arab allies, who—as the battle developed—were in urgent need of a cease-fire, it had to accept a resolution calling for a cease-fire which was not linked with any withdrawal from territories occupied during the war, let alone with compensation from the so-called Israel aggressor to his supposed victim. What it had failed to achieve in the Security Council, the Soviet Union hoped to achieve, following the precedent created in 1956, from the General Assembly of the UN, which— on Soviet initiative—was duly called into special session. Prime Minister Kosygin himself came to New York to lend the session his own personal weight. The Arab and Soviet aim was to force Israel to give up all the territories occupied during the war without the conclusion of permanent peace nor the negotiation of secure boundaries. Israel's government declined to accept this course; its intention was to maintain the cease-fire lines until they could be replaced by peace treaties establishing territorial boundaries by ne- gotiations.

The debate in the Special Session of the General Assembly started with a violent Soviet attack, accusing Israel of "treacherous" aggression and even calling on her to pay compensation to the Arab "victims". Israel's Foreign Minister Abba Eban replied: "You do not come here as accusers but as a legitimate object of international criticism for the part you have played in the somber events leading up to the war. . . . Never has armed force been used in a more righteous cause." Israel's right to use force in self-defense was as unquestionable as that of the Russians defending Stalingrad, the British expelling Hitler's bombers from their skies, and the uprising of the Warsaw Ghetto.

The U.S. lent its support to Israel's basic position. President Johnson, in a broadcast, called for a departure from the armistice to which there should be no return. Although he admitted that there should be a withdrawal, he considered it as part of a negotiated settlement, to secure borders, not to "fragile and oft-violated armistice lines." He insisted that the nations of the Middle East must sit together to work out the conditions of their coexistence. He called for free use of inter- national waterways and a just settlement of the problems of refugees. Opposition to the Soviet-Arab campaign was widespread in Europe, Latin America and in Africa. Nasser's boasts of victory and his threats to destroy Israel were still fresh in their memories. The withdrawal resolution was defeated; beyond the Arabs and the Soviet bloc only eight members of the UN supported their position. At the same time a Latin American resolution, calling for withdrawal from all the territories occupied during the war in exchange for a permanent and just peace, also failed to gain the required support. The only outcome of the Special Session was a resolution, adopted on 4 July, to oppose the union of Jerusalem, which Israel had decreed a few days earlier That resolution remained without effect. The dividing walls had come-down after almost 20 years, and there was no power in the world in a position to reestablish them.

Soviet failure to redress the balance by diplomatic means increased Egypt's insistence that its army should be re-equipped by the Soviets so as to enable it at least to exert military pressure. An unprecedented stream of Soviet equipment reached Syrian and Egyptian arsenals. Together with armaments, thousands of Russian experts and advisers began to arrive in the two countries. The Soviet Union explained to the Arabs that sophisticated and up-to-date weaponry was not sufficient: it was necessary to learn how to use it. The reason for the defeat, according to the Russians, was not in the faultiness of Russian equipment or doctrine, but in the level of Arab commanders and fighters. That came in reply to criticisms and scepticism which were heard after the war, both in Arab countries and in the armies of the Soviet bloc, concerning the quality of Russian equipment.

In Egypt alone about 3,000 Russian advisers arrived within a few months. They penetrated into all units. Although officially they were not in command, nothing was withheld from them. In ground forces the advisers went down to battalion level. More than once they told Egyptian commanders what to do, sometimes even in the presence of their soldiers, thus humiliating them publicly. Although they did not directly issue firing-orders, they were instructing the Egyptians how to shoot and when. In the air force they were to partici-pate together with Egyptian pilots in joint flights; they were omni-present in all signal and control centers, and in units responsible for particularly sophisticated weapons systems, such as ground-to-air missiles and radar equipment. Subsequently, complete Russian units began to arrive in Egypt, and certain airfields were set aside for their exclusive use.

In order to divert attention from the grave responsibility from the highest political level—his own—Nasser instituted a number of show trials for the top commanders of his armed forces, as well as for his Minister of Defense, Shams Badhran. They were accused of carelessness and of treasonable behavior. At first the trials were open. Only when General Amer, the Commander-in-Chief of the Egyptian armed forces, declared to the court that he had warned Nasser long ahead of time that the closure of the Straits of Tiran would be considered by Israel as a *casus belli* and would practically compel her to take military action, were the doors of the courtroom closed.

The newly-appointed Egyptian General Staff now devoted its serious attention to the analysis of errors made, and to their correction. Special emphasis was laid on the problem of how to avoid surprise in the future. Radar systems were reconstructed and reinforced; a closely-knit anti-aircraft system was established, including dozens of SAM 2 batteries and many hundreds of AA guns. The Egyptians realized that the destruction of their air force had been decisive for the outcome of the war. They soon engaged in an effort to find substitutes for the airfields that had been lost in Sinai, and for other airfields which now found themselves within Israeli artillery range. New airfields were established and landing strips constructed. In some places in Egypt main roads were enlarged, so that in an emergency they could become landing fields. Aircraft were dispersed over a wide area, and underground hangars were constructed for their protection. Some of the Egyptian bombers were sent to Algeria and to Sudan. Jordan engaged in similar methods, and some of the few planes which had remained in Jordanian hands were sent to airfields in other Arab countries.

Lessons were also learned in Arab countries concerning the professional operational level of their armies. A more intensive training system was inaugurated. Infantry and armor were now being trained in larger frameworks. Many hundreds of officers and pilots were sent for training to the Soviet Union and to other Soviet bloc countries. Their training included new subjects such as the crossing of water obstacles, the employment of chemical and biological weapons, and defense against them. Beyond a purely military analysis, some Arab writers and thinkers probed deeper into the character of their own people—finding evidence of superficiality, a tendency to self-illusion, and an exaggerated individualism. Arab society would have to be reformed—backward communities could not be forged into modern armies.

For the replenishment of the formations, which had been decimated by the war, and the establishment of new ones, a new mobilization policy was instituted in Egypt. In the past most students had their military service deferred, or were called up for one year only; following the Six-Day War the graduates of secondary schools, as well as students and teachers at universities, were to serve for three years. For special units the length of military service was extended up to five years. In order to provide concentrated control, divisions were grouped together in armies. From 1970, two army staffs were set up on the banks of the Suez Canal, with a 3rd Army in the rear, in the Cairo region. The improvement in armament was not only quantitative but also qualitative. In armor—for the rather outmoded T–34, T–54 tanks were substituted. Syria and Iraq as well as Egypt received more batteries of 130mm. guns, with a longer range. MIG–21s were substituted for the MIG–17s and MIG–19s, many of which had been lost during the war. Many Sukhoi 7s were dispatched, which are particularly suited to bombing and low-level penetration. The Egyptian navy was equipped with Komar rocket boats, and outmoded submarines were replaced by more modern ones.

The retraining and re-equipment of Arab armed forces was perforce a prolonged process, and it started soon after the termination of the war. With new equipment came renewed confidence. If there were any Israeli leaders who were waiting to receive a call from President Nasser—a call which would initiate direct negotiations—they waited in vain. Rather than a serious effort to negotiate a final peace settlement, the Arab leaders, assembled in a summit meeting in Khartoum in September 1967, reiterated the slogans of the old irredentist policy: "No peace with Israel; no recognition of Israel; no negotiation with Israel; no territorial bargaining with Israel." The old anti-Israel ideology was not to be changed; on the contrary, it was to be more systematically and intensively applied. It was in that vein that President Nasser declared that what had been taken by force would be returned by force. He realized that he was not ready for another round in the immediate future. He therefore outlined a three-stage program: the first phase was to be one of a firm stand, of steadfastness, to be followed by the phase of active deterrence. Ultimately, when everything would be ready, with the Egyptian armed forces reconstituted and close co-ordination instituted between it and other Arab armies, the phase of the final liberation would begin.

When the UN Security Council convened in New York in October 1967 to pick up the pieces where the Special Session of the General Assembly had left off in June of the same year, it failed to be intimidated by the intransigent stand taken by the Khartoum conference. Although the Soviet Union had not changed its position by a hairsbreadth, it realized that any effective resolution required the support of the U.S.; in addition, it had to consider the U.K., Canada, Denmark and two Latin American states, which had opposed the Soviet proposals in June for immediate withdrawal without the establishment of peace. The U.S. representative, Ambassador Goldberg, pointed out that there had never been any agreements on any lines as permanent territorial boundaries between states in the Middle East; that the armistice demarcation lines of 1949 had been specifically defined

by the signatories as provisional lines based on purely military considerations, that according to the armistice agreements could be
revised in the transition to peace. He pointed out that neither the
armistice demarcation lines in force on 4 June 1967, nor the cease-fire
lines that had emerged from Israel's victory, could be regarded as
permanent territorial boundaries: "Since such boundaries do not
exist, they have to be established by the parties as part of the peace-
making process." The text ultimately adopted, known as Resolution
242, was based on a British draft. In its preamble there is a reference
to the principle of "the non-admissibility of acquisition of territory
by force," however, it did not speak of a need to return to the armistice
lines, and did not rule out the determination of new boundaries by
agreement. It called for the establishment of a just and lasting peace
to be based on the principles of withdrawal from occupied territories—
not all the occupied territories—and the renunciation of all forms of
belligerency, blockade or organized warfare. It was stated that peace
should include "the right to live in peace within secure and recognized
boundaries." A special representative of the Secretary-General would
be appointed to "promote agreement" between Israel and the Arab
states, and to achieve a mutually acceptable settlement. The principle
of an externally imposed solution had been ruled out.

The Security Council resolution was necessarily vague, as the
result of the need to secure the support both of the U.S. and of the
Soviet Union, and the acquiescence of the Arab states and of Israel.
For the Arabs, there was the omission of the words negotiation,
recognition. For Israel, withdrawal was linked with the establishment
of peace; the establishment of secure and recognized boundaries;
the omission of the word "the" before occupied territories; and the
inclusion of agreement, to the exclusion of external adjudication.

The question whether the Security Council resolution of 22 November 1967 envisaged territorial revision, was discussed endlessly in the
years to follow. The Arab interpretation was—and is—that no territorial revision was envisaged, that withdrawal should take place
from all the territories, and should be unconditional. The Israel interpretation, based on statements made by the authors of the resolution,
was emphatically that the withdrawal envisaged by the resolution
would not be from "all the territories" but only from those which
lay beyond whatever boundaries would be ultimately agreed upon
between the parties, under the peace settlement. In 1968 the British
Foreign Secretary Michael Stewart pointed out that the omission of the
words "all the" before "territories" had been "deliberate".

However differently interpreted, Resolution 242 was ultimately accepted by Israel, Egypt and Jordan; Syria did not accept it, and the P.L.O. rejected it outright, since it mentioned the Palestinian people only under the category of refugees whose problem must be solved. Ambassador Gunnar Jarring of Sweden was appointed as Special Representative of the Secretary-General to promote agreement in accordance with the Resolution, which has served as the basis for the various, and so far futile, attempts to bring about a just and permanent peace, in the years that have passed from 1967 until the moment of writing.

El-Fataḥ Terrorism

Whilst Arab governments were still trying to find their bearings in the entirely new situation which had been created in the wake of the Six-Day War, a month before the Khartoum Conference and before the Security Council had adopted Resolution 242, El-Fataḥ had decided on its policy. On 23 June 1967, just two weeks after the cease-fire, Fataḥ's central committee met in Damascus. As they evaluated the situation, they had to admit that to the extent that their policy of "entanglement" had led directly to the war, it had indeed borne fruit—but of an unexpected sort. If, indeed, they were responsible for the outbreak of war (it has been shown above that this was at best partially true), they also shared responsibility for the crushing defeat which had been suffered by Arab armies at Israeli hands. Having been defeated, the Arab governments—including even the Syrians—had not adopted the doctrine of a popular war of liberation, which would have dictated a refusal to accept a cease-fire, and a determination to continue warfare by any possible means, even after defeat, with the concomitant risk of losing additional territory. El-Fataḥ—as well as Algeria, which was protected by distance from the risks involved in its stance—had in fact urged Syria to do so.

It would seem that at the meeting there were some who advocated a pause in sabotage activities; raids carried out across the border might provide Israel with a pretext of undertaking military operations against neighboring countries at a time when they were completely unprepared, and operations from within the occupied territories might provide the military government with an excuse for adopting stern counter-measures, which might result in a renewed exodus from these territories. Ultimately, at the urging of Yasser Arafat,

THE YEARS OF 242   139

an activist course was decided upon. Arafat argued that a revolution that ceases to act is doomed to extinction. "It is a young shoot that one must continue to cultivate."

Indeed, the fact that one million Arabs now found themselves under Israel military government seemed attractive to the protagonists of a popular war of liberation. To the extent that their models were the Viet Cong operating in Viet Nam, the F.L.N. operating against the French in Algeria, and the Mao Mao operating against the British in Kenya—here, for the first time, circumstances had been created which, at least superficially, were comparable. The attempts to involve Israel Arabs in the struggle against Israel before 1967 had proved a failure; the Arab population of the occupied territories should provide a more promising hunting ground. They had been exposed to Arab nationalist propaganda throughout all these years. Moreover, it was expected that military government would prove harsh, and by adopting counter-measures, the harsher the better, would arouse resentment amongst the population, which would play directly into the hands of El-Fatah. The fact that the Palestinians were no longer subject to Jordanian or Egyptian authority was an additional reason for Fatah to think that now was the time to seize control more easily by inciting them against Israel occupation. The fear that the UN might impose a solution, an armistice or even a peace agreement, which would ignore the nationalist aspirations of the Palestinians, provided an additional element of urgency.

The first few weeks immediately after the war provided El-Fatah with a golden opportunity. If any additional proof was required that Israel had not planned the war, it was to be found in the fact that the capture of the Gaza Strip and the West Bank, with almost one million inhabitants, found Israel's security services totally unprepared in terms of planning and preparation of manpower. Thus, when Yasser Arafat, accompanied by some of his top aides, left Damascus in July 1967, and infiltrated the West Bank to set up his headquarters in Nablus—in the casbah—he was able at first to operate practically without any hindrance. His plan of operation was two-pronged: on the one hand, the organization of a network of saboteurs, who could undertake terrorist operations, preferably within Israel itself, so as to avoid any possible linkage and subsequent retaliation against the local population; and, on the other hand, the stirring up of the local population so that it would engage in a campaign of civil disobedience to the occupation authorities.

Taking to heart the words of Mao Tse-tung that resistance fighters must feel like fish in water amongst the local population, he aimed at the quick organization of a local government that would place Fataḥ in command of the villages, granting it control, at least at night, over whole sections of the West Bank. He believed that he would be able to create a terrorist enclave in the West Bank that would defend itself against Israel and slowly expand until it encompassed the entire country. In the middle of September 1967 sabotage activities were initiated. From then on, there was a rise of sabotage operations—13 in September, 10 in October, 18 in November and 20 in December 1967. Early efforts were directed mainly against civilian targets—factories, private homes and cinemas in Israel: in the Sharon, in Jerusalem, and once even in Tel Aviv, the first and largest all-Jewish city. When the Israelis reinforced their vigilance along the green line, Fataḥ began to operate within the occupied territories.

At first, Fataḥ was backed only by Syria. Egypt was busy stabilizing its government and was preoccupied with its problems along the Suez Canal. Jordan openly opposed the terrorists. Pro-Egyptian notables publicly adopted a reserved stand towards Fataḥ, repeating the old argument that its activities might lead to another untimely war. It was only in October, when a Fataḥ delegation visited Cairo, that Egypt began to change its position. Having adopted the three-phase policy, Nasser found that terrorist activities—particularly as long as they did not entail the risk of retaliation against Egyptian territory, since by now they could not possibly have operated from within territory under Egyptian control—might be helpful in filling the military gap in the first phase, that of the firm stand, and the second, that of active deterrence.

The policy adopted by the Israel military government, however, failed to play into Fataḥ's hand. On the contrary, the first encounter with the Israeli—whether he be soldier, tourist, buyer or seller—was a traumatic experience in the opposite sense. The average Israeli failed to live up to the stereotype which had been inculcated into Arab minds during the previous decades. Arab administrators, teachers and policemen were called upon to continue their functions as before. The Jordan bridges had been dynamited on the fourth day of the war. Just a few days later new bridges were established alongside the old ones. A policy of open bridges was initiated, with two objectives: to enable the population to continue its life as heretofore, as much as possible, through maintaining commercial and family ties with the East Bank of the Jordan, and through Jordan—with the rest of the Arab world. On the other hand, it was designed to prevent the terrorists from feeding on the discontent of the local population, and thus to isolate the terrorists so that the struggle against them would not injure the attempt to create peaceful coexistence between the Palestinians and the Israeli administration. Moshe Dayan, the Minister of Defense, stated his views during a visit to a farm near Jericho: "We do not demand that you fight the terrorists: that is our responsibility. Only you must understand what Fatah means for you. You will be hurt indirectly by any deterioration in the situation, and anyone personally involved in these activities will suffer direct consequences."

In September 1967 the military government instituted a selective policy of demolishing the homes of terrorists and their collaborators, in accordance with the Emergency Regulations in force under the previous Jordanian rule. Altogether some 500 houses were demolished as a result of that policy. It provided El-Fatah with an outstanding propaganda plank against Israel, which was to be echoed at the UN and elsewhere for years to come. However, it proved effective in isolating the terrorists from the local population. The terrorists soon found that they could not count on support from villages: on the contrary, some of the villages actively organized in order to keep terrorists out of their domain. The terrorists had to move into caves in the mountains. When the Israelis conducted a survey of caves throughout the West Bank, the terrorists were forced into the cities, particularly into the casbah of Nablus. Captured terrorists soon led the investigators onto the trail of their former colleagues. By November, Fatah leaders were forced to admit in public that their organization had suffered "relatively great losses" in killed and captured. By the end of the year, it had become clear that the attempt to instigate a popular war of liberation from inside the occupied territories had proved a failure.

Village notables—the traditional leaders—and the merchant class which was keen on reaping profits from the increasing commerce with Israelis banded together to curb the terrorists. Fatah threats against such leaders proved of no avail. Sheikh Jaberi, the mayor of Hebron and the outstanding leader in his region, made it clear that he considered it his responsibility to prevent a repetition of what had happened in 1948 as a result of the mistaken policies of Arafat's predecessor and relative, the Mufti of Jerusalem. He considered it his main task to prevent another exodus. In order to achieve that, he considered it his duty to maintain quiet in his region, and to establish a working relationship with the military authorities for the benefit of the population of the region. Hebron, the scene of the massacre of 1929, would (he claimed) have been exposed to particularly violent Israeli counter-measures if it had provided the Israel government with even the slightest pretext.

The Fataḥ leadership came to realize that sabotage activities required political backing. Passive resistance in the form of boycotts and strikes, and political resistance headed by some party or movement to direct the public and to channel its emotions, were necessary conditions for the success of sabotage activities. Lacking those two conditions, sabotage activities from within the West Bank could never develop into a large-scale movement with a lasting military and political impact. Towards the end of 1967, the center of Fataḥ activities therefore moved from the West Bank to bases beyond the Jordan. The emphasis was shifted to raids and sporadic fire from across the Jordan, directed at settlements in the Jordan Valley and the Aravah. Fataḥ groups, which were still active sporadically in the West Bank, rather than serving as the nucleus of a popular revolution, continued activities at a low level in order to keep the flame of revolt from dying out, hoping for better times.

Yasser Arafat managed to escape the fate of many of his men. Towards the end of his stay on the West Bank, following a major raid into the casbah of Nablus, as a result of which 33 terrorists were captured and large quantities of arms discovered, he had transferred his headquarters from Nablus to the villa of a supporter in Ramallah. One night in the fall, Israel security forces encircled the villa and broke into it. They found a warm bed, and boiling tea, but Arafat had managed in the nick of time to jump through the window and to hide in a private car parked on the road. Once the investigators had departed, Arafat turned east and crossed the Jordan for the last time. He left behind him about 1,000 terrorists detained and 200 dead. To justify the disaster, Fataḥ's organ, the *Palestinian Revolution*, claimed that "every revolution is measured by the number of its casualties".

Some time later an Arab writer summed up the differences between Palestine (Israel) and Algeria, which according to him account for the failure of the Popular War of Liberation on the West Bank. In Algeria, he stated, there were eight Algerians to one Frenchman; in Israel, one Palestinian to two Israelis; there was one French soldier to sixteen Algerians, and one Israeli soldier to every four Palestinian fighters; Algeria has 1,000,000 square km., Israel only 70,000; Algeria has forests and mountains, whereas all parts of Israel are easily accessible; the French did not wish to drive out the Arabs, unlike the Israelis;

Algerian rebels had strong outside bases, while Palestinian terrorists had none.

The last two statements are obviously incorrect. Whilst the Jordanian government was not inclined to be hospitable to terrorist organizations prior to the Six-Day War, following that war it did co-operate, though reluctantly, with their organizations. Humiliation, the desire for revenge, the pressure of other Arab countries, as well as the increasing influence of Palestinians in Jordan combined to strengthen the links between the Arab Legion and the terrorist organizations. The Arab Legion, assisting terrorists in their attempts to infiltrate into Israel and covering their withdrawal, gradually lost control over considerable parts of the Jordan Valley. The presence of Iraqi forces, who maintained autonomy in Jordanian territory, lent additional weight to terrorist organizations. Even though the Legion was in no hurry to cross swords with the Israel army it was dragged into confrontations under these circumstances.

Local incidents with terrorists soon developed into tank and artillery battles. The Israel air force also joined the fray, but casualties inflicted on the Arab Legion did not deter the terrorists from their activities. Mortar fire from across the Jordan against Jewish settlements in the Beisan and Jordan Valleys became a common occurrence. Shelters had to be constructed in all border areas. In February 1968 mortar fire against two kibbutzim in the Beisan Valley soon escalated into an artillery battle raging all along the Jordan River. Israel fighter planes hit Jordanian artillery batteries, military bases and outposts. A major irrigation project was damaged in a number of places, and put out of action. Jordanian villagers deserted their villages in the valley. A state of emergency was decreed throughout Jordan. The King, now finally aware of the danger to his government resulting from the unbridled activities of the terrorists, published a warning that in the future he would sternly react, if the terrorist organizations would undermine his authority. However, he was no longer a free agent, but rather a prisoner of his own commitments to other Arab countries. Two days later, he went back on his word and once more supported the terrorists—a move for which he was to pay dearly.

Parallel to these developments, infiltrations across the Jordan into Israel-held territory were stepped up. Israel took counter-measures. As time went on, it perfected a defensive system all along the border, which included barbed-wire fences separated by mine fields; various electronic warning devices and booby traps; machine-guns operated automatically by infra-red rays; dust roads which facilitated the detection of terrorist tracks; fortified strongholds capable of holding their ground independently for long periods of time; and patrols all along the front line and ambushes along the saboteurs' presumed axes of movement. As time went on, not only did it become increasingly more difficult to infiltrate into the West Bank, but the likelihood that those few who managed to infiltrate could escape undetected became smaller and smaller.

However, such defensive measures were not sufficient. Active operations against terrorist bases in the Jordan Valley were decided upon. The main base was the village of Karameh. When the terrorists moved in, the population of that refugee town was about 7,000 out of its former 17,000 inhabitants. Arafat and his assistants set up shop in a primary school for girls in the heart of the village. All services including water and electricity were operated by the terrorists themselves. Karameh and its neighborhood were split into separate camps, each with its own supplies and equipment. The terrorists dug a number of underground bunkers and built large storehouses. The entire area was surrounded by a system of interconnecting trenches and dugouts. Nearby a dry riverbed was used for exercises with live ammunition. Thus Karameh had become a supply and training base, a headquarters, and a point of departure for infiltration.

On 21 March 1968 Israel forces forded the Jordan River with the aim of liquidating this terrorist base, the largest operation undertaken by the I.D.F. since the war. Tanks, parachutists, artillery, engineers and air force participated. The advancing forces crossed the bridges at dawn, and liquidated the forward positions. Artillery moved further east in order to isolate the battle area. The capture of the village itself was the mission of a parachute unit, supported by armor. An additional parachute unit, helicopter borne, blocked the approach and escape routes to and from the village. The capture of the village and the outlying camps was completed around 8 a.m., and detained terrorists were being transferred into Israel. The disengagement, however, took a number of hours until evening fell. Resistance was stronger than had been expected. The Israel force had suffered 28 casualties killed, and 69 wounded; Arab casualties amounted to 150 terrorists and 25 Arab Legion soldiers killed, and 130 persons were detained and brought back to Israel.

A parallel operation took place southeast of the Dead Sea. The objectives were the village of Safi and the adjoining police station, locations which had been well known to the Israel army ever since the War of Independence. Enemy casualties here amounted to 74 killed, with no casualties for the Israelis. The blow inflicted on the terrorist base in Karameh forced Arafat to move his base further east to a mountain area, and to disperse his forces further away from the Jordan River. It also served as a further demonstration to the Jordan government, that in the absence of effective counter-measures on its part, it might itself be the victim of the train of events started by the terrorists.

On the other hand, the battle at Karameh was exploited to the full by Fataḥ propaganda. For a whole day they had engaged considerable Israel army forces, and they had inflicted considerable casualties. For the first time, an Israel tank was left behind when the Israelis withdrew, a trophy which was publicized throughout the Arab world. In Fataḥ's struggle for recognition as a military factor to be reckoned with, distorted versions of the battle of Karameh, which made it seem that the Israeli withdrawal was forced by the Arabs, rather than part of the original battle plan, henceforward played an important part.

Some months later, in July 1968, the Palestinian National Council convened in Cairo for its fourth session in order to amend the Palestinian National Covenant originally adopted at a meeting in 1964, at which the P.L.O. had been established. The number of delegates had been reduced from some 400 to 100. Ahmed Shukeiri and his fellow dignitaries, who had been thoroughly discredited as a result of the Six-Day War, were conspicuously absent. Their place was taken, to a large extent, by men who, in Arafat's words, were sitting in trenches rather than in offices. Representatives of almost all the Palestinian organizations existing in Arab countries, including all the *fedayeen* outfits, participated. Fataḥ and the *fedayeen* organizations affiliated to it had 37 representatives; the Marxist Popular Front, led by George Habash, had ten. Fataḥ's style was recognizable in the new covenant. The amended version was seriously considered and weighed.

The main principles set down in the covenant now adopted were as follows. In the Palestinian state only Jews who lived in Palestine before 1917 will be recognized as citizens; only the Palestinian Arabs possess the right of self-determination, and the entire country belongs to them; any solution which does not involve total liberation of the country is rejected, and this aim cannot be achieved politically, only militarily; warfare against Israel is legal, whereas Israel's self-defense is illegal. This covenant remains the basic charter of the Palestine Liberation Organization at the time of writing.

Whilst the covenant proclaimed military action as a *sine qua non* for the liberation of Palestine, the military position of the P.L.O. and its affiliates was weak. The Israel attack against Karameh had forced Fataḥ into the mountains; the Israel Air Force pursued it into that area; and from August 1968 onwards Fataḥ could no longer feel safe in its bases further east. Thenceforward, the terrorists mingled with the population of Jordan, avoiding major separate concentrations, which provided perfect targets for Israel's Air Force. They established their bases in refugee camps, in cities and in villages, or in caves and groves. The control of terrorists by their commanders became more complicated. Successful operations diminished, and invented victories widely broadcast often took their place. The absence of capital punishment in Israel now helped to save blood, since many terrorists, once discovered, preferred to surrender rather than fight to the bitter end.

It was to a large extent as a result of Fataḥ's failure to incite the popular war of liberation inside the occupied territories, and to conduct a war of attrition from bases in neighboring countries, particularly from Jordan, that, soon after the Cairo meeting, it began to resort to new tactics, which have been prominent ever since—that of hijacking airplanes. On 22 July 1968, an El Al plane en route from Rome to Lydda was taken over by Arab terrorists and landed in Algeria. Public opinion in the west was practically unanimous in the condemnation of this new extension of the Israel-Arab conflict, but international organizations—primarily the UN—proved ineffectual. Algeria held on to the crew and to the Israeli passengers, pending an arrangement through the mediation of the Italian government. The plane and its passengers were finally released on 31 August 1968. Fifteen Arabs detained in Israel were set free as a "gesture" to the mediators.

The War of Attrition

Throughout this period, from the end of the Six-Day War to the end of 1968, the armistice lines with Egypt and with Syria were, on the whole, quiet. As on previous occasions, before and after wars between Israel and its Arab neighbors, the Palestinian terrorist movement held the center of the stage. The quiet, however, was broken on a number of significant occasions. As early as 1 July 1967, the first exchange of fire took place between the I.D.F. and Egyptian forces. Although the dividing line between Israel and Egypt along the Suez Canal was clear, its delineation in the northern sector was still nebulous.

North of Kantara, there is a marshy area, where water and dry land are not clearly distinguishable, and along the Suez Canal there is only a narrow strip of land, along which there is a single dirt road leading north to Port Said. Since it was impossible for Israel to establish strongholds along that strip, Israel control was exercised primarily through patrols. Egypt established a position east of the Canal, and local fighting broke out. On 8 July Egypt brought planes into action, in addition to artillery. The intervention was ineffective, but it was an obvious reminder that Egypt was not willing to accept the status quo established following the battle. Later that month two Egyptian torpedo boats were sunk by an Israel ship.

On 11 July Israel and Egypt agreed to the stationing of UN observers on both sides of the Suez Canal, but the problem of the dividing line in the Canal was still open. Israel's position was that the line would pass in the center of the Canal, and shipping would be based on reciprocity: if one side could use boats in the Canal itself, the other side would have the same right. Since Egypt was using small boats in various sectors of the Canal, Israel did the same. Egyptians opened fire, which soon brought about Israel retaliation. The Israel Air Force participated, and attacks soon moved further south. In the city of Suez, the refineries were set on fire, and in Port Ibrahim coastal artillery batteries were hit. Several Egyptian planes were downed whilst attempting to intercept Israel planes. A new wave of refugees began, comprising residents of the Egyptian cities on the west bank of the Canal who now decided to abandon their homes. At the end of July an agreement was reached for mutual abstention from shipping along the Canal.

Local firing continued in the following months. Although the cumulative result was a steady increase in refugees, Egypt continued firing, in an evident effort to prevent a freezing of the situation along the Suez Canal. On 21 October 1967 an Israel destroyer, the *Eilat* was sunk by an Egyptian torpedo boat using sea-to-sea missiles. Of the 199 crew members, 47 were either dead or missing. In a clear warning against a repetition of similar actions, a massive Israel attack paralyzed the Egyptian refineries, petro-chemical industries, and oil tanks in Suez. There followed a lengthy period of quiet in the south. The prisoners of war of the Six-Day War were exchanged in the course of January 1968—6,000 on one side, and a handful on the other. The Egyptian prisoners had been more than well treated by Israel's authorities during their captivity, in the hope that by letting them know what Israel really represented, they would go back to their own country in a different mood and with a different attitude towards Israel.

In February the Israel submarine *Dakar* was lost *en route* from Portsmouth to Haifa. Until this day no-one knows where and how she was lost. Its 69 men have no tomb.

It would seem that in September 1968 Nasser felt that he was ready for the second phase—that of active deterrence, which was conceived as the preliminary for the third and final phase, that of liberation. Egyptian artillery opened up fire against Israel air forces along a front of 65 miles (100 km.). This fire was not only designed to give Egyptian soldiers a renewed feeling of self-confidence; its objective was to kill Israeli soldiers. It was based on the assumption that Israel, wishing to defend itself, would be compelled to devote forces and means over and above its capacity. The Egyptians, advised by the Russians, had concluded that Israel's successes in the past involved quick and decisive moves, and wars which lasted for a few days, for which Israel was able to mobilize its maximum forces. The assumption now was that Israel's army, being mainly based on reserves, would not be able to withstand a lengthy war of attrition, along more or less static lines. Not only would the economic burden be unbearable but—above all—constant casualties would undermine morale. This new concept indeed showed an understanding for Israel's mentality. In Israel each soldier killed was the occasion for national mourning; each man belonged to the national family; his picture and his epitaph were published in all the newspapers. Egypt, with its tremendous superiority in manpower, and its different concept, was much better able to withstand continuous casualties in a war which subsequently became known as the War of Attrition.

The results of the first artillery duels were indeed not unfavorable from the Egyptian viewpoint. Ten Israeli soldiers killed and 17 wounded on the first day; 15 killed and 34 wounded in a subsequent incident, about one month later. Israel artillery reacted against the Egyptians, showing up once more the vulnerability of the Egyptians on the west bank of the Suez Canal, with its concentration of population, and of oil and other installations.

It soon became clear that fortifications which had been set up on the east bank of the Canal were not sufficient to withstand a concentrated artillery barrage. The winter months of 1968–69 were dedicated to a concentrated effort to reinforce those fortresses; the rails of the abandoned railway line leading from Kantara to El-Arish were used to provide each fortress with bomb-proof roofs; together with sandbags and concrete they provided constructions which subsequently proved their ability to withstand continuous and concentrated artillery fire.

It was clear from the outset that merely returning fire was not the answer to this new tactic. The I.D.F. thereupon embarked on raids deep into Egypt, in order to prove to the Egyptians that once they opened fire the I.D.F. was not bound to react in the same method, time or place. The first raid was directed against Naj Hammadi, on 31 October 1968. Some 236 miles (350 km.) from the nearest Israeli area, a bridge, a dam, and a transmission station on the Aswan-Cairo high power line were blown up. In order to defend military objectives in the interior of Egypt, Nasser now established a popular militia. Once he felt that his rear areas were safe, in the spring of 1969, he embarked on a continuous War of Attrition. The first incidents caused few casualties to the I.D.F. The newly fortified fortresses proved able to withstand the fire. This did not deter Egypt. From now on, for 16 months until the standstill cease-fire in August 1970, there was continuous war with Egypt—no longer isolated incidents, but a war with the objective of causing casualties to the I.D.F., to lower its morale, to cause despair and sow confusion among civilians, to destroy war matériel, and to impose on Israel an insufferable economic burden.

Egyptian fire varied in intensity—sometimes it came like hail, in order to shock Israeli troops; at other times, it came in trickles, in order to wear them out; or it latched on to anything found moving in the area, in order to interfere with normal life. Although the fortresses themselves were hardly affected, movement between them was often difficult; and if that was the situation along the asphalt roads, wherever they existed, it was even more so along the mud tracks. There, every moving vehicle immediately indicated its position by a cloud of dust, particularly in the northern sector, with its single track, leading to Israeli positions, within artillery range of the Egyptians. In order to minimize casualties, Israeli fortresses were constructed only in a number of selected positions, facing the main invasion routes to the interior of Sinai. The area between the fortresses was covered by patrols, and by armor, which now had to get used to a new role. No longer was it engaged in fast movement and fire; Israeli tanks had to dig in at prepared positions in order to face the possibility of Egyptian raids. Such raids were not infrequent.

A major objective of Egyptian armor at the time was to capture at least one Israeli fortress; most likely there were no illusions that they could thereby achieve a significant change in the military situation, but it was considered vital for recovering the national honor, and wiping out the humiliation of the Egyptian army. A series of raids with that objective took place during the following months. All of them were repulsed, and not a single Israeli fortress fell in the course of the War of Attrition.

Israeli raids had become more frequent and bold. Power lines in the interior of Egypt and coastal stations along the west coast of the Gulf of Suez were the main targets, attacked either by airborne or by naval units. The artificial and well-fortified Green Island, just west of Port Tuwfiq in the Gulf, was attacked in July 1969, in one of the most difficult and daring operations of the war.

The Egyptians were unable to achieve their main objective. Israeli soldiers coming home on leave were sometimes shocked by the sheer normality of life in the rear—but they soon realized that it was precisely this normality that they had been fighting for so successfully. On the other hand, Israel's objectives were not achieved either. Successful defense of the line of fortresses combined with daring raids into Egyptian territory were not sufficient to force the Egyptians to give up the war. Thus, on 20 July 1969, Israel's Air Force was brought into play in an unprecedented attack against Egyptian positions along the Suez Canal. Anti-aircraft installations, fortifications, headquarters, munitions and petrol dumps were attacked. Attempts to intercept Israeli planes ended in failure.

This type of operation entailed a calculated risk. As has been seen, there were thousands of Russian advisers dispersed throughout Egypt, particularly active in signals and anti-air installations. The extent of the Russian commitment to Egypt was an open question; the risk, however, had to be taken, in order to enable the I.D.F. to continue to defend its positions along the Suez Canal with a minimum of casualties.

The intervention of the I.D.F. caused havoc and confusion amongst the Egyptians, but they continued the war. In September additional Israeli raids were undertaken. After Israeli frogmen had sunk 2 Egyptian torpedo boats which might have endangered the success of the main operation, Israeli landing craft moved across the Bay of Suez, and—for the first time—Israeli armor was landed on the opposite, Egyptian side of the Gulf. The armored column set out south, and along dozens of kilometers of coastal road, it destroyed 12 Egyptian outposts, raided an Egyptian army camp, and hit other military targets, including radar installations. Following the Israeli raid, some senior Egyptian officials, including the chief of staff and the commander of the navy, were relieved of their posts. Whilst the foreign press was announcing

Israel's invasion of Egypt, the Egyptian authorities had only nebulous information concerning the raid, because, in their shame, the local commanders did not give accurate reports to their superiors. Egyptian attempts to raid Israeli positions resulted in the loss of 11 of their planes on the following day.

Further Israeli raids took place during the remaining weeks of 1969, culminating, on Radar Night, in the most spectacular raid of all. This time the objective was not to destroy Egyptian radar stations, but to take the equipment of one of them back to Israel. The weight of the installation was in the neighborhood of seven tons. The area of operation was effectively isolated by air force bombardments of a neighboring army camp, to gain the considerable time which was necessary to carry out the complicated operation. The radar wagons were anchored in the ground, and it was very difficult to cut the steel cables without damaging the installation itself. Finally its two radar wagons were secured to the belly of two helicopters. For the first time, sophisticated Soviet radar equipment had fallen into alien hands.

These raids, coupled with Israel Air Force attacks, which had become more deadly and effective ever since the first Phantoms started to arrive in September 1969 on the basis of an agreement reached between Prime Minister Golda Meir and President Johnson, brought Egypt, towards the beginning of 1970, to a watershed. Its anti-aircraft installations, artillery, radar and SAMs had been severely damaged, and the interior of Egypt was no longer sealed against Israeli air penetration. An Israeli plane overflying Cairo and creating a supersonic boom brought this reality home to millions of Egyptian civilians, Egyptian propaganda concerning fictitious victories notwithstanding. President Nasser was faced with a choice between stopping the war and talking to Israel, or inviting deeper and more widespread Soviet involvement. Early in January he flew to Moscow, on a secret mission. He had evidently decided on the second course.

At the same time, Israel's Air Force began attacks against targets in the interior of Egypt, including ammunition dumps, supply bases, headquarters, and military installations in the Cairo region, where the preparations for war against Israel were being made. The citizens of Cairo witnessed with their own eyes how Israel's attacks came closer and closer to the city without reaching the city itself. The Egyptian army no longer contemplated the third phase—that of liberation, liquidation of aggression; it was concerned with the outcome of the second phase. Egyptian army bases in the Cairo region were evacuated; the pilots' school, the naval academy, and the cadet course moved to Sudan or Libya. Israel's aerial superiority was now being recognized and Egyptian planes avoided direct encounters with Israel rivals. Simultaneously, Egyptian artillery activity along the Suez Canal gradually died down. Another Israeli raid was carried out in January, this time against the Island of Sadwan near the entrance to the Gulf of Suez, some 19 miles (30 km.) from Sharm el-Sheikh—an important base for the Egyptian navy and commandos.

The 9th of March was the nadir of the War of Attrition, from the Egyptian viewpoint. From this time, Egyptian defenses on the west bank of the Suez Canal were no longer effective, with the result that Israel planes could penetrate Egyptian air space at will. Nasser once more turned to his Soviet allies, who now undertook to reconstruct the anti-aircraft system, but this time, in view of their shaken confidence in the ability of Egyptian experts, the system was to be manned by Soviet crews. The new system was made up of improved SAM–2 missiles, and SAM–3s, to intercept low-flying aircraft. Israel was fully aware of the risk involved, but could not turn back. A determined effort was made to prevent the reconstruction of the anti-air system by daily raids. Now the Soviets went one step further and, committing themselves to the defense of the Egyptian heartland, Soviet squadrons were brought into play for the first time in the history of Israel-Arab warfare.

In April 1970 Israel's Minister of Defense, Moshe Dayan, declared that from then on Israel would have to find a *modus vivendi* with the Russians—but in Egyptian skies, not in Israel skies. "I do hope that they will be located in places where we will not be compelled to attack them."

Egypt, with its newly-found sense of confidence and security, in that its rear was protected, once more attempted to take the initiative. Egyptian planes penetrated into Sinai, dropping bombs in various places; the effectiveness of these attacks was limited, and Egyptian losses in planes not inconsiderable. Artillery fire was stepped up; an Israeli fishing boat was scuttled; 14 Israeli soldiers were killed and two kidnapped by an ambush in the northernmost sector of the Suez Canal line. Israel retaliated with fierce air strikes.

The Soviets, in their attempt to reconstitute some sort of anti-aircraft defense system, no longer used previous positions. They now brought forward a number of missile batteries up to 15 miles (25 km.) from the Canal, in a narrow sector which was only 44 miles (70 km.) long, but the missiles were so placed that they covered each other, and penetration became more difficult. Five Israel planes were brought down in attempts to neutralize the new system.

In July the Russians finally arrived at the conclusion that it was no longer enough to use Russian pilots for the protection of Egypt's heartland; they now brought Russian pilots into the frontline to intercept Israel planes. In the one and only air encounter between Israeli and Russian pilots, four planes piloted by Russians were brought down. Both the Soviet Union and Israel, each for its own reasons, refrained from publicizing the battle. However, the Russians were fully aware of the fact that they could not continuously commit their prestige in Egypt to a lost war. As late as 14 June Nasser had declared that he was willing to accept a cease-fire provided Israel would undertake to withdraw from all occupied territories. About a month later, he was prepared to accept an American initiative which called for a cease-fire and a stand-still along the Suez Canal, coupled with the acceptance by Israel of the principle of withdrawal, within the framework of Resolution 242.

That American initiative, started a few months earlier by Secretary of State William Rogers, came about as a result of the American realization that Ambassador Jarring's mission, in the course of which he had shuttled back and forth between Middle Eastern capitals throughout 1968 and 1969, had been a failure; on the other hand, increasing Russian involvement in the War of Attrition had increased the risk of a concomitant American involvement and a Big Power confrontation, in which neither the U.S. nor the U.S.S.R. was inter- ested.

Thus, on 19 June 1970, Secretary of State Rogers formally approached Israel, Jordan and the U.A.R. with a three-point proposal: the appointment of representatives to confer through Ambassador Jarring on the establishment of a just and lasting peace; indication of their acceptance of the Security Council resolution of 1967; and observation of the cease-fire resolution for at least 90 days. Whilst Syria remained intransigent, President Nasser reluctantly accepted. His War of Attrition and siege had failed. He had not been able to persuade the U.S. to impose an embargo on Israel, while arms from the Soviet Union continued to flow into Arab states. For Israel the acceptance of the American initiative was difficult; it involved a compromise of principles which had been continuously upheld in Israeli policy up to that time. The proposed negotiation would be indirect, at least in its first phase; the cease-fire would be temporary; and any prolongation might have to be bought by additional concessions. On the other hand, the majority found it urgently necessary to start a dialogue, and what might have been more important, to maintain U.S. dedication to the maintenance of Israel's strength, and to the deterrence of external intervention. On 4 August 1970, the Israel government therefore accepted the American initiative. This brought about the break-up of Israel's government of national unity. Menaḥem Begin, leader of the center-right Gaḥal party, and former commander of the I.Z.L., led his six ministers out of the cabinet, objecting primarily to Israel's acceptance of the principle of withdrawal without any evident return.

The events of the first few days after the cease-fire came into effect, on 8 August 1970, seemed to bear out Begin's premonitions. Within a few days the Soviets and the Egyptians re-established a complete system of anti-air missiles along the Suez Canal, contrary to the terms of the agreement, something they had been unable to do during the weeks and months preceding the cease-fire. The U.S. for a while denied the facts, and a public debate ensued between Israel and the U.S.; however, the evidence was too clear to be ignored. The Israel Cabinet unanimously decided to suspend participation in the Jarring talks with Egypt until the previous situation west of the cease-fire line was restored. Ultimately the U.S. called on the Soviet Union for rectification of the violated status in the stand-still zone. When this brought no response, the U.S. expedited increased arms supplies to Israel in an effort to restore the equilibrium.

Although the cease-fire was originally limited to only three months, it was prolonged for another six months; then, without official prolongation, it lasted for a number of years—in fact until the outbreak of the Yom Kippur War.

The Northern Borders

While the main burden of fighting had been on the Egyptian front, the Syrian front was relatively quiet. Syria had reluctantly accepted the cease-fire of June 1967; it had rejected the Security Council resolution of November of the same year. While giving continuous support to the terrorists, both in terms of propaganda and by providing bases for training and supplies, it evidently preferred the terrorists to operate somewhere else, in order to avoid the risk of Israeli retaliation. However, the deterioration in Egypt's position presented Syria with a dilemma. Continued abstention from action would diminish its prestige and open it to attack for leaving its ally in the lurch. Thus, in April 1969, a terrorist attack inspired by Syria took place against an Israeli position in the Golan. It was repulsed. Subsequently, infiltrators from across the Syrian border undertook sabotage and mining operations in the Golan, in which by now a number of Naḥal settlements had been established. They caused little damage. In July 1969 Syrian planes attempted to penetrate into Israel skies, and in an air battle above Kuneitra, seven Syrian MIG–21s were downed. Operations on a similar scale continued in the first months of 1970, culminating in a Syrian MIG overflying Haifa, and creating a supersonic boom. About one hour later, Israel planes caused a similar boom in the skies of Damascus, Haleb, Homs and Latakia. Syria now declared that it had completed the reconstruction of its army, and that it was preparing for an all-out war against Israel to return the occupied territories and to liberate Palestine.

Incidents along the Syrian front increased throughout the winter of 1969–70. Naḥal Golan alone was shelled ten times within a few weeks. Thus it was that on 15 March 1970 the I.D.F. undertook deep penetrations into Syrian territory, its targets being an army camp, high power lines, and a bridge. A few weeks later, a combined operation was undertaken against Syrian frontline positions along more than 12 miles (20 km.). The Syrian air force withdrew from the battle after three planes had been downed. However, Syrian artillery fire against Naḥal settlements on the Golan continued. In June the Syrians attempted an isolated attack against another Israel position; on the following day, a series of Syrian frontline positions were captured and destroyed by the I.D.F. In the course of three days of fighting, hundreds of Syrians were killed and 38 taken prisoner, and 5 planes and 30 tanks were destroyed. A congratulatory cable from the Soviet Minister of Defense, Marshall Grechko, testified to Russia's concern for Syria more faithfully than it reflected the outcome of the battle.

Ultimately Egypt's withdrawal from active fighting as a result of the cease-fire of 7 August 1970 gave Syria the welcome excuse to follow in its ally's footsteps.

Syria's western neighbor, Lebanon, fared differently. Its relatively open society and democratic institutions, the weakness of its position among Arab states resulting from its religious structure, and the nature of its southern terrain, adjoining Israel—combined to make it a haven for terrorist activities, from the summer of 1968 onwards. Members of El-Fataḥ from Jordan and Syria congregated in the southeastern corner of Lebanon, in the sector between Mount Hermon and the Hatzbani River which subsequently came to be known as Fataḥland. Although the government of Lebanon, which had not participated in the Six-Day War, had no interest in joining the conflict now, it could or would not prevent others from using its territory as a base for fighting against Israel. An agreement reached in Cairo in November 1969, according to which terrorists would not be permitted to shell Israel settlements from Lebanon, but would only be permitted to operate within Israel itself, was not honored by the terrorists. Following a series of katyusha attacks against Jewish settlements in the north, particularly Kiryat Shemonah, Israel's Air Force started systematic bombings of terrorist bases in Fataḥland, and its ground troops raided a series of bases on the western slopes of the Hermon. The Jewish population along the northern frontier was compelled to adjust its life to the circumstances, constructing the shelters in which many a night was subsequently spent. However, the terrorists continued both the shelling from across the border and infiltrations, which resulted in the destruction of a bridge here, an electric pylon there, and civilian houses in *moshavim* along the northern border. Attempts by the Lebanese army to restrain the terrorists were of little avail; they brought about increased tension among different sectors of the Lebanese population which, in the summer of 1970, verged on civil war.

The Jordanian Border

A similar situation prevailed on the Jordanian front. Although the terrorists had been displaced from their bases in the Jordan Valley, and subsequently further east, they had established bases in the main towns and refugee camps. King Hussein vacillated between stern action to reimpose his authority, and giving free rein to the terrorists who reflected the mood of many of his subjects. In the winter of 1969–70 a royal decree was published prohibiting the terrorists from carrying arms in the cities. Under the combined pressure of terrorist organizations and Arab governments, he appointed a new government to appease the terrorists. They were not, however, satisfied. The moderates amongst them wanted active participation in the new government; the extremists wished to overthrow the king altogether.

By now Israel's frontier along the Jordan River had been almost hermetically sealed, and infiltration across it became less and less rewarding. However, the terrorists found a chink in Israel's armor south of the Dead Sea, and early in 1970 they attacked the Potash Works at its southern tip, in Sedom. By a series of raids and patrols, the I.D.F. gained control of the area of Safi and eliminated terrorist bases on the east bank of the Dead Sea. Rubber dinghies and other equipment captured near the mouth of the Arnon witnessed to the preparations that had been made for raids across the Dead Sea. Once more the king was compelled to enter into an agreement with the terrorists, which resulted in the renewed firing of katyushas into Israel settlements in the Jordan and Beisan Valleys, and—in June 1970—in the first shelling of the city of Tiberias by Iraqi forces, which were still stationed in Jordan. It was in that month that the first clash occurred between the Jordanian army and the terrorists. This, however, was a half measure; other Arab Legion units, and Iraqi and Saudi troops stationed in Jordan, continued their collaboration with the terrorists, who stepped up their attacks against Israel settlements in the valleys. No settlement was abandoned, and normal daily activity was continued; however, a good deal of the life of the adults, and even more of the children, was forced underground. Israel land and air forces reacted not only against terrorist bases, but also against Jordanian military targets, including headquarters of army units which had facilitated terrorist activities against Jewish settlements. Jordan's acceptance of the cease-fire in August 1970 did not change the terrorist attitude.

Finally, now that President Nasser had relinquished armed combat, King Hussein decided to put an end to the anomaly of a terrorist "state within a state", in his own kingdom. El-Fataḥ had by now openly defied his authority. Its units moved freely throughout the country, armed in full daylight. They had their own courts, their own system of extracting contributions from the inhabitants, their own license plates. The king realized that it was not the security of Israel, but his own throne which was at stake. Early in September 1970 he therefore decided to clamp down on the terrorists. In order to minimize casualties amongst his own troops, he used artillery and armor against refugee camps, causing thousands of casualties, both amongst the terrorists and among the civilian population, particularly of refugee camps. El-Fataḥ subsequently claimed that 20,000 casualties had been inflicted, more than the total number of Palestinian Arabs killed in the course of all the clashes with Jews and with Israel, from the early 1920s onwards. Unable to resist the counterattack of King Hussein's army, the terrorists called upon Syria for aid. In the

third week of September 1970, the Syrian forces invaded Jordan
in the area of Irbid. It seemed likely that they would move southward
to overthrow the Jordanian government and install a regime composed
of the terrorists and their supporters. This would have brought about
Soviet control over Jordan, displacing Western influence. Accordingly,
Israel and the U.S. indicated to Syria and to the Soviet Union that
any attempt to take over Jordan would have grave results. Israeli
armor was concentrated, without any attempt at camouflage, on the
Syrian frontier. This, together with effective actions of the Jordanian
Air Force, caused the Syrian troops to retreat. Many of the terrorists,
aware of the fate which awaited them at the hands of the Arab Legion,
preferred to cross the Jordan River unarmed and surrender to Israel
troops. King Hussein had taken a calculated risk, and it had paid off.
In spite of the bloodshed which his troops had caused amongst the
Palestinian population of the east bank, he had asserted his authority
during the "Black September", and earned the grudging respect of his
subjects and of other Arab governments.

Towards the end of September 1970, President Nasser called an
Arab summit meeting in Cairo to consider the new situation which
had been created by the cease-fire, and particularly to heal the rift
between Syria and Jordan which, for all practical purposes had broken
up the eastern front. It was at the end of that conference that President
Nasser died of a heart attack. For almost 18 years he had dominated the
Arab scene, and had become the best known Arab leader and the most
recognized Arab spokesman in world councils. His obsession with
Israel had diverted his energies, and condemned his other ambitions
to failure. He was succeeded by Anwar Saadat, his deputy.

New Terrorism

From the beginning of 1969 until the outbreak of the Yom Kippur
War, and in fact beyond that date until the present date of writing,
the competing terrorist organizations did their best to assert their
presence and their continued activity by acts of sabotage and terrorism
both inside the administered areas and in Israel itself. Having failed
in their attacks against military targets, they decided on a policy of
indiscriminate killing and wounding, with the objective of gaining
maximum publicity, and causing maximum confusion and dislocation
of normal life. The cafeteria of the Hebrew University in Jerusalem,
supermarkets, marketplaces, cinemas, and other public venues were
preferred targets. Israel had to adjust to this new menace. It was clearly

impossible to protect every citizen during all hours of the day; however, the civil defense organization was now given the task of searching all those who entered public places. This, together with the increased vigilance of the population and the increasing efficiency of the security forces, minimized the damage caused by this new tactic. Most of the terrorist squads responsible for these outrages were eventually appre- hended. In the course of time the terrorists resorted to more devilish devices—booby-trapped fountain pens, and explosive charges in the shape of buttons which would attract the attention of children. The identification and treatment of suspicious objects became part of the regular curriculum in all Israeli schools.

Although the terrorist organizations did obtain a good deal of publicity, and did compel Israel to dedicate a concentrated effort to the prevention of sabotage, they failed in their main objective—the dislocation of normal life in Israel, and the disruption of peaceful co-existence between Jew and Arab both within Israel and in the administered territories. Except for one isolated incident, following the blowing up of a car loaded with explosives in Jerusalem's oriental marketplace, the Jewish population failed to react as the terrorists had anticipated—by indiscriminate attacks against the Arab population. Such attacks would have played directly into the terrorists' hands, by poisoning the atmosphere of mutual tolerance which the Israel Government did its best to foster. Life in Israel and in the administered territories continued its normal flow: schools, cinemas and market- places continued their operations, and Jews and Arabs continued to intermingle at work sites, in the streets and in market places.

A good deal of the terrorists' efforts were devoted to the prevention of Arab workers from the administered territories from coming to Israel to work. Buses loaded with Arab workers became regular targets. For a while the Gaza Strip became a center for terrorist activi- ties. The refugees in the Strip were worse off than those on the West Bank; many former Egyptian soldiers were still hiding in the Strip; the vast refugee camps with their narrow lanes were largely inaccessible to motorized patrols of the I.D.F. However, a concerted effort made by the security forces to identify terrorist leaders and centers, as well as a program of road building in the refugee camps, and an ambitious project for providing new and more spacious housing for those refugees who were dislocated—these together almost put a complete stop to terrorist activity in the Strip. Although it was never completely uprooted, it never became an unbearable menace, and thus failed to achieve its major political objective.

The greater Israel's success in curbing terrorist activities within the territory under its control, the greater the temptation for the terrorists to try their luck abroad. It was there that they gained their major successes. Beginning with the hijacking of an El Al plane en route from Rome to Lod on 22 July 1968, which has been described above, airplanes became a favorite target. Since El Al soon took the necessary precautions, the hijacking of El Al planes was abandoned; the planes of other airlines, to and from Israel, were considered easier prey. When that also became difficult, planes were hijacked indiscriminately. Simultaneously, Israeli institutions abroad were sought out; when these institutions had taken the necessary precautions, the net was widened to include Jewish firms and personalities. Such attacks and hijackings inevitably attracted a good deal of attention, and gave even the smallest organizations huge headlines, magnifying their image in world public opinion far beyond their actual strength. At the same time, there was little risk involved in such operations. Although world public opinion condemned the widening of the Israel-Arab conflict beyond the borders of the region, governments were unwilling or unable to curb such activities. A good many European governments did little to prevent the organization of terrorist cells in their territory. Terrorists who had been apprehended, were in most cases subsequently released as a result of another hijacking, combined with blackmail directed at the release of terrorists previously detained.

At the end of December 1968, terrorists attacked an El Al plane in Athens. The presence of mind of the crew and the exemplary behavior of the passengers prevented a disaster. One man, however, was killed; and the two terrorists who were apprehended were subsequently released in 1970, following the hijacking of another plane. Two months later, in February 1969, an El Al plane was attacked in Zurich. An Israeli security man killed one of the terrorists, and three others were detained. They, too, were released—following the hijacking of a Swissair plane in September 1970.

In May of the same year, a number of terrorists were detained in Denmark, en route to Latin America where they intended to assassinate Ben-Gurion, who was visiting there. They were released after three weeks on the pretext that intention to kill was not a sufficient reason for trial.

Israeli targets in Brussels, The Hague, and Bonn were attacked in September of the same year. Two terrorists were apprehended in Belgium and in Holland, but were released following a brief inquiry. Again, in November 1969, a hand grenade was thrown into an Israeli office in Athens. The two terrorists detained were released after the hijacking of an Olympic Airways plane in July 1970. Three terrorists apprehended in Athens a few weeks later, in an unsuccessful attempt to hijack a plane, were similarly released.

On 10 February 1970 an El Al plane was attacked in Munich; a week later an attempt was made to hijack an El Al plane in the same city. All those detained were subsequently released following the hijacking of a plane to Jordan in September 1970—"Black September." On 4 May 1970, the Israel Embassy in Asunción, capital of Paraguay, was attacked, and the wife of the first secretary murdered. The two terrorists detained there are amongst the very few who are still in jail at the time of writing.

Hijackings culminated, as has been mentioned, in September 1970, when a series of planes en route neither to nor from Israel, were hijacked and brought to Jordan, where they were subsequently destroyed. No less a terrorist personage than Leila Haled was captured by the security men of an Israeli plane, and handed over to British authorities. She, too, was released as part of a package deal.

Early in January 1971, a suitcase filled with arms was discovered in an Italian airport. The terrorist carrying the suitcase was, however, soon released: the Italians feared complications. In April of that year, a number of attacks against hotels in Israel were thwarted, and five French citizens were detained. An elderly couple was released because of illness and age, and three young women were condemned to lengthy sentences, and released after completing a substantial part of them. This was one blatant example of terrorist organizations using non-Arabs, particularly young women whom they persuaded by various means, to carry out their murderous intent.

Following "Black September," Jordanian targets came increasingly to the fore. Towards the end of 1971 a Jordanian plane was hijacked, and the Jordanian Prime Minister was assassinated in Egypt. The Egyptian Government, which had played host to the Jordanian Prime Minister, detained a number of terrorists, but released them subsequently: it, too, wanted to avoid complications. The year 1972 witnessed an acceleration of this type of activity. A Sabena plane was hijacked and brought to Lod airport; the terrorists were overpowered by Israeli commandos, and subsequently detained and sentenced.

The most brutal and indiscriminate terrorist killing took place at Lod airport on 13 May 1972; it was carried out by a Japanese suicide group, members of the Red Front in Japan, which by that time was collaborating closely with the Democratic Front for the Liberation of Palestine, one of the more leftist terrorist organizations. Most of the

Lod airport after terrorist attack, May 1972.

victims of the Lod massacre were Catholic pilgrims from Puerto Rico. A few months later 11 Israeli sportsmen were assassinated in Munich, whilst participating in the World Olympic Games. The three terrorists detained at the time were subsequently released, following the hijacking of a Lufthansa plane in October of the same year.

The year 1973 witnessed the addition of another target to the list of previous targets: a number of terrorist operations were aimed at Jewish immigrants from the Soviet Union. The first attack against the Schönau camp in Vienna in January of that year, was thwarted, and the terrorists detained at the time were expelled from Austria—in order to avoid complications. On 28 September 1973, a train coming from Czechoslovakia to Austria, and carrying Jewish immigrants, was attacked. The terrorists had boarded the train inside Czechoslovakia, and it is reasonable to assume that they could not have done so without the acquiescence of the local authorities. It was as a result of this attack that the Austrian government decided to close down the Schönau camp, but—following lengthy negotiations which occupied a good deal of the attention of the Israel Government in the days immediately prior to the Yom Kippur War—an alternative camp was opened and procedures were streamlined, so that Jewish immigrants would spend a minimum of time in Austria en route to Israel. This attack is also significant in another respect. It was carried out by E-Saika, the terrorist organization which, as had been proven, was and is a branch of Syrian Intelligence. The hypothesis has been formulated that this attack was in the nature of a diversionary attack, instigated by the Syrians in order to divert attention from the impending attack on Yom Kippur.

As Israeli targets in Europe became better protected and less penetrable, terrorists searched for suitable targets still further abroad. The Israeli Embassy in Bangkok, seized for a while by terrorists, was one; the Israel Embassy in Nicosia was another. However, the terrorists soon branched out, attacking Arab embassies as well. In the Saudi Arabian Embassy in Khartoum, two American diplomats and one Belgian were assassinated; others were seized in the Saudi Arabian Embassy in Paris, some months later.

Altogether, from the middle of 1968 until the end of 1973, 137 hijackers were apprehended in different countries, the vast majority of them being either released immediately, or after a short time. By the end of 1973, only 27 of them were still in jail—seven in Israel.

Most of the terrorist organizations had their headquarters in Beirut,

the permissive capital of Lebanon. When Israel authorities realized
that in this battle, too, merely protective measures were not sufficient,
it was against Beirut that counteractions were directed. Beginning
with a spectacular raid against the Beirut airport, which resulted in the
destruction of 14 planes belonging to Arab airlines, at the end of
December 1968, and ending in raids against terrorists' headquarters
in the city of Beirut, resulting in the death of some of the most notorious
leaders, Israel undertook a series of operations designed to convince the
Lebanese government that it was in its own interest to curb terrorist
activities emanating from its territory. While these operations disrupted terrorist activities for a while, the Lebanese government did not
find the courage to expel terrorist headquarters from its territory
altogether. To the extent that wide-ranging indiscriminate terrorist
operations beyond the boundaries of the Middle East have been
curbed, this was largely due to the pressure of Arab governments, who
realized that ultimately such operations were damaging to the Palestinian cause, and who applied pressure, including financial sanctions, on
the terrorist organizations, to direct their operations against Israel,
alone. Terrorist operations in Europe were, at the same time, dampened
when some of the key operators in various European capitals were killed.

While the Lebanese capital served as the headquarters of the terrorist
organizations in general, its southern tip—Fataḥland—was the center
of guerrilla activities against Israel, across the border. Between 1970 and
1973, in monotonous repetition, shelling and infiltration took place
across the border, followed by Israeli warnings to the Lebanese government; when such warnings remained unheeded Israeli ground and
air forces undertook raids and attacks against terrorist bases. From
time to time the UN Security Council would meet at the request
of Lebanon—either blandly resolving to condemn all violence, or
condemning Israel for its military acts (ignoring previous Arab attacks
which had provoked them), or dispersing without adopting any
resolution at all. From time to time, Syria entered the fray, permitting
guerrilla activities from bases on Syrian territory; here, too, Israel
took appropriate counteraction.

Peace Initiatives

As has been seen, the cease-fire standstill agreement which came
into effect on 7 August 1970 was only part of a plan designed to bring
about a peaceful solution to the Israel-Arab problem. The Jarring

THE YEARS OF 242   165

talks, which were to have been renewed immediately thereafter, collapsed as soon as Egypt broke the agreement by moving its anti-air missiles forward from their previous positions. It was only about six months later, in January 1971, that a formula was found under which Israel agreed to resume the Jarring talks. Ambassador Jarring came back from Moscow to New York, visited Israel, and summed up his efforts in a memorandum directed to Egypt and to Israel. He soon found that the positions of both sides were unbridgeable—Egypt insisting on withdrawal from all the territories as a pre-condition for negotiations, Israel making it clear that it would not return to the vulnerable 1967 lines. From then on, Jarring's mission went into limbo.

It was substituted in the spring of 1970 by an initiative of U.S. Secretary of State, William Rogers, which envisaged a return to the 1967 armistice lines without substantive alterations, cemented by an international peace-keeping force. That initiative, too, came to naught. Another initiative, for a partial agreement involving the withdrawal of Israel forces from the east bank of the Suez Canal and the opening of the Canal itself, which for a time looked like the most hopeful of all, was also stillborn—when it became clear that the Egyptians would not agree to any partial agreement unless they had a prior commitment from Israel that it was part of a plan which would ultimately culminate in the evacuation of all the territories captured by Israel in the course of the 1967 war.

In the autumn of 1973, just prior to the Yom Kippur War, the newly appointed Secretary of State of the U.S., Dr. Henry Kissinger, sounded out Egypt and Israel on the possibility of renewed negotiations. Subsequently it became clear that Egypt's participation in these talks was only camouflage, part of a plan to deceive Israel and to lure it into a sense of security.

★ ★ ★

From the very first days of his rule, President Saadat adopted the slogan of his predecessor, that what had been taken by force could only be returned by force. Even if he had considered a political settlement possible—and, in effect, the interim agreement concerning the Suez Canal mentioned above was not basically different from the separation of forces agreement to which he agreed subsequent to the Yom Kippur War—he did not consider it desirable. Wiping out the humiliation suffered by the Egyptian army in 1967 became an end in itself; it was, in fact, his major ambition.

Egyptian forces were being built up with a major offensive against Israel in view. Saadat loudly declared the year 1971 to be a year of decision; when nothing happened in the course of that year, he was held up to ridicule both within Egypt and beyond. There is no doubt now that that ridicule proved to be an incentive for him to try even harder.

In a speech little noticed at the time, broadcast on the anniversary of Mohammed's birthday over Cairo Radio in April 1972, Saadat stated: "[The Jews] proved that they were men of deceit and treachery, since they concluded a treaty with his [Mohammed's] enemies, so as to strike him in Medina and attack him from within . . . they are a nation of liars and traitors, contrivers of plots, a people born for deeds of treachery. I declare here and now that their dreams, those that they speak of today out of the lust of victory that they think they achieved in 1967 and will preserve forever—I tell them today from this place that we shall not give up a single inch of our soil, that we shall not negotiate with Israel, whatever the circumstances, and that we will not bargain with them over a single one of the rights of the Palestinian people. I promised you this last year, and I promise you this year that, on the next anniversary of the birth of the Prophet, we shall celebrate in this place not only the liberation of our country, but also the defeat of Israeli arrogance and rampaging so that they shall all return to be as the Koran said of them: 'condemned to humiliation and misery.' We shall not give in on this. The matter is no longer one of freeing our country, but one linked with our honor, in that destiny of ours in which we believe. We shall send them back to their former state."

Following that speech Saadat went once more to Moscow. He asked the Russians for offensive weapons, and he insisted on a free hand in using them. The Russians refused. They did not want a Superpower confrontation and, following the débacle of 1967, they had little faith in Egyptian ability to use weapons. In order to give himself complete freedom of maneuver, Saadat therefore decided to expel all Russian experts from Egypt. Their presence, he felt, had given Russia a veto of any military plans. On 17 July 1972 all Soviet military personnel and their families—about 40,000 persons in all—were ordered to leave Egypt immediately. They included 4,000 to 5,000 advisers with the Egyptian forces; 10,000 to 15,000 other personnel, some manning the 50 SAM–2 and SAM–3 missile sites; 200 pilots with ground crew for the MIG–21, MIG–23 and Sukhoi–11 fighter and bomber planes; and heavy Russian contingents at four Egyptian ports, and virtually in control of seven airfields.

Israel's evaluation of the move indicated primarily that as a result of the expulsion of Russian personnel, Egyptian potential for making war had been considerably weakened; in Saadat's view, his ability to decide upon a war had been increased. In fact, it was a few weeks thereafter that planning for the Yom Kippur War started in all seriousness.

The Yom Kippur War

At 2:00 p.m. on 6 October 1973—on the afternoon of Yom Kippur, the Day of Atonement, while many Israelis were in synagogue and the entire country was at a standstill—the Yom Kippur War broke out. Just a short while earlier, as part of the *Mussaf* service, the medieval prayer had been chanted in which the Day of Atonement is vividly described as the day on which it is finally decided who shall live and who shall die, who by water and who by fire. People were preparing for the afternoon prayer which includes the reading of the Book of Jonah, and the prophet's miraculous escape from the whale.

Until that very day, war was unexpected. Only at 4:00 a.m. that morning had the possibility of war turned into a certainty; even so, the simultaneous massive onslaught of Syrian forces in the north and Egyptian forces in the south constituted a surprise to the troops in the frontline, by its dimensions and its timing. This was the first time in many years of intermittent warfare, that the Arabs were able to exploit the element of surprise, in an operation which in military annals will no doubt stand with Pearl Harbor and the German invasion of the Soviet Union, during World War II.

Tactics and Timing

Egypt and Syria had been preparing and planning for this moment for many months. Unlike previous wars, in which Egyptian and Syrian participation had been explained primarily as an act of solidarity with the Palestinian Arabs, this time there were specific Egyptian and Syrian motivations for the war: the recapture of territories taken by Israel during the Six-Day War of 1967. President Nasser had declared that what had been taken by force could only be recaptured by force. Saadat had adopted his philosophy; now, finally, he felt that he was ready to put it into action.

It has been seen that it was soon after the expulsion of Russian advisers from Egypt in July 1972 that planning for the war started in all seriousness. In October of that year Saadat had appointed as War Minister and Commander-in-Chief one of his oldest army colleagues and supporters, General Ahmed Ismail. In November of that year, following the election of President Nixon, Saadat received a letter from Brezhnev, First Secretary of the Central Committee of the Communist Party of the Soviet Union, advising Egypt to support the policy of détente, and informing him that normal arms supplies would not be increased. According to his own subsequent testimony, Saadat now arrived at the definite conclusion that the situation of "no peace, no war" was in the interest of both Superpowers, and that only a violent initiative from the Arab side would change that situation.

On the basis of Egypt's experience in wars with Israel in the past, Ismail decided that a repetition of the 1969–70 War of Attrition would be disastrous. It would meet with a more violent reaction on Israel's part, greater than the political and military importance of any action Egypt might take. Nor did he consider an imitation of what he called Israel's swift-strike—*blitzkrieg*—tactics as the way to beat the Israelis. Hence, he concluded, "Our strike should be the strongest we can deal." The solution: to "chop the Israelis up," in what General Shazli, the Egyptian Chief of Staff, called "a meatgrinder war."

Early in 1973, General Ismail was made Commander-in-Chief of the armies of the so-called Federation of Arab Republics: Egypt, Syria and Libya. Since the relations of the first two with Libya were ambivalent, and Libya was in any case far removed from Israel, its inclusion in the joint command seemed somewhat pointless; but the inclusion of Syria gave General Ismail hope that he might be able, in the forthcoming war, to activate two fronts simultaneously: the Syrian and the Egyptian one. At the same time Saadat rejected another American initiative based on "negotiations of a Suez Canal agreement," on the grounds that this would allow Israel to perpetuate her occupation of Sinai.

In March 1973, in an interview with an American journalist, Saadat announced "everything in this country is now being mobilized in earnest for the resumption of battle, which is now inevitable." He complained: "Everyone has fallen asleep over the Middle East crisis—but they will soon wake up." At the same time he announced that the Russians were now providing Egypt with everything that it was possible to supply.

On 21 April, the Arab chiefs of staff met in Cairo to examine Israel's military situation. General Ismail later formulated his conclusions: "My appraisal was that Israel possessed four basic advantages: its air superiority; its technological skills; its minute and efficient training; its reliance on quick aid from the United States, such as would ensure . . . a continuous flow of supplies. This enemy also had his basic disadvantages: his lines of communication were long and extended to several fronts, which made them difficult to defend. His manpower resources do not permit of heavy losses of life. His economic conditions prevent him from accepting a long war. He is, moreover, an enemy who suffers the evils of wanton conceit."

To exploit these points of weakness, Israel should be forced to distribute her counterattacks widely. But this presupposed a common Arab strategy exerting pressure on many fronts, which in April was still far from assured. Indeed, it was just a few days later that fighting broke out once more between the Lebanese army and Palestinian guerrillas. It was a direct result of the Israel commando raid on Beirut on 10 April, in the course of which three noted Palestinian leaders had been killed in their residences. The Lebanese army had stood by passively during the raid, and it was resentment at this which brought the Palestinian terrorists into direct confrontation with that army. There was a possibility that Syria would intervene on the terrorists' behalf in Lebanon, and that Egypt might join in the fray. It was for this reason that early in May, coinciding with Israel's 25th anniversary, Israel forces were put on alert. As will become apparent later on, that alert—costly in terms of manpower and finance, and subsequently proved to have been unnecessary—had a decisive influence on I.D.F. conduct five months later.

At about the same time, Syria was receiving huge quantities of armaments from Russia. According to American estimates, arms shipments in the first half of 1973 were considerably larger than the shipments throughout the whole of 1972. In addition to T–62 tanks, the most modern Soviet model, President Assad of Syria received from the Soviet Union a complete air defense system of SAM missiles and an additional 40 MIG–21 fighters. To install the air defense system, Russian experts were sent to Syria.

Throughout May and June Egyptian military and political leaders exchanged visits with those of Syria. It would seem that during Saadat's visit to Damascus for talks with Assad on 12 June, a joint attack was finally agreed upon, the objective being—for the first phase, at least— not the destruction of Israel and its final liquidation, but the more limited one suggested by Egypt: the recapture of territory taken by Israel during the Six-Day War.

The tentative date for the attack was set, according to Ismail, a month before the war actually began. "There was the general consideration that the situation had to be activated when Arab and world support for us was at its highest," he explained subsequently. "More particularly we needed: first, a moonlit night, with the moon rising at the right time; second, a night when the water current in the Canal would be suitable for crossing operations; third, a night on which our actions would be far from the enemy's expectations; and fourth, a night on which the enemy himself would be unprepared. These particular considerations suggested 6 October. On that day, astronomical calculations gave us the best times for moon rise and moon set. Our scientists examined the records of the old Suez Canal Company to assess the speed of the water currents and that day was by far the most suitable. In addition, the Israelis would not expect any action from our side during the month of Ramadan [a month of fasting]. For their part, they would be preoccupied with a number of events, including their forthcoming general election." Although Ismail does not mention it, obviously Yom Kippur, a day of fasting for the Jews, during which Israel would be at a standstill, also seemed an auspicious date.

6 October also had a specific appeal for the Arabs, because it coincided, according to the Moslem calendar, with the day on which the Prophet Mohammed began preparations for the battle of Badr, which opened the door to the capture of Mecca and the spreading of Islam. The operation was therefore code-named Operation Badr, literally "lightning".

The precise hour of the attack was the subject of some dispute with Syria; the Syrians preferred an attack at dawn, with the sun in the eyes of the Israelis; the Egyptians would have preferred sunset, because of the necessity of setting up bridges and moving tanks across the Canal under cover of night. The compromise adopted was an attack in the afternoon.

Having reached an agreement with Syria, Saadat now concentrated his efforts on Jordan. Relations with Jordan had been broken after "Black September" in 1970. Relations between the Palestine Liberation Organization (P.L.O.) and the Jordan Government were at a low ebb, and Egypt was reluctant to resume diplomatic relations with Jordan. However, the military advantages which might accrue from drawing Jordan into a three-front war against Israel outweighed all other considerations. After lengthy talks, in which King Feisal of Saudi Arabia exerted his maximum influence on Jordan, most of the diplomatic and military differences had been ironed out by the time King Hussein and President Assad arrived in Cairo on 10 September for their summit meeting with Saadat. Jordan was brought back into the alliance, even though because of military weakness its task was merely to pose the threat of a third front for Israel. For a start, it would tie up Israeli forces and prevent a flank attack through Jordan into southern Syria.

The first phase of Operation Lightning aimed at restoring the Golan Heights to Syria, and part of Sinai to Egypt. The Superpowers were to be drawn into the conflict and they would subsequently draw concessions from Israel, as a result of which the rest of Sinai and the West Bank of the Jordan River would also be given up by Israel. Israel would be subjected to a meatgrinder war for weeks, even for months, until from the sheer exhaustion of money and lives it would have to sue for a settlement. The P.L.O. had been left out of the summit, which was bitterly attacked by its radio station, and which was considered by some of its leaders as a sell-out of the Palestinians.

It would seem that although most of the groundwork had by now been completed, Saadat still left his options open, and still hoped that the war aims could be achieved by a mere threat of war. In any case, neither King Hussein nor President Assad were told of the precise date of the attack at that time. In Egypt itself, only a handful of senior officers were properly informed. Of 18 senior officers captured subsequently, during the War, only four had any advance knowledge; of these, one had been informed on 3 October, the other three even later.

On the day following the summit, 13 September, thirteen Syrian MIGs were brought down by Israeli planes in the course of an aerial battle over the Mediterranean off the Syrian coast. This new demonstration of Israeli's air superiority, which according to one Israeli spokesman was expected to demonstrate once more Israel's deterrent capability, in fact had the opposite result. President Assad now urged Saadat to take action, and Saadat gave the order for the countdown to war.

The Egyptian army had been in the habit, ever since 1967, of organizing its main maneuvers in the autumn. From year to year the maneuvers increased in size and complexity. The preparations for the war were so organized as to appear like just another maneuver. Although, for the first time, American Intelligence noticed that formations up to the division level were being exercised, and communications networks were being spread out beyond what had been customary in the past, the final assessment of both American and Israel Intelligence did not indicate that this was a preparation for actual war. Most of the Egyptian army—a regular army—had been stationed alongside the Suez Canal all along; whatever additional movements had taken place during the last days before the war were interpreted as being part of the annual maneuvers.

Simultaneously, the Syrians built up their armored formations close to the cease-fire line in the Golan Heights, and this was duly registered by Israeli Intelligence. However, the formations were defensive, and although certain precautions (which will be described later) were taken, the build-up was not considered ominous enough to justify a mass call-up of reserves. Thus, both the Egyptian and Syrian build-up for war was interpreted incorrectly, and did not trigger off the necessary preparations—until 4:00 a.m. of Y-Day itself.

The Element of Surprise

The question why Israeli authorities had been misled, at all levels, until it was too late to prepare adequately for an onslaught of the dimension which was to occur on Yom Kippur, constituted a major heading in the terms of reference of the Agranat Commission which was appointed after the war. In the published part of its report, referring to the period before the war, the Commission gives three main reasons for the failure of Israel's Intelligence: The first was blind belief in the preconception that the Egyptians would not go to war until they were able to stage deep air strikes into Israel, particularly against Israel's major military airfields, in order to neutralize Israel's Air Force, and the related belief that Syria would not go to war without Egypt. While this may have been true in the past, the Commission felt it was outdated, particularly in the light of new evidence, which reached army Intelligence with regard to new weapons purchased by Arab states, "evidence which made the conception obsolescent." The reference here is clearly to the dense, closely interlinked, and effective network of SAM missiles of various types, on which the Egyptians and the Syrians relied as a shield against the Israeli Air Force, without the need for another weapon which would neutralize Israel's Air Force on the ground, or by interception in the air.

Secondly, the Commission notes that the officer in charge of Intelligence had made a firm undertaking to provide I.D.F. with adequate warning should war become a certainty, an undertaking on which the I.D.F. based its call-up procedures. That undertaking was based on exaggerated self-confidence, and left no margin for error.

Thirdly, in the days preceding the war the Army Intelligence Research Department possessed a vast amount of divergent information which had been supplied both by military field intelligence and other bodies. Because of their refusal to budge from preconceived ideas, Israel Intelligence had not appraised this information correctly, claiming that the military build-up was of a defensive nature in Syria, and that Egyptian forces, amassed in the area of the Canal, were holding annual maneuvers.

It was only on the morning of 5 October that the Intelligence chiefs began to reassess their previous conclusions, and that was only after very specific additional information had reached their head-quarters. Even then, they still claimed that the possibility of war was "extremely low" and it was only on the following morning, at 4:30 a.m., that they finally concluded that the enemy actually intended to attack—after yet more information had been received.

Even so, the Agranat Commission concludes, the Chief of the General Staff (General David Elazar) should have requested a call-up of reserves in the week preceding the outbreak of hostilities, to maintain a realistic balance between enemy forces in the field and Israel forces along the borders. At the least, he should have ordered a call-up on the morning of 5 October, even if enemy intentions were not entirely clear. During the tension in May 1973, the Chief of Staff had taken a more severe view of the situation than the assessment of the Chief of Intelligence. But the latter's "victory" regarding this tension, which passed peacefully as he had assessed, apparently weakened the alertness of the Chief of Staff in the days preceding the Yom Kippur War so that "he failed to make a real effort to reach his own assessment as a commander," concludes the Agranat Commission.

Success in May thus contributed to failure in October. Moreover, despite the warnings of impending war, no steps had been taken to deploy the armored force in the vicinity of the Canal to block an Egyptian attack. According to plan, two-thirds of the armor in the southern command should have been deployed close to the Canal, and one-third in the rear. But when the war broke out the deployment was reversed. The correct deployment was to have been carried out at 4:00 p.m. on Yom Kippur—but war had broken out two hours before. Not even the forward forces were deployed in their proper positions in time. When Israel armor started to move forward, it already encountered ambushes from enemy infantry who had managed to take up positions between Israel tanks and the Canal, and on the Canal ramparts from which the tanks were to have covered any crossing.

When on the morning of Saturday 6 October it became certain that there would be war that day, the Chief of Staff, after consultation with senior officers, gave additional orders for calling up reserves and left for a meeting with the Defense Minister, Moshe Dayan. At that meeting the Chief of Staff recommended that the state's entire reserve potential be called to arms to enable a counterattack once the enemy had been checked. Dayan, however, authorized only a limited call-up which would enable the I.D.F. to check the enemy's attack. The issuing of call-up papers was delayed for two additional hours while the Chief of Staff waited for the Prime Minister, Golda Meir, to resolve the differences between himself and the Defense Minister. Immediately upon being informed of the army's desire to call up reserves. Mrs. Meir authorized Dayan's estimates at 9:05 a.m., and 20 minutes later agreed to the figures requested by the Chief of Staff. It was only at that time, that total mobilization was finally ordered— less than five hours before Egyptian and Syrian zero hour. At the same meeting it was decided, for political reasons, not to allow the I.D.F. to stage a pre-emptive air attack on the Egyptians and Syrians, The government's decision was immediately brought to the notice of the U.S. Government through its ambassador in Israel.

The situation was somewhat different in the north. The commander of the Northern Command had warned the General Staff about Syrian troop concentrations some days earlier; although there, too, no reserves had been mobilized prior to Yom Kippur, an additional regular armor brigade had been brought up to the Golan Heights in the days just prior to the war, and existing forces were in a high state of alert. These two factors were to be of vital importance in the days to come.

Although the Intelligence Branch of the army had been found to be vindicated in its assessment of the events of April and May, on 21 May 1973 the Minister of Defense had issued guidelines to the General Staff as follows: "I now speak as the representative of the government and on the basis of information. We, the government, say to the General Staff: 'Gentlemen, please prepare for war, and those who are threatening to begin war are Egypt and Syria.' . . . A renewal of war in the latter part of summer must be taken into account."

In spite of that guideline, when war did break out on 6 October 1973, it came as an almost complete surprise to I.D.F.

The Onslaught from the North

At 1:58 p.m. on the afternoon of Saturday 6 October, five Syrian MIG–17 fighters came in low over the Israel positions in the northern-most sector of the Golan Heights. The tank crews, some of whom were engaged in afternoon prayer, jumped into their tanks. As the MIGs swept north, they fired on civilian residents of the Druze village of Majdal-Shams at the foothills of Mount Hermon; a young mother was killed—the first casualty of the war. Immediately thereafter, 20 MIGs, part of an initial strike of 100 aircraft, swooped over the Israel brigade headquarters, ten miles behind the frontline at Naffakh.

Then, at precisely 2:00 p.m., at the moment when 400 miles to the southwest, Egyptian commandos were scrambling down the Suez banks to launch their rubber assault dinghies, a barrage of artillery fire crashed down from Syrian batteries massed on the Golan plain. As the Syrian gunners were "walking" the curtain of fire towards the squadrons of Israeli tanks hastily assembling at their firing stations, at least 700 Syrian tanks went into action—300 in a thrust down towards Kuneitra, another 400 from the south, up the long and utterly exposed road from Sheikh Miskin to Rafid. Two Syrian armored divisions participated in that first assault; a third was held in reserve. Syrian armor was supported by as many as three infantry divisions. Facing them were fewer than 180 Israeli tanks—two armored brigades, one of them under strength: the 7th Armored Brigade, moved up on the very eve of Yom Kippur, held the northern sector, whilst the 188th Brigade was deployed in the southern sector.

The Israel line was held by a series of fortifications acting as outposts and observation points, and supported in each case by a small force of tanks. With the opening of the assault, helicopters landed in the area of Mt. Hermon and infantry forces transported by them attacked the Hermon positions—"the eyes and ears of the State of Israel." Within a matter of hours, the position which had barely a section of fighting troops in it, apart from specialist troops, such as Intelligence and air force personnel, was overrun and captured.

Soon after the extent of the concerted onslaught in the north and in the south became clear to the Israel General Staff, a crucial decision was taken: to concentrate everything possible, both the Air Force and the reserves which were hurriedly being called up, in the north—whilst attempting, in the south, to contain the enemy assault. In Sinai, geography favored Israel: the 125 miles (200 km.) of desert between

Israel air-ground support, October 1973.

the Canal and the heartland of Israel enabled the I.D.F. to give ground
to gain time. On Israel's northern front, however, the geography of
Golan presented its forces with none of the possibilities of Sinai.
From the frontline to the cliffs overlooking Israel, Golan is just 15
miles (25 km.) deep; to hold it, Israel forces had to fight virtually
where they stood. This was done. The Golan was, however, bare of
natural features for the Syrians to exploit as fixed strategic positions.
To succeed, they had to fight a war of continuing movement and
unceasing assault, a type of warfare at which Israeli tank crews excelled.
Following five days of bitter fighting, not one of the Syrian tanks
which had crossed the cease-fire line on Yom Kippur made its way
back into Syria.

As they crashed through the high wire fences of the cease-fire line,
the first Syrian tanks did not pause by Israel bunkers, but passed them
by. Some miles west of the cease-fire line, both Syrian thrusts
divided. The attack on Kuneitra separated out into a classic pincer
movement; the other attack separated even more sharply: 200 tanks
wheeled southwards along the Golan border, where the cliffs drop
away steeply down towards the Yarmuk River; the other 200 continued straight on through Kushniya towards Naffakh. For both
main thrusts, Naffakh was a key objective. It was the headquarters
of the two defending Israeli brigades. It also controlled the main
route from Golan to Israel, through the Bridge of the Daughters
of Jacob.

The western edge of the Golan Heights is rugged, and there are
only four roads leading into Israel; one, at the extreme north, running
from the foothills of Mt. Hermon into Dan; the one leading from
Naffakh to Mishmar ha-Yarden, over the aforementioned Bridge of
the Daughters of Jacob; another one a little to the north of that bridge;
and, finally, a road winding down towards the Sea of Galilee, towards
Zemaḥ at its southern tip. Of these, the main thrust of the Syrian
attack seemed to concentrate on those in the center, possibly with the
idea of achieving in 1973 what they had failed to achieve in 1948:
to isolate and subsequently to overrun the Finger of Galilee. The
thrust towards the south, following in the footsteps of the Syrian
attack at the beginning of the invasion of 1948, would in retrospect
seem more in the nature of a diversion, although, had the Syrians
known it at the time, the chances of success there were not inconsiderable; there was little if anything to stop the Syrian tanks from
descending towards the Sea of Galilee and advancing along its edge,
if they had tried.

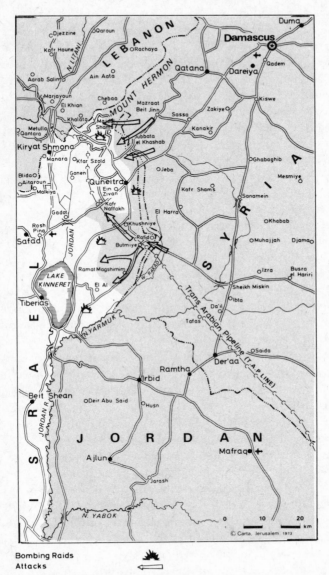

Bombing Raids
Attacks

Yom Kippur War, Syrian attack, Oct. 6, 1973.

Israel's "fortified settlements," designed to hold the gains of 1967, did not prove effective. Two of them were overrun by the Syrians; others, it was decided to evacuate. Against a motorized and armored enemy, as Rommel had written as early as 1942, infantry troops could prove of little value.

In the north, defending the narrowest, and therefore presumably the most vulnerable sector, the 7th Armored Brigade stood fast. The brigade commander was able to maintain his tanks in closed formations, so that they could cover each other. The 188th Brigade covering the central and southern sectors—roughly from the Kuneitra-Daughters of Jacob road and southward—fared much worse. Its task was to stop both thrusts of the column from reaching Rafid. One now pressed northwest to cut the plateau in half, the other swept towards Tiberias. The odds were stupendous: an overall average of five to one, and in some local battles as much as twelve to one. Israeli platoons fought against entire battalions, and again and again the battle was decided by the sheer weight of numbers. Incredible acts of heroism were performed by Israeli defenders, but the Syrians moved on. Having broken through the first defenses, the Syrian tanks fanned into line abreast. To avoid being outflanked and swamped, the Israeli tanks—many by now almost out of ammunition—had to abandon their prepared positions and began a fighting retreat. As dusk fell they were losing the battle.

The loss of the Mt. Hermon position meant not only that it was difficult now for Israel to read the battle, and target its artillery and aircraft: it enabled Syrian artillery to target in on the Israeli tank positions far below.

From mid-afternoon Israel's Air Force concentrated on counter-attacking in the north. The Skyhawks played the heaviest role, with Phantoms and Mirages giving air cover. Targeting was so precise that tank commanders could call down air strikes only a few yards from their own positions. Losses, though, were heavy. For incorporated in the defense screen which the Syrians had moved up to their Golan lines were the latest Russian mobile anti-aircraft missiles, the SAM–6. On the first afternoon Israel lost 30 Skyhawks and about 10 Phantoms, mostly over Golan, and almost all to SAM–6s or the devastating flak of the mobile CSU–23 anti-aircraft batteries, likewise Russian, which shot up pilots flying at deck level in an effort to beat the SAMs. Few managed to parachute. The losses were so high that for a couple of hours, the Chief of the General Staff abandoned air strikes, while the Air Force worked out what to do when they resumed.

By that time, the O.C. Northern Command, General Hofi, had decided to divide the Golan into two commands, placing the north under the command of a veteran parachutist, "Raful" Eytan, and the south under the command of Dan Lanner, a member of kibbutz Neot Mordekhai, situated just below the Golan Heights, who had recently returned to civilian life from his post as Commander of the Armor in Sinai. The first trickle of reservists, called up that morning, had by now begun to arrive. The situation on the Golan was so critical that they were not deployed in organic formations; once a tank had been prepared, and manned with its crew, it was sent up to the plateau to participate in the fighting. Because of lack of time, one of the major advantages of Israel's reserves—that of coherence within each unit—had to be foregone.

As night fell the Golan plateau was a confused world of individual tank battles and ferocious hand-to-hand infantry fighting, as the Israeli defenders slowly retreated. Syrian forces were on the routes leading to the Sea of Galilee, and their advance elements had reached within half a mile (800 meters) of *moshav* El-Al, overlooking the Sea of Galilee.

Sunday 7 October was the hardest day in the north. Contrary to their practice in previous wars, the Syrian tank crews had not wasted the hours of darkness. Using the infra-red night vision equipment with which many of the Russian tanks were equipped, they had redeployed through the night and at sunrise were waiting to attack in a long line abreast. The major battle was joined in the area of Naffakh. Part of the battle was fought at such close range that Syrian and Israeli tanks intermingled. In the extreme south the Syrians were now faced with newly called-up reservists; some of their tanks—Shermans—were of World War II vintage, though they had been equipped with modern 150 mm. guns. Ranged against them were large numbers of Russian T-54 and T-55 tanks, dating from the 1950s and 1960s, and even some of the latest T-62s, which had been driven off from transporters straight into battle.

By Sunday afternoon Israel's 188th Brigade had, for all practical purposes ceased to exist. Both the brigade commander and his deputy had been killed, the former while reconnoitering from one of the extinct volcanoes which are a common feature on the Golan Heights; both battalion commanders had been wounded. Some 150 men of the brigade had been killed, and most of its tanks disabled. By that time, Syrian lead tanks had come down the Kuneitra road, passed Naffakh, to the old customs house at the top of the ridge above the

Jordan River. Less than five miles (eight km.) down the road lay the
Daughters of Jacob Bridge; all that lay between were scattered squadrons of reserves coming up the road towards them: as fast as they
were collected and equipped they were sent up the road to stop the
Syrians. Phantoms and Skyhawks used the last minutes of light to
make low-level runs across the Jordan Valley and up over the Golan
ridge, to strafe the advancing tank formations. According to one
commentator, this was the supreme effort of Israel's Air Force.

It was decided at this stage that the Northern Command be reinforced
by a division commanded by General Moshe Peled, which had hitherto
been held in reserve in the Central Command, in view of the possibility
of Jordan opening an additional front. Peled's division took over
responsibility for all the forces on the El-Al route and the route parallel
to it, both leading to the Rafid crossroads.

At 5:00 p.m. on Sunday, the Syrians made their last attempt to
destroy the 7th Armored Brigade as well. Over the cease-fire line
rolled the main Syrian reserve force, 300 tanks of a crack armored
division commanded by the brother of the Syrian President Assad.
Because of the nature of the terrain and the 7th Brigade's dispositions,
they were unable to spread out over the plateau, and most of them
were picked off one by one.

Less than 48 hours after the beginning of fighting, the Syrians
reached their maximum penetration—half a mile (800 meters) from
El-Al, and five miles (eight km.) from the Daughters of Jacob Bridge.
Their attack had evidently run out of steam, in view of the ferocious
Israel defense; additional forces were brought in to roll them back.
The immediate crisis was over. The Syrian advance had been halted,
and there was no immediate danger facing the heartland of Israel.

The victory had been bought at a heavy price: over 250 killed on
the Golan; over one-half of the tanks of 7th Brigade destroyed, and
188th Brigade practically liquidated. Even more disturbing was the
price that had been paid in pilots and planes; although Israel had been
aware of the existence of modern SAM land-to-air missiles, this was
the first encounter with the mobile SAM–6 and SAM–7, and the Air
Force had paid a heavy price learning how to deal with them.

The Assault from the South

The Northern Command had been taken aback by the scope and the
timing of enemy operations when war broke out; however, its units
had been in a relatively high state of alert, reinforcements had been

sent, and although the number of units was fewer than what could be considered necessary for the defense of the Golan Heights in the event of an overall war, the imbalance was not intolerable. The command had been aware that hostilities might break out and had taken appropriate measures.

In the south, on the other hand, the surprise was complete both in time and method of attack, so that no effective steps had been taken beforehand. When the assault came, many soldiers were washing their clothes and others were at prayer. General Elazar later ascribed this unpreparedness to "a serious failure in observing the order for full alert at some of the lower echelons."

The battle for Sinai was heralded by four crashing waves of artillery fire from 1,000 guns concealed among the dunes behind the west bank of the Canal. The assault that followed was concentrated along three stretches: below Kantara in the north, around Ismailia in the center, and south of the Bitter Lakes, from Shalufa to El Kubri. Opposing them were less than 600 men, reservists from the Jerusalem Brigade, manning the fortifications of the Bar-Lev Line.

The first wave of Egyptian troops was composed of 8,000 infantry, who made their way across the Canal in rubber dinghies, scrambled up the ramparts on the east bank of the Canal, bypassing the fortifications of the Bar-Lev Line, and took up positions facing the approach roads to the Canal. They were equipped with the launchers of an advanced Russian-built bazooka called RPG–7, as well as by another weapon, considerably more deadly: the Sagger Russian anti-tank guided missile, directed all the way to its target by signals which the soldier firing it transmitted down hair-fine wires unreeling behind the missile in flight. As Israel tank forces under General Mandler rushed to occupy the positions which they were due to reach at 4:00 p.m., they were met by a hail of anti-tank missiles fired by Egyptian troops already in position on the east side of the Canal, from the very same positions which had been prepared for Israel tanks. These missiles caused heavy casualties to the Israel tanks meeting the initial assault.

An Israel device, designed to cover the Canal with a thin layer of oil and set it afire the moment an invasion would start, which had caused the Egyptian planners considerable headaches, had in fact been abandoned some time earlier, and was not activated.

At 2:07 p.m. Cairo Radio announced that Egyptian forces had succeeded in overrunning the Suez Canal in several sectors, seizing enemy strongpoints and raising the Egyptian flag on the east bank of the Canal. Immediately thereafter a second wave, crossing under heavy

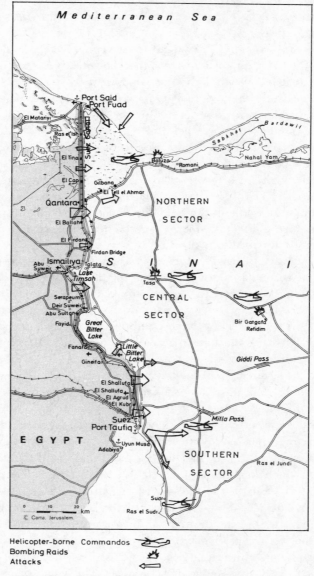

Yom Kippur War, Egyptian attack, Oct. 6, 1973.

fire, began the assault on the Bar-Lev bunkers themselves with grenades, smoke and submachine guns, and savage hand-to-hand fighting ensued.

Meanwhile the first wave, equipped with small buggies to carry equipment, fanned out into the desert for a number of miles. There they dug in and, in addition to their anti-tank missiles, produced the most sophisticated of all their new infantry weapons: the portable Russian anti-aircraft missile, the SAM–7. The task of the missile infantry was now, according to the Egyptian Chief of the General Staff, to hold their ground against counterattack by tanks and aircraft for a period of 12 to 24 hours while tanks and heavy weapons were brought across.

One of the major problems facing the Egyptians was the steep sand barrier on the east bank of the Canal. The Egyptians had calculated that they needed some 60 holes on the east bank in order to be able to move tanks and heavy equipment further east, once they had crossed the Canal. For this purpose they employed water cannons, fed under high pressure from pumps floated on pontoons to the middle of the Canal. By this device, which had been tried out on model ramparts in Egypt, they managed to cut the time necessary for boring the holes by at least one-half. Most of the holes were open within a period of three to five hours.

At the same time, bridges were being laid across the Canal. For this purpose the Russians had supplied the Egyptians with a new type of bridging equipment, the PMP bridge, made of box shaped pontoons, each carried on a tracked vehicle. Hydraulic arms on the vehicle lowered the pontoon into the water. A second vehicle then drove on to this in order to lower another pontoon which was clipped to the first, and so on. By this means, a bridge could be constructed at a rate of 15 feet a minute; a bridge across the Canal in just under half an hour. The Egyptian Second Army, laying its bridges for the northern assault around Ismailia and Kantara, was on schedule. The Third Army further south hit trouble, the sand barrier being thicker than the Egyptians had expected. All the same, within nine hours, according to General Shazli, the Egyptian engineering corps had carved out 60 holes, established 10 bridges, and set up 50 ferries. By dusk on Saturday, the way was clear for the crossing of the Egyptian armor. By midnight, after ten hours of war, Egypt had assembled on the east bank of the Suez Canal 500 tanks and a forward missile defense system. The crossing, under cover of night, had been meticulously rehearsed; signal cables had been strung across the Canal from the beginning, with different colors being used to indicate the route of each unit. Altogether, in the course of the night of 6–7 October, the Egyptians ferried five divisions of infantry across the Canal, together with their armor, and set up three major bridgeheads, according to their original plan.

Israel's reserves were in the meantime being mobilized. Mobilization did not proceed according to plan. Many of Israel's tanks were being serviced; others had their gun-barrels coated in grease to preserve them against the desert grit. Stocks of shells close to the frontline were low, and many tanks finally drove into combat with only half a load of ammunitions. There were not enough tank transporters to carry tanks to the front, so that many tanks had to drive hundreds of miles to the frontline on their own tracks, arriving in poor shape.

Even though the extent of the Egyptian-Syrian assault was obvious by nightfall, and the effects of Israel's lack of preparedness were by now evident, the Defense Minister, speaking on television that night, promised victory in the coming few days. These and similar statements reduced the credibility of Israel's spokesmen during the Yom Kippur War to a point below the high standards they had achieved in all previous wars.

The early Israeli counterattacks had been flustered and reckless—individual tank squadrons gallantly rolling forward, only to be blown apart, sometimes each tank by several missiles simultaneously. The element of surprise resulted in lack of co-ordination in the early counterattacks.

The first Egyptian air strikes—from 100 aircraft—had hit Israel's main Sinai airfields and communications centers in Bir Gafgafa, Bir el-Thamada and the forward headquarters in Tasa; thus Israeli counterstrikes had to operate mostly from bases back inside Israel. Moreover, the Air Force concentrated its efforts on the Golan, so that the first serious counterblows to the Egyptian attack had to be made by Israeli tanks. To face more than 500 Egyptian tanks assembled by the early hours of Sunday, Israel had in Sinai some 230 tanks, mostly Pattons, of which many—those stationed on the Bar-Lev Line itself—had by now been wiped out.

During the years before the war, Israel had constructed two roads parallel to the Canal—one about six miles (ten km.) from the Canal, the other about twice as far on the average. This second road ran through the headquarters at Tasa. The Israel defense plan had always been to use the forward road for its heavy artillery, with the road behind being used for ammunition supplies and for reserves of armor.

THE YOM KIPPUR WAR 187

The main efforts of Israel's forces on Sunday 6 October were directed towards holding a line along the artillery road, and preventing the Egyptians from enlarging their bridgeheads. Egyptian tanks overran the artillery road in places, but the Israelis destroyed their advance before the rear supply road fell.

Beyond the roads were the three strategic passes, the only access through the parched and otherwise impassable mountains of central Sinai: the Mitla Pass in the south, the Giddi Pass in the center, and the Khatmia Pass further north. Apart from these passes the only other way across Sinai is by the coast road, and the Mediterranean on the one side and the soft sea sand on the other virtually ruled that out for tank formations. To advance across Sinai the Egyptians thus had to capture at least one of the passes. From the southern bridgehead, the Egyptians tried to thrust the mere 20 miles (35 km.) to take the Mitla pass; they were stopped, however, before they reached the pass itself.

Egypt was trying meanwhile to disrupt Israeli attacks from the rear. Helicopters ferried Egyptian commandos on raiding expeditions deep behind the Israeli positions; although they were Egypt's crack troops, many of them were wiped out before landing, or immediately after landing; those who managed to survive were a nuisance, but were unable to disrupt Israel's deployment for counterattack.

Attempts to reinforce the isolated fortifications of the Bar-Lev Line were of little avail. One by one these fortifications fell, or else were evacuated under cover of night. Only one fortification, at the extreme northern end, near Baluza, succeeded in holding out throughout the whole war, and was never taken by the Egyptians. The southern-most position, at Port Tewfiq, held out for most of a week, fighting bravely and surrendering only when it had run out of ammunition, food and medical supplies. It was then ordered to surrender, in order to save the many wounded who were in the fortification.

An Egyptian effort was mounted on a number of occasions south-wards along the Gulf of Suez in the direction of the oilfields of Abu Rodeis, but in each case this effort required that Egyptian armor leave the cover of the anti-aircraft missile system. Israel's Air Force drove the Egyptian armored forces back, inflicting heavy casualties. Commandos, helicoptered to the same area, were brought down in midflight.

On Monday 8 October the area of the Southern Command had been divided into three divisional areas: the northern division commanded by Major-General Adan, the central sector by Major-General Sharon, and the southern sector by Major-General Mandler. It was on that day that the Chief of Staff ordered a counterattack, for which preparations had been made from the outset. The intention was to recapture a sector of the Suez Canal, and if possible exploit to the west bank of the Canal itself. General Adan's forces mounted an attack towards the area of the Firdan bridge, opposite Ismailiya. This attack was held by the Egyptians, and Adan's forces were unable to advance. An armored brigade, the 190th, was practically wiped out, and its commander, Colonel Assaf Yaguri, was taken prisoner—the highest-ranking Israeli prisoner captured during the war.

While Adan's forces were engaged in battle, Sharon was moving further south. When he was recalled to the central sector to reinforce Adan, not only was it too late to intervene, but the positions previously occupied by his division had meanwhile been overrun by the Egyptians. The counterattack on Monday 8 October, possibly the most hotly contested and widely debated action of the war, was a costly failure. As one critic of the operation put it: it had been made with insufficient preparation and insufficient strength. General Elazar's words on television that night, to the effect that we are already "at a turning point, that we are already moving forward"—in a speech which was to become famous, and which ended by saying "we shall strike them, we shall beat them, we shall break their bones"—were, to those who had followed the fighting from close quarters, premature.

Forces under General Sharon managed to reach the water's edge at the northern end of the Great Bitter Lake, but—in view of the heavy casualties and the limited reserves—the Israel General Command now chose to remain in a holding position, in preparation for the major armored Egyptian assault which was expected to develop as soon as the remaining armored divisions held back in Egypt, the 4th division in the south and the 21st division in the north, would move across the Suez Canal.

Challenges to the Air Force

By Monday 8 October, the casualties which most concerned the Israel high command were pilots and planes. It had become clear during the first two days of the war that, in combating two deadly types of anti-aircraft missiles employed by the Arab armies, Israel's Air Force faced potential losses as harrowing as those already inflicted on Israel's armor.

In the past, during the War of Attrition, the Israel Air Force had encountered—and learned how to deal with—the SAM–2 and SAM–3 missiles; their mobility was limited, since it took eight hours to dismantle the missile and move it elsewhere, and certain electronic countermeasures proved to be effective against them. However, the SAM–6s and SAM–7s, now encountered for the first time, provided challenges of a different order. The SAM–6s were mounted in threes on a track launching-vehicle which could travel over sand; the launcher and its accompanying radar vehicle could drive to new positions immediately after firing a missile. Camouflage and concealment was relatively easy, and the Syrians, in particular, exploited this cleverly. For most Israeli pilots the first sign of danger was the thin white smoke trail of a SAM–6 as it climbed towards them in a shallow curve at twice the speed of sound. By the time the Israelis could call down artillery fire or bring in support aircraft for a diving counter-strike, the launcher and radar vehicle had moved and reappeared elsewhere.

The SAM–7 was even more mobile. Apart from the infantry-carried version—so light that it could be fired from the shoulder—the Israeli pilots realized by the second week of war that they were also confronted by SAM–7s of a different mode. The Egyptians and Syrians put into action new vehicle-mounted launchers, each capable of firing a salvo of up to eight SAM–7s—called Strellas—simultaneously, thus reducing the possibility of evasive maneuvers. There were many hits by SAM–7s, though these were not always lethal because its explosive charge is smaller than in other SAMs.

In their attempts to avoid the missiles, Israel planes dived low—and there many were caught by the CSU–23 anti-air guns, each capable of firing 4,000 shells a minute, which were deployed between the SAM batteries. Over the following week, Israel was to lose 80 planes on the two fronts, the vast majority downed by SAM–6 and CSU–23s as they flew close support missions for Israeli armored assaults. About two-thirds of these losses were over Golan. Out of the 115 planes lost throughout the war only four were downed in dogfights. Israel's assessment of the potential of Arab air forces had proved to be correct: they were no match for Israel's Air Force. But the conclusion based on that assessment was proved wrong: the Russians and the Arabs were well justified in assuming that the new generation of SAM missiles would at least be able to neutralize the air space over the battle zone. It was only subsequently that effective counter-measures were developed to enable Israel's Air Force more freedom of action, with a far lower casualty rate.

Counterattack on the Golan

On the Golan, Israel's counterattack began as soon as the Syrian assault had lost its momentum. On Monday 8 October General Peled's reserve division launched a counterattack along the El-Al road, against two Syrian tank brigades which had reached to within a few miles of the Sea of Galilee. It lasted for two days, and by 10:00 a.m. on Wednesday, Israel forces had driven the Syrians back to the cease-fire line in that sector, inflicting very heavy casualties on them.

On the 7th Brigade front in the north, both sides had fought to a standstill and were wavering, when one of the Israel positions behind enemy lines which had held out intact throughout the fighting, although surrounded by the Syrians, reported that the Syrian supply trains were withdrawing. The Syrian attack had been broken. In the area facing 7th Brigade, known as the Valley of Tears, north of Kuneitra, some 300 Syrian tanks and armored personnel carriers, abandoned and burnt out, bore testimony to the incredible bravery which had given this victory to Israel arms.

General Lanner's division maintained the pressure around the area of Naffakh and along the TAP-line oil route, which was the axis of the main Syrian effort. Gradually his division cleared the area around Naffakh and between it and the village of Kushniya, by now established as a major Syrian supply base and headquarters. Pushed in a south-eastern direction, the Syrians were gradually driven back from Naffakh

I.D.F. artillery barrage on the Golan Heights, October 1973.

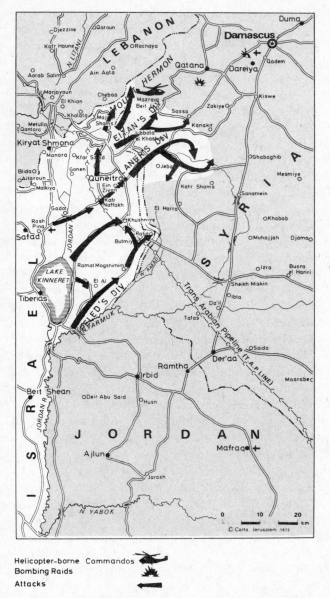

Yom Kippur War, Israel counter-offensive, Syrian front.

towards Kushniya. During the early hours of Tuesday morning, the Syrians launched a series of determined and co-ordinated counter-attacks. Simultaneously a division had broken into Israel lines in front of Kuneitra. Only at 4:00 a.m. on Tuesday did the Kuneitra action ebb away as the Syrians retreated again. The battle to contain the southernmost Syrian counterattack, near Kushniya, took the I.D.F. all of Tuesday 9 October. A large part of that Syrian column had been cut off during the early hours; at dawn the Israelis called in air strikes to destroy the clustered Syrian formations of tanks, mobile guns and armored personnel carriers. A two-divisional effort, by General Lanner from the north and General Peled from the south, boxed in the Syrian forces in that area and destroyed a considerable number of tanks in very heavy fighting. By Wednesday 10 October, General Lanner's forces too had reached the purple line, the original 1967 cease-fire line on the Golan Heights, and the Syrian forces had either been destroyed or driven out of his divisional area.

On Monday 8 October, units of the Golani Brigade had attempted to recapture the Mt. Hermon position which had been lost on the 6th, but the attack failed with very considerable losses.

On Tuesday 9 October the Israel Air Force for the first time bombed strategic targets in the Syrian capital of Damascus, the headquarters of the air force and ministry of defense, wreaking havoc inside both. This was Israel's reply to the launching of Russian Frog–7 rockets against civilian targets in Israel ever since the beginning of the war. One Frog rocket, presumably aimed at a nearby airfield had landed amid the buildings of kibbutz Gevat, in central northern Israel. Some of the buildings were wrecked, including the fortunately empty dormitories for the 270 children of the kibbutz. Israel continued its bombing of airfields, and now added Syria's heavy industry to the list of targets. Two oil refineries at Homs were hit, as were fuel tanks in Der'a and Latakiya. More oil tanks at the port of Tartus were destroyed, together with a loading terminal. Power stations in Damascus and Homs were bombed. The costliest blow of all was to Banyas, the Mediterranean terminal for Iraqi crude oil: it was devastated. Inevitably, civilian casualties did occur during these attacks, but the targets were of a strategic nature. Israel had been aware all along of the vulnerability of its civilian population against indiscriminate attack, and it was bound to do everything possible to show the Syrians that the escalation of war in that direction would be costlier for them.

By Wednesday 10 October the Syrian forces had been driven

out entirely from the Golan Heights, and Israel forces had closed in on the cease-fire line along its entire length. On the following day, 11 October, Israel counterattacks were launched into Syria itself. The operation began at 11:00 a.m., when General Eytan's division in the north, including the remnants of the 7th Brigade, broke into the Syrian positions along the foothills of the Hermon, while General Lanner's division in the center attacked along the heavily fortified main route to Damascus. The attack in the north developed according to plan; in the center, however, General Lanner's division ran into a very heavy anti-tank screen which had remained undetected in the broken terrain. When the leading brigade was held up, the support brigade followed through and took the village of Khan Arnaba. On the following day, General Eytan's forces in the north reached the village of Mazrat Beit Jan and established defensive positions there. The 7th Brigade was repulsed in its attempt to take the strategic feature of Tel Shams, which granted a commanding view of the plains below, most of the way towards Damascus, about 25 miles (40 km.) away. To the south, General Lanner's division widened its area of penetration and advanced towards Kanaker. As the division moved in that direction, Iraqi forces which had entered Syria at the beginning of the war finally reached the battle area.

The first of the two armored divisions moved forward towards the flank of General Lanner's advance. The General, directing the battle from his vantage-point on the hill, saw the Iraqis advancing in a massive cloud of dust across the plain from the southeast. He withdrew his division from the attack and prepared to meet the Iraqis. With an additional brigade from General Peled's division which he received just in time, he created an armored box into which the Iraqi forces unwittingly moved. The battle began during the night, at 3:00 a.m. The unsuspecting Iraqis, who had taken up positions between Israeli forces, were smashed and withdrew. Israel's forces exploited their success and reached the area near Kafr Shams; on the following day, parachute forces captured the vital hill of Tel Shams, suffering only four wounded in the battle.

The Syrians developed a counterattack in the area of Beit Jan, on the main route linking the vital juncture of Sasa with Tel Shams. In the meantime, the 40th Jordanian armored brigade, Jordan's contribution to the joint war effort—its compromise between doing nothing and opening a seperate, third front, along the Jordan River—had entered Syria and, basing itself on Tel Hara, one of the extinct volcanoes so prominent on the Golan Heights, supported the Iraqi forces on their left flank in the counterattacks which were mounted. General Lanner's division counterattacked and captured two dominant positions, two of the tells. Combined Syrian, Iraqi and Jordanian counterattacks, mounted in turn, were of little avail.

The Israelis now held a very strong line, which Arab forces failed to penetrate. In the battle which raged in the Iraqi sector approximately 100 Iraqi tanks were hit, with some 80 destroyed, and about 40 Jordanian tanks were hit, of which 30 were destroyed. After incredibly hard fighting, in which the Syrians had enjoyed all the possible initial advantages, the threat to the heartland of Israel had been wiped out, and was substituted by a very real threat to the capital of Syria.

Egyptian Objectives

The original scenario of Saadat for the Yom Kippur War and its outcome is still under discussion. There is no doubt that the war was intended to break the deadlock—to interrupt the process by which Israel control of the territories became a *fait accompli*, to undermine the Israel-American gentlemen's agreement for the preservation of the status quo as the lesser of evils, and to prevent the détente from crystallizing into an arrangement, freezing the existing situation in the Middle East.

According to Saadat himself, he had explained to Brezhnev as early as in April 1972 that "things will not move except by means of a military operation, a major Arab offensive," which would compel Israel to participate in an international conference and to implement the arrangement which would be decided upon there, just as the North Vietnamese offensive of January 1972 compelled the U.S. to return to the Paris Conference and to accept the evacuation agreement.

But what was the specific objective of this offensive? There are those who claim that the offensive had far-reaching territorial objectives. Others believe that Saadat hoped to gain a foothold along the east bank of the Suez Canal and, at best, to reach the passes, at an average depth of 19 miles (30 kms.). Testimony published by Egyptian commanders after the war would indicate that they were mainly concerned with the question of how to prevent the crossing of the Canal from developing into an additional military defeat, rather than the question of how to capture the whole of Sinai.

However, even the minimum objective was still far from being achieved towards the end of the first week of fighting. The Egyptian line now extended along the entire Suez Canal, but its penetration had reached a mere six miles (10 kms.), too little to enable Egyptian forces to withstand determined Israel counterattack. Egypt's Minister of War, General Ismail, whose planning had so far dictated developments, was willing to wait and see how Israel would react, before he would engage in a break-out. Specifically, he was reluctant to move the remaining tank forces—some 500 tanks—to the east bank, because of the possibility of an Israel airborne assault on the west bank, which would leave the heartland of Egypt exposed. On the other hand, General Shazli, the Egyptian Chief of Staff, pressed for a quick exploitation of success, a break-out from the bridgehead, either in the north, along the coastal road, or towards the passes further south, supported by helicopter-borne commando raids which would strike at the eastern ends of the passes. General Shazli was overruled, and Ismail's strategy—that of halting, consolidating, waiting for the Israelis to react—prevailed.

Thursday 11 October brought a decisive change in Egyptian deployment. Reluctantly, the Egyptians now brought into Sinai the 500 tanks they had held on the west bank of the Canal to protect the rear of their armies. Egypt was under intense pressure from Syria to take some of the Israeli weight off Golan. Politically, General Ismail had little choice but to prepare for a fresh assault in Sinai.

This Egyptian move triggered a violent debate on the Israeli side. There were those who argued that now was the time to strike against the rear of the Egyptians, by crossing over to the west bank. "By carrying the ball to the west bank," said General Sharon "we would be in our element, fast-moving armor in open, classic tank country." He was overruled, and a more cautious strategy prevailed, that advocated by General Bar-Lev, who—although a Cabinet Minister—had been mobilized and appointed to a supervisory capacity of the entire southern front, and by the Chief of the General Staff. It was decided to wait for the Egyptian break-out, which was bound to come, before Israel would engage in a decisive counterattack. Israel's dwindling reserves, its high rate of casualties, and the massive resupply operation undertaken by the Russians, by air and by sea, of the Egyptian and the Syrian armies—so far unmatched by any resupply by the U.S. for Israel—dictated the decision not to commit Israel's major remaining reserves before Egypt's momentum had been exhausted.

The Role of the Navy

Israel's navy, relegated to an auxiliary role in previous wars, came into its own during the Yom Kippur War. In fact, it was the only arm which came close to the "quick and elegant victory" of which General Bar-Lev had spoken in the past. This was because the navy had recognized the revolutionizing impact of missiles on warfare, possibly before other arms. It will be recalled that on 21 October 1967, the Israel destroyer Eilat was sunk off Port Said by a Styx missile launched from a Russian-built Comar-class missile boat of the Egyptian navy. As a long-term response, Israel built up its own fleet of a dozen fast missile boats—five of them smuggled out of their French construction dockyard at Cherbourg, on Christmas Day 1969, in defiance of De Gaulle's embargo on arms sales to Israel. These Sa'ar boats, plus two homemade models named Reshef, are armed with a missile designed and manufactured by Israel itself, the Gabriel. This has a range of only 12 miles, half that of the Styx missiles used by the combined Egyptian and Syrian missile fleets of 28 boats. But the Gabriel's guidance system is highly sophisticated.

Israel navy anti-aircraft gunner, October 1973.

From the first day of the war, when Israel wiped out four Syrian craft, mostly with the Gabriel, the Israel navy had the battle all its own way. On the first Wednesday of the war, 10 October, three Egyptian missile boats were sunk near Port Said and Israel tackled Syrian missile boats actually lying in Tartus harbor, sinking four, although at the same time damaging Greek, Russian and Japanese cargo vessels anchored in the port.

From then on, Israel had the run of the coastline. Its boats were out 24 hours a day, rocketing and shooting up "anything that moved." Its 76-mm. guns played a part in the destruction of the Syrian coastal oil installations, as well as damaging several radar stations, military complexes and supply depots on both the Syrian and Egyptian coasts. The navy evidently also tackled some of Egypt's northernmost SAM sites. It was thus Israel's navy which of all the military arms did best during that bitter war.

Superpower Patronage

There is no doubt that the Russians had prior knowledge of the Arab assault on Yom Kippur. The timely evacuation of the Russian advisers, as well as the launching, on 6 October, of a Cosmos reconnaissance satellite, together point to that conclusion. By Monday the Soviet leader of the Party, Leonid Brezhnev, was urging other Arab states such as Iraq and Algeria to join the battle. From that day onwards, the Russian resupply effort gained momentum, until on Friday 12 October as many as 60 flights to Damascus and to Cairo were recorded.

Israel's reserves of certain types of ammunition were running low; its losses in planes and in tanks compelled it to ask for a parallel American resupply effort. At first this was in vain. Some members of the Intelligence community had believed at the beginning in a swift Israeli victory which would make an airlift unnecessary. But there is reliable evidence, *inter alia* from the not unsympathetic biographers of the American Secretary of State, Dr. Henry Kissinger, that he held back because he wanted a limited Israeli defeat—big enough to satisfy the Arabs "humiliated pride"; modest enough to preclude a propaganda triumph for the Russians; sobering enough to bring Israel to the conference table, on the basis of the Arab interpretation of Resolution 242; bearable enough to avoid the collapse of Mrs. Meir's government and its replacement by another, which would be more intransigent. It was in pursuit of that strategy that Dr. Kissinger envisaged a cease-fire *in situ*, with the Egyptians in full possession of the east bank of the Suez Canal. Saadat, however, rejected such a solution. The only cease-fire he would accept would be one linked with a long-term solution—the full evacuation of all territories captured by Israel in 1967, and the recognition of the legitimate rights of the Palestinians. The Russians seemed to have supported Kissinger's initiative, pressing on Saadat the argument that he had made his political point.

It was only when that initiative had failed that the U.S. decided on a massive airlift to Israel, which began on Sunday 14 October. A major difficulty faced by that airlift was a logistical one. On Tuesday, the third day of war, the Kuwait Council of Ministers had announced the organization of a meeting of Arab oil producers to discuss the role of oil in the conflict. The following day, Egyptian and Saudi Arabian oil experts were discussing ways in which the oil weapon might be used. Europe obtained over 70% of its oil from the Arabs, and the Europeans were reluctant to enable the Americans to use bases for the airlift, and thus endanger their oil supplies. Ultimately, the U.S. had to channel its airlift to Israel through the base leased from Portugal in the Azores.

Suez: Offensive and Counteroffensive

On Sunday 14 October the Israel Ministry of Defense announced that 656 Israeli soldiers had been killed so far during the war. It later emerged that at least 100 of those listed as missing were in fact dead. It was on that day, at 6:00 a.m., that Egyptian armor began developing an offensive eastwards—the break-out which had been expected by the I.D.F. The Egyptian attack was concentrated at four different points. The major battle was mounted in the central sector against General Sharon's forces, where some 110 Egyptian tanks were destroyed in the course of the day. The northern division commanded by General Adan and the southern division commanded by General Mandler were likewise engaged in battle, with a determined attempt being made by the Egyptian Third Army to break out southeast along the Gulf of Suez, towards the oilfields of Abu Rodeis. This attempt was foiled by the Israel Air Force which destroyed the greater part of an Egyptian brigade. In all, during 14 October, the Egyptians lost over 200 tanks in the assault, which failed to achieve any advance.

It has been calculated that more tanks were engaged in the battle of that day than the 1,600 British, German and Italian tanks which fought the battle of El Alamein, 200 miles on the other side of Cairo, during the same month in 1942. It was a classic tank battle; infantry-operated anti-tank weapons, which from carefully chosen positions had proved so effective in the first days of fighting, were of little avail in the fluid battle that now developed. Moreover, the Israel army had by now taken the measure of Egyptian anti-tank missiles, and had developed tactics to avoid them. Israel's Patton and Centurion tanks were at a slight advantage as compared with Egyptian Russian-made tanks, as their wider vertical firing angle enabled them to shoot downhill with only their turret being exposed, thus taking better advantage of the undulating territory of western Sinai.

Basically, though, the victory was won by the side whose tank crews were more skilled and better trained. By the afternoon of 14 October the Egyptian attack had been so badly broken that many of the attacking units faced difficulty even finding their way back to the bridgehead. Israeli tank forces now attempted to cut off Egyptian retreat. One commander reported that in the battle, which lasted until 3:00 a.m., his forces lit about 55 bonfires—half of them tanks, the rest artillery pieces and personnel carriers—without suffering a single loss. General Ismail subsequently claimed that he had been forced to launch a wide offensive before the suitable moment in order to relieve the pressure on Syria. He now tried to go back to the bridgeheads to proceed with their consolidation, to render them "a stubborn rock over which the enemy's counterattacks could be smashed."

On the afternoon of Monday 15 October, when it was apparent beyond doubt that the Egyptians would not attempt again to break out of their constrictive bridgeheads, clearance finally came through for the crossing of the Canal westwards—the Israeli counter-offensive for which the Chief of the General Staff, General Elazar, had been planning from the moment war had become a certainty, which had been attempted prematurely one week earlier, and which was now designed to decide the outcome of the war. The task of spearheading the crossing was given to General Sharon. Well before the war, when he was O.C. Southern Command, General Sharon had picked out a spot for a Canal crossing, between the two Bitter Lakes, near the entrance of the Canal into the Great Bitter Lake, at a point where two side roads branch off and link up at the side of the Canal, and whose left flank would be protected by the lake. At this point, about

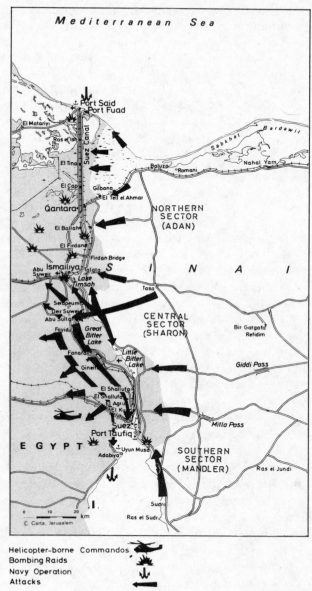

Yom Kippur War, Israel counter-offensive, Egyptian front.

12 miles (20 km.) south of Ismailia, the massive ramparts of the Canal bank had been thinned down and the weakened section had been marked out with red bricks. Nearby a vehicle park had been laid out, 100 yards by 400 yards, protected by high earth walls. The original force consisted of three armored brigades, originally of 90 to 100 tanks each, but somewhat decreased by a week's fighting—a brigade of infantry, including paratroops, and a special force of engineers with earthmoving equipment, self-propelled barges, and bridging equipment. Facing that division was the Egyptian 21st Armored Division, with about as many tanks as Sharon's—the core of Egypt's Second Army, commanded (from Ismailia) by Major-General Sa'ad Mamoun.

It was obvious from the outset that the success of the operation would depend on speed and surprise. If surprise had been lost, a considerable number of tanks could have been assembled by the Egyptians waiting on the west side of the Canal. Unlike the Egyptians, who had been in undisturbed possession of the west side of the Canal before making their crossing, General Sharon's problem was how to reach the water and establish a bridgehead in the same night. The point of penetration was chosen, at the gap between the Egyptian 2nd and 3rd Armies. Starting at dusk on 15 October, one of the three armored brigades launched a diversionary attack to the west, while another swung southwest towards the Great Bitter Lake. From the lake's shore it raced north to the crossing point. As it did so, the brigade split into three: one group headed for the Canal, another to the east to link up with the third brigade, and a third went north to establish a secure perimeter. By midnight the link-up had been achieved with the third brigade's paratroopers, and an hour later General Sharon himself was over the Canal, with about 200 paratroopers.

But the crucial objectives were not achieved: by dawn the bridge was not established, and even the roads leading to the crossing-point were not secure. And the northbound group had run into heavy Egyptian fire after a few kilometers: it was now deployed for a battle which was to last most of the next two days.

At noon on Tuesday 16 October, evidently unaware of the Israel crossing into the west bank and of its potential significance, Saadat made a public speech in which for the first time he outlined the aims of the war.

He promised to go on fighting to liberate the land which was seized by Israel occupation in 1967, and to find the means towards the restoration and respect of the legitimate rights of the Palestinian people. He declared his readiness, once the withdrawal from all these territories had been carried out, to attend an international peace conference at the United Nations. Most significantly, he announced that he was prepared to accept a cease-fire on condition that the Israeli forces withdrew forthwith from all the occupied territories to the pre-5 June 1967 lines, under international supervision. Just a few days later President Saadat would be ready, in fact anxious, to accept a cease-fire on conditions far different from these.

A few hours later Mrs. Meir spoke to the Knesset, which had been called into special session in Jerusalem. Replying to President Saadat, she said: "There is no doubt in our minds that war was launched once more against the very existence of the Jewish state: our survival . . . is in the balance. The armies of Egypt and Syria, with the help of other Arab states . . . went to war with the aim of reaching the lines of 4 June 1967 on their way to achieving their main purpose—the conquest and destruction of Israel."

She attacked the Soviet Union for supplying offensive weapons to the Arabs, and denounced the embargos on Middle Eastern arms exports announced by Britain and France—theoretically even handed, but undoubtedly of more help to the Arabs than to Israel. Concerning Israel's war aims, she said: "The time for a cease-fire will be when the enemy's strength is broken. I am certain that when we have brought our enemies to the verge of collapse, representatives of various states will not be slow in 'volunteering' to try and save our assailants. . . . " The most important line in her speech was a brief announcement that the Israel army was already on its way to the military resolution of the issue with Egypt: "An I.D.F. task force is operating on the western bank of the Suez Canal." It was the first news of Arik Sharon's bridgehead. Originally, Mrs. Meir had thought of announcing the establishment of a bridge. That vital part of the operation, however, had not yet been accomplished.

For, whilst Sharon, with his handful of men, encountered no opposition on the west bank, one of the most ferocious and costly battles of the entire war developed about two miles (three km.) from the eastern bank, behind them, around the so-called Chinese Farm road junctions. Egyptian infantry had managed to infiltrate the T-junction area to the north, and with rocket launchers and wire-guided missiles made that junction impassable, and had brought the Y-junction further to the south under attack from time to time. The entire operation was now behind schedule. By 9:00 a.m. on Wednesday 17 October, only about 30 tanks and about 2,000 men had crossed the Canal. By that time, Egyptian artillery had zeroed in on the area of the junctions, making the passage of the cumbrous, slow-moving convoy a costly affair. The main cargo to be transported was the bridge—rectangular steel floats carried on flat-bed trucks. Some of the bridge sections were damaged by shells on the way through, which meant that there was no chance of establishing a bridge within the next 12 hours. Had a force, of any kind of strength, turned up on the west bank, there would have been nothing whatever the Israelis could have done about it. To get a division-strength force across the water by barge ferry, the I.D.F. would have required about 1,000 trips.

The original plan of the operation had been for General Sharon's forces to secure the bridgehead, while General Adan's division would move through for exploitation. Of the different options open for that phase, a northward move towards Ismailiya was ruled out because of the complex system of canals, the "agricultural barrier," which would make any progress in that direction cumbersome, and presumably costly. It had therefore been decided instead to move south, towards Suez, and cut off the Third Army. The route lay over firm open sand where Israel columns could make maximum speed. For well over 19 miles (some 30 km.) the Israelis would have one flank protected by the Bitter Lakes—a barrier which neither side could cross in strength. Once in position to the south, the I.D.F. would only need to control a front of about 12 miles (20 km.) between Shalufa and Suez, in order to have the Third Army trapped.

On Tuesday morning that plan seemed to be in ruins. General Adan's forces, rather than crossing over at once to begin the long

The "Baruch" bridge with the cultivated area of the west bank of the Suez Canal in the background.

sweep southwards, were engaged in the bitter battle of the Chinese Farm, designed to secure a corridor of approach to the crossing.

Meanwhile, the forces of General Sharon, following a bitter debate between Sharon and his superiors, were engaged in raiding the soft belly of the Egyptian forces—blowing up fuel dumps and, what proved to be of primary importance, wiping out SAM sites, thus clearing a landing strip for Israel's planes and an aerial corridor for them to penetrate.

When President Saadat failed to mention the Israeli invasion in his speech, it was assumed in Israel that this was deliberate. It did not occur to the Israeli command that perhaps President Saadat and General Ismail just did not know what was happening. Yet, according to General Ismail's version, the first he knew of the invasion was "information which he found waiting after his return from the People's Assembly session, concerning the infiltration of a small number of amphibian tanks." The message had added that in the estimation of the local command "it was possible to destroy them quickly", and a storm battalion had been moved to face them. Not until after dark on Tuesday 16 October, well over 24 hours after the beginning of the operation, did the Egyptians mount a co-ordinated attack on the eastern approaches to the crossing point.

All night a savage tank-to-tank conflict raged. Darkness cut down the value of the Egyptian infantrymen's anti-tank missiles. But because ranges close in at night, it also cut down the Israel tank crews' advantage in long-range gunnery. It was a complicated battle, in which the outnumbered Israeli tanks were under fire from two and sometimes three directions at the same time. Slowly and bloodily the Egyptian resistance at the Chinese Farm was reduced and the fire at the crossing points slackened enough for the Israeli engineers to get the pontoons in position for the much-delayed bridge. Following the war well over 1,500 burnt-out vehicles, half of which were tanks of both sides, were counted in the limited area of the Chinese Farm. Around mid-Wednesday, 30 hours behind schedule, the first bridge was in place, and the first of Adan's three tank brigades began to roll across. Soon afterwards a second bridge was thrown across the Canal. By this time, surprise had been lost completely; Egyptian artillery had zeroed in on the crossing points, and both the construction of the bridges and their crossing involved heavy casualties.

The Demand for a Cease-Fire

The Soviet Union had become convinced of the need for a cease-fire after a very few days of fighting; it would seem that its experts were profoundly pessimistic about the ability of the Egyptian army to deal with a powerful Israeli counterattack, which would require rapid improvisation, rather than the execution of a set piece battle, well planned and rehearsed in advance. On Tuesday Kosygin decided to see the progress of the war for himself. He flew to Cairo, arriving there soon after Mrs. Meir had announced the news of Israel's bridge-head. According to Russian sources, the Egyptians concealed the true state of affairs from Kosygin until Thursday morning. Once the extent of the débacle facing Egypt had become clear to the Russians, Secretary-General Brezhnev sent an urgent request to President Nixon that Secretary of State Kissinger be sent to Moscow to conduct negotiations to speed an end to hostilities that might be difficult to contain if continued. The Russians stressed that they could not allow Egypt to be defeated, even if they had to take drastic steps. Thus, at 5 a.m. on Saturday 20 October, Kissinger and a team of officials left for Moscow.

By that time, the division commanded by General Magen (replacing General Mandler who had been killed in action) had also crossed the bridges; thus, there were already three Israeli divisions on the west bank of the Suez Canal. General Sharon's force, in the north, was obliged to fight through the cultivated area created by the sweet water canal, in the general direction of Ismailia, while at the same time endeavoring to remain parallel to the Israel forces on the east bank of the Canal, which encountered heavy opposition from the Egyptian Second Army. General Adan's forces were directed in the direction of Genifa-Suez, while clearing the area to the west of the Bitter Lake and the west bank of the Canal itself. General Magen swept inward in a broad sweep to the west of Jebel Genifa in an arc towards the port of Adabiya, on the Gulf of Suez.

On Sunday 21 October the Egyptian High Command in Cairo, at the first press conference of the war, admitted that there were two small pockets of Israelis about six miles (ten km.) into Egypt in the Deversoir area, but claimed that both were hopelessly besieged by thousands of Egyptian troops. The truth was that by that time Israel's forces had not only advanced most of the way towards Suez, but had dismantled the missile sites, the last of those that had provided the Egyptians with their air umbrella for their original advance. The comparative freedom of the skies enjoyed by the Israeli Mirage and Phantoms on that day manifested itself in the aerial battle. The Egyptians, obliged to commit their MIGs in an effort to halt the Israel advance, lost 17 fighters in the course of one day. Israeli troops, rapidly advancing towards the Cairo-Suez road, threatened to cut the main lifeline of the Egyptian Third Army; that army, numbering some 20,000 men, and with an estimated 300–400 tanks still intact, was highly vulnerable.

As Mrs. Meir had predicted, once an Israeli victory was imminent the Superpowers quickly agreed on a cease-fire. Now, finally, the rusty machinery of the UN Security Council was brought into motion. Shortly after 10:00 p.m. on Sunday in New York (just after 4:00 a.m. on Monday morning in the battle zone), the Security Council was called to order by its president, and after a brief debate adopted Resolution 338, co-sponsored by the U.S. and the U.S.S.R. The resolution called upon the parties to the present fighting to cease all firing and terminate all military activity immediately, no later than 12 hours after the moment of the adoption of this decision, in the positions they then occupied. The fact that President Saadat, who but a few brief days earlier had promised not to accept any cease-fire which would not entail the complete withdrawal of Israel from all territories captured in 1967, was now relieved by a cease-fire *in situ*, testified more than anything else to the decisive turn the fighting had meanwhile taken. The resolution also called upon the parties concerned to start immediately after the cease-fire on the implementation of Security Council Resolution 242 in all of its parts, and concluded with the provision that "immediately and concurrently with the cease-fire, negotiations will start between the parties concerned under appropriate auspices aimed at establishing a just and durable peace in the Middle East." While the second paragraph, calling for "implementation" of Resolution 242, could be considered as a concession to the Arabs, the last one, calling for negotiations between the parties concerned, was considered a concession to the Israelis. However, the cease-fire resolution contained a gap: the agreement contained no proposals for observation or enforcement of the cease-fire. It was to come into effect at 5:58 p.m. on Monday 22 October.

Mount Hermon Recaptured

The last week of the war saw a considerable amount of fighting also in the north, but few territorial changes. Israeli forces had driven into Sasa but, exposed to counterattacks and concerned about their supply lines, withdrew from that junction and took positions further to the west. Israel had achieved its major objectives on that front: the entire Golan had been cleared and a considerable amount of territory to the east of the previous cease-fire line was securely under Israeli control. Beyond lay the capital of Syria, clearly visible from Israel positions. Its capture would have entailed considerable military difficulties and casualties (the ring of defense around the capital itself was still intact); moreover, it was considered politically unwise for a number of reasons, primarily the assumption that the Russians, in view of their commitment to Syria, could not possibly stand idly by while the capital of their ally fell to the Israelis. Meanwhile, the main effort of the I.D.F., including that of Israel's Air Force and armor, had been moved to the south, to the Egyptian front, where the decisive battle of the war was in progress.

However, there was one Israeli position which had not yet been recaptured—that on Mt. Hermon, which had fallen to Syrian hands during the first hours of the war. It was vital not only to deny the Syrians the visual and electronic observation capacity of that outpost; it was important to secure these facilities for Israel itself, so as to be able to observe the heartland of Syria. It will be recalled that a previous attempt to recapture the Mount Hermon position, which was mounted hurriedly under the assumption that a number of Israeli soldiers were still holding out within the captured fortress, had been repulsed by the Syrians with heavy Israeli casualties. Now, with the cease-fire in sight, another attempt was made—by parachutists being landed from helicopters, and by infantry men climbing up the craggy side of the boulder-strewn mountain to its peak, 3,000 meters above sea level, supported by artillery, armor and the Air Force. Syrian snipers, who had taken up positions around the fortress, fought obstinately, supported by Syrian planes, nine of which were shot down. By 11:00 a.m. on Monday 22 October, eight hours before the cease-fire was due to come into effect, the Israelis successfully completed the operation; the Israel and Golani flags were once more fluttering from the radio antennae on top of the fort—"the eyes and the ears of Israel."

From Cease-Fire to Cessation
of Hostilities

The Government of Israel had accepted the cease-fire reluctantly, since it realized that after almost three weeks of bitter fighting and of grievous casualties, the price of victory was about to be snatched from its hands. President Saadat had also accepted, hoping to save the Third Army from complete containment. Ultimately, even Syria announced its acceptance, although on "the basis that it means the complete withdrawal of Israeli forces from all Arab territories

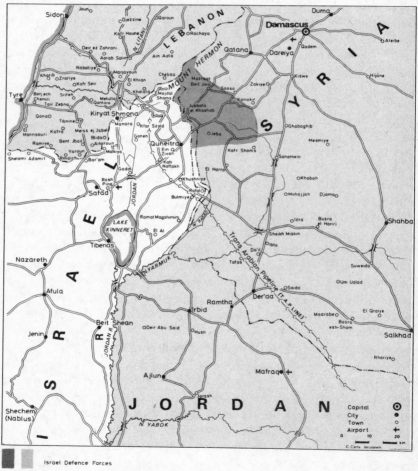

Israel Defence Forces

Situation at time of cease-fire on Syrian front, Oct. 1973.

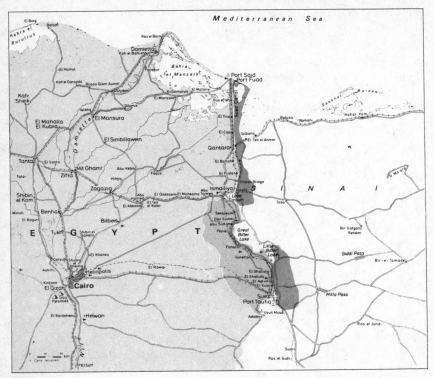

Israel Defence Forces

Egyptian Forces

Situation at time of cease-fire on Egyptian front, Oct. 1973.

occupied in June 1967 and after . . . "—a condition which was clearly contrary to the resolution itself. All the same, the fighting continued. Between the time the resolution had been adopted, and the time it was about to come into force, Israeli forces had completely cut off the Suez-Cairo road. The Egyptian Third Army tried desperately to break out from encirclement, and Egyptian artillery pounded Israeli forces both near the road and further north. Since Egypt had not stopped firing, the I.D.F. saw no reason why it should unilaterally withhold fire, and it utilized the additional hours in order to strengthen the ring around the Third Army by taking the Red Sea fishing port of Adabiya on the Gulf of Suez. General Adan cleared the entire water edge and reached the outskirts of the town of Suez where bitter fighting continued.

At the request of President Saadat the Security Council convened for another emergency session on Tuesday 23 October, and once more it was the two Superpowers who proposed a joint resolution. This resolution, Number 339, adopted by 14 votes to none, with one abstention, whilst confirming the decision on an immediate cessation of all kinds of fire and all military action, urged "that the forces be returned to the positions they occupied at the moment the cease-fire became effective". Since those positions were in dispute, and the very fate of the Third Army hinged on which of the conflicting versions was adopted, this clause did little to clarify the issues. The Security Council now also requested the Secretary-General to take measures for the immediate dispatch of UN observers to supervise the observance of the cease-fire.

In spite of this new resolution, firing continued. The Soviet Union, in a desperate attempt to bail out its client Egypt, and re-establish its credibility in Arab eyes, now engaged in a series of diplomatic and military moves which indicated a willingness to intervene unilaterally, with considerable force, in order to save the Third Army. Party Secretary Brezhnev sent a strong note to the U.S. Government urging that the two Superpowers send forces to enforce the cease-fire, and if the U.S. did not agree, the Soviet Union would be obliged to consider acting alone. Simultaneously, American Intelligence indicated the presence of seven Soviet landing craft and two ships with troop helicopters on their decks, in eastern Mediterranean waters; moreover, seven divisions of Soviet airborne troops were on a stand-by alert, with one division on a high alert level ready to move on call. A new element in the situation was the evidence that the Soviet air force had pulled back most of the large transports which had been used in airlift supplies to Egypt and Syria, to their home bases in the Soviet Union. They might be used for transporting Soviet troops into the battle zone.

To prevent any precipitate move by the Soviet Union, the U.S. Government now decided on a worldwide alert, all commands being ordered to assume defensive condition 3—one above the normal peace-time defensive condition, a situation in which troops were placed on stand-by and awaiting orders, with all leave cancelled. It was subsequently rumored in Washington, D.C., that this worldwide nuclear alert was occasioned more by internal considerations, since the Watergate scandal reached another climax at about the same time as a result of President Nixon's decision to fire his special prose-cutor, Archibald Cox, who had been investigating the scandal. This allegation has been violently denied by all those directly concerned. In any case, the "Superpower debate on a nuclear footing" disappeared as quickly as it had emerged. Within the Security Council a compromise was evolved, which would exclude the permanent members of the Council, and therefore the two Superpowers, from the immediate peace-keeping operation. The Secretary-General of the UN, Dr. Kurt Waldheim, received unanimous approval to transfer forces of Austria, Finland and Sweden, then serving the UN in Cyprus, to the Middle East war zone.

The U.S. nuclear alert brought to a head a latent tension between the U.S. and its NATO allies, who protested that they had not been consulted beforehand. The U.S. retaliated by putting on record its irritation at Europe's failure to rally to the Americans in the Middle East. Except for Portugal, which had granted landing rights in the Azores to U.S. planes resupplying Israel with war matériel, none of the Europeans had co-operated with the U.S. during the Yom Kippur War. The real reason for this European dissociation from American policy was economic: unlike Europe, the U.S. was dependent on the Arab countries for only 11% of its oil consumption, while the Europeans feared an oil ban which might bankrupt many of their economies.

The accommodation reached by the Superpowers was not immediately reflected in the battle zone. On Thursday there was renewed fighting in the Suez area, and once again the UN observers sent from Cairo failed to establish any satisfactory cease-fire line. The plight of the 20,000 men of the Egyptian Third Army was desperate. They had been cut off for four days and on the most generous estimate could not be expected to hold out for another week. Israel permitted a shipment of blood plasma for the treatment of the wounded there, but refused to permit provisions including water to go through, since such provisions would help to turn it into a well consolidated base from which future aggression could threaten.

So far, Egypt had reported only 48 Israeli captured, and Syria, which had exhibited captured Israeli soldiers on television, had reported none, whilst Israel, on the morning of 24 October, held 1,300 prisoners of war—988 Egyptians, 295 Syrians, 12 Iraqis and five Moroccans. It now became evident that commitments under the Geneva Convention notwithstanding, the Arabs were preparing to use the emotional issue of POWs and of missing soldiers as a bargaining card. Another card which was being used was the maintenance of a naval blockade in the Bab-el-Mandeb Straits at the southern entrance to the Red Sea, considered by Israel as an act of war and a violation of the cease-fire.

While the other fronts remained quiet on Friday 26 October,

the encircled Third Army made a desperate last attempt to improve its position. Under cover of tank and artillery fire, the Egyptians attempted to take control of the pontoon bridges south of the Little Bitter Lake and to lay a new one across the Canal south of Port Suez. After a battle lasting three hours, in which the Israel Air Force played a prominent part, the attempt to establish an east-west link-up between the Egyptian forces was foiled and the Arabs' new bridge lay in ruins. That day also brought more positive evidence of the disintegration of the Third Army's morale as the Israelis rounded up numerous small bands of soldiers, often without a fight, who had detached themselves from the main force and were trying to make their own way back to the Egyptian heartland.

The U.S. Secretary of State now initiated an intensive round of diplomatic negotiations to prevent the collapse of the Third Army. Whether motivated by concern over the possibility of direct Soviet involvement and the concomitant danger of Superpower confrontation, or by his own desire to avoid a total Egyptian humiliation and to salvage something of the "limited defeat" which he had envisaged from the outset, the Secretary of State leaned hard on the Israel government to permit a regular resupply of the Third Army. On Saturday 27 October, 21 days after the outbreak of hostilities, the guns fell silent on both fronts. A few hours later Israeli and Egyptian military chiefs, meeting at the 101-kilometer milestone on the Suez-Cairo highway (63 miles from the Egyptian capital), finally ironed out the details of the supply operation.

From a military point of view, the war which had begun under the worst possible circumstances that Israel could have envisaged and under the most promising ones that the Arab forces could have hoped for, and for which they had prepared, resulted in a victory for Israel's forces. Although Egypt maintained two major bridgeheads on the east bank of the Suez Canal, Israel forces held about 625 square miles (1,600 sq. km.) on the western bank of the Canal, with its westernmost forces about 44 miles (70 km.) from Cairo; the Egyptian Third Army had been trapped, and but for Superpower and UN intervention, would have been doomed. In the north, Israel held 234 square miles (600 sq. km.) of territory beyond the 1967 truce line, reaching up to 25 miles (40 km.) from Damascus. According to American estimates, the combined Arab forces had lost about 2,000 tanks and some 450 planes, compared with Israel's loss of 800 tanks and 115 aircraft. Many of the Egyptian and Syrian disabled tanks were left in territory controlled by Israel, and were subsequently reconditioned. As against

THE YOM KIPPUR WAR   213

over 8,800 prisoners held by Israel, Egypt and Syria held fewer than 400 Israelis.

While the feeling in Israel was one of profound relief, a sensation of having been saved from immense danger, there was no celebration of victory. Israel had lost 2,522 killed—almost one pro mil of its population, an average of 105 per day up to 27 October, when fighting stopped. The fact that Arab armies had lost many times more—the Syrians an estimated 3,500 killed, and the Egyptians an estimated 15,000—was no comfort to Israelis.

On 11 November the cease-fire agreement was signed between Israel and Egypt at Kilometer 101 on the Suez-Cairo road. This agreement made arrangements for the supply of food, water and medicine to the beleaguered town of Suez, and for the provision of non-military supplies to the Third Army on the east bank of the Suez Canal. It also made initial provisions for the exchange of all prisoners of war.

The Geneva Peace Conference opened on 21 December 1973 with the participation of Egypt, Jordan and Israel, under the auspices of the U.S. and the Soviet Union. The chair reserved for Syria was conspicuously empty. After a ceremonial opening and an exchange of speeches it adjourned *sine die*. On 18 January 1974 a separation of forces agreement was entered into between Egypt and Israel, and by 1 March 1974 it had been fully implemented. Israel agreed to withdraw all its forces from the west bank of the Suez Canal and a UN force manned a belt nearly seven miles (11 km.) wide between Egyptian forces on the east bank of the Canal and Israeli forces. On either side of that UN belt defense zones of a similar width were established, in which Egyptian and Israeli forces were each limited to a force of 7,000 troops, 33 tanks and 36 artillery pieces. Similar negotiations with Syria took considerably longer, and were accompanied by heavy, though localized, fighting. A major stumbling block was the Syrian refusal to hand over lists of Israel POWs, after a considerable period during which visits had been denied to them. Bodies of Israeli soldiers who had been killed, with their hands tied behind their backs, had been found on the Golan, and as long as complete lists were not available, the fear that a similar fate awaited other prisoners turned this into an issue of national importance for all of Israel. Finally, on 31 May 1974, a disengagement agreement was signed with Syria. Israel agreed to give up all the territory it held east of the 1967 cease-fire lines, and a belt held by UN forces was established, faced on each side by defensive zones in which thinned-out forces

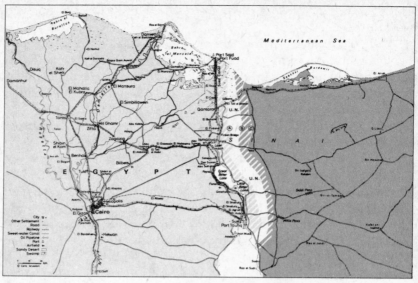

Israel–Egypt agreement on separation of forces, Jan. 18, 1974.

A–Line of deployment of Egyptian forces. The area between this line (shaded) and the Suez Canal is limited in armament and forces. B–Line of deployment of Israel forces. The shaded area between B and C is limited in armament and forces. The white area between A and B is the position of the U.N. emergency force.

were permitted. These were rather narrower than those in the south, considering the nature of the terrain.

These were purely military agreements, signed by commanders from both sides—the Egyptian agreement at Kilometer 101, the Syrian agreement in Geneva.

After prolonged shuttle talks conducted by Secretary of State Kissinger, which were deadlocked in March 1975 and resumed in August of that year, an additional Interim Agreement between Israel and Egypt was initialled in Geneva on 4 September 1975 and signed on 10 October. Israel undertook to return to Egypt civilian control the important oil fields at Abu Rodeis, which, since 1967, had supplied about 60% of Israel's petroleum requirements. It also agreed to withdraw from the strategic Mitla and Gidi passes and from territory further north, which from then on would become a buffer zone under UN supervision. Israel would maintain its electronic early warning system at Um Hashiba, to the west of the passes, a position from which a wide area reaching well into the heart-land of Egypt could be electronically surveyed; Egypt would be permitted to establish a parallel station to the east, giving electronic access to a large area under Israel control. For the first time in the history of the conflict—an innovation widely discussed in the U.S. and elsewhere—an American presence would be established, 200 technicians manning an independent electronic surveillance facility whose findings would be reported to both sides. The former UN belt was now to be occupied by Egyptian troops—another, wider UN belt being established further east. In return for Israel's concessions, Egypt joined Israel in an undertaking that they would not resort to the threat or use of force or military blockade against each other; Egypt also commited itself to permit the passage through the Suez Canal of non-military cargoes to and from Israel. The pledge of non-renewal of fighting was hedged, however, by an exception made in case Israel were to attack another Arab country. (The question as to who is the attacker has always been a difficult one to decide. It will be remembered that even in October 1973 the first Egyptian and Syrian communiqués referred to an Israel attack repulsed by Arab forces.) The agreement was to remain in force until superseded by another agreement. In a separate document the Egyptian government undertook to agree to automatic renewal of the mandate of the UN forces for a period of three years. Egypt also pledged to moderate its political propaganda and boycott warfare against Israel.

To make up for the imbalance between Israel's strategic, territorial and economic concessions, and the Egyptian *quid pro quo*, which is a far cry from the non-belligerence which had earlier been stipulated as a *conditio sine qua non* for withdrawal from the passes, the U.S. government made certain commitments to Israel, including guarantees for oil supplies in case of embargo and their financing, as well as arms supplies and political consultations in the future. These commitments demonstrated the U.S. interest in bringing about the agreement, as part of a strategy designed to displace the Soviet Union in Egypt and to assert U.S. primacy in the Middle East. In the course of subsequent Congressional hearings it was made clear that, barring the first mentioned undertaking, concerning oil, the remaining commitments were not to be considered "legally binding." The agreement was signed by both military and diplomatic representatives. By the end of February 1976 all the military and civilian dispositions resulting from the agreement had been accomplished.

𝟡

Comparisons

In the period from 1947 to 1974, five full-scale wars were fought between Israel and its Arab neighbors; in Arab eyes they are campaigns within a single war, within one long war. For the Arabs the war has never stopped, regardless of truce decisions, armistice agreements, and cease-fires which intervened from time to time. The intervals between the bouts of fighting were often filled to overflowing with terrorist operations. The first episode was Israel's War of Independence in 1947–49. The second war was the Sinai Campaign of 1956. The third was the Six-Day War of 1967. The fourth, the War of Attrition, lasted from 1968 to 1970. Fifthly, the Yom Kippur War of 1973, with the subsequent War of Attrition lasting for three months on the Egyptian front and seven months on the Syrian front.

The purpose of this chapter is to compare these wars from a number of angles. Just as before 1947, the political initiative for the employment of force was in Arab hands, so after 1947 all five wars were launched, on the political level, by the Arab side. It has been said that, for the Arabs, in the context of the Israel–Arab conflict, war is not a continuation of diplomacy by other means, as Clausewitz pronounced, but just the opposite: diplomacy is the continuation of war by other means.

Objectives

A comparison of the objectives of the respective wars entails certain difficulties, not only because the declared aims are not necessarily the real ones, but because the starting point of each war was different. It may be said that, from the beginning of the War of Independence early in December 1947 until the end of the British Mandate in Palestine and the establishment of Israel in May 1948, the political objective of the Arab side was to prevent the emergence of a Jewish State, primarily by compelling the United Nations to realize the "mistake" that it had committed in adopting the Partition Resolution, and forcing the Organization, and its senior members, to alter it. It does not seem that at that stage the objective was to occupy by force the area designated for the Jewish State. As long as the British were in the country and their military forces dominated the scene, the Arabs probably assumed that even if they could occupy the Jewish territory there would be intervention by the British or by an international agency to prevent any such occupation. Even though it is now known, from various sources, that the British authorities had made preparations, or at least established contacts in certain countries, with a view to the setting up of refugee camps for Jews from Palestine, it still seems likely that, at that juncture at least, the British would not have permitted the complete destruction or subordination of the *Yishuv*.

The Arab objective then was first and foremost a demonstration of force, to prove to the world that a Jewish State could not possibly be created except by a continuing struggle—which the Great Powers would and could not permit. In fact, the Arabs came perilously near to achieving their aim. In March 1948, the U.S. went back on its support for the Partition Resolution, and advocated a trusteeship, which, for all practical purposes, would have implied postponement *sine die* of the establishment of a Jewish State. This was, no doubt, an Arab political triumph won by military means. It was their greatest triumph ever in the unbroken chain of struggle. Jerusalem was cut off from the coast; Jewish settlements in the vicinity of Jerusalem—the Ezyon Bloc, Neveh Ya'akov, Atarot, the Dead Sea Works—were severed from the city; the Negev was cut off from the center of the country, Western Galilee from Haifa, Upper Galilee from the Jordan Valley. These military successes had led to a political accomplishment of the first order. Thus, for military and for political reasons, it became necessary for the Haganah to take the initiative and, for the first time in almost three decades of existence, to go over to a large-scale offensive; the ongoing British evacuation and the reduced likelihood of inimical British intervention made that offensive feasible.

It was early in May 1948, after a resounding Jewish military performance—after phenomenal progress in carrying out what was called Plan D, designed to gain control of the territory allotted to the Jewish State and to establish corridors to Jewish settlements which would be left outside its boundaries—that the Arabs realized that

all hope of preventing the establishment of the Jewish State had
vanished. It was then decided that the regular Arab armies would
enter the war. The Arab intent from the middle of May to the first
truce on 10 June 1948 was, undoubtedly, to destroy the infant Jewish
State, through occupation of its entire area by force. The idea was not
wholly utopian. It is well known, from secondary sources, that Field-
Marshall Montgomery, then Chief of the Imperial General Staff,
expressed the view that a Jewish state could not last longer than a
fortnight against the onslaught of the regular armies of five neighboring
countries. The Jews had no heavy armament, no artillery, no tanks
and no fighter planes: they would not, he was persuaded, be able to
resist. However, the Arab invasion failed. After two weeks of fighting,
and in spite of grievous losses in men, equipment, and territory, the
Haganah, soon to be reconstituted as the Israel Defense Forces, was
able to halt the invaders. Once the Arab offensive had lost momentum
and equipment for the Haganah, already purchased abroad, began
to arrive (as soon as the British blockade was lifted), the Arabs relinquished their no-longer-realizable objectives of destruction and,
from the eve of the first truce onward their military ambition seems
to have been circumscribed. It was no longer the wiping out and
occupation of the Jewish State as a whole.

   The impression that emerges (which is rather difficult to substantiate)
is that after the first truce the Arabs had ceased to think in terms of
"a meeting in Tel Aviv," and instead each Arab army concentrated
on its own limited objectives. The Syrians, in the north, aimed at the
isolation and seizure of the "finger of Upper Galilee," and therefore
shifted the main thrust of their offensive from Deganyah northward
to Mishmar ha-Yarden. When they attacked Deganyah, they no
doubt hoped to advance toward Haifa; once they attacked Mishmar
ha-Yarden, they probably wished to reach Rosh Pinnah, and thus
amputate the "finger". In the south, too, the Egyptians gave up their
attempt to advance northward from Ashdod toward Tel Aviv;
they concentrated on their move eastward, and on consolidating
their positions further south, so as to cut off and ultimately occupy
the Negev. The Arab Legion, the army of Transjordan, which from
the outset aimed at the occupation of the Arab parts of Palestine, now
set itself almost exclusively to that task; the army of Iraq, which had
crossed the Jordan near Gesher, in a thrust parallel to that of the Syrians,
now deployed further southward to assist the Transjordanians, whose
king was related to the Iraqi monarch.

   To sum up, the Arab objective changed from 1947 to 1949. In the first phase, it was to prevent the establishment of a Jewish State; in the second—to occupy and destroy the State; in the third—to truncate its area.

In 1956, the timing of the Sinai Campaign was determined by the Israel side, and it is difficult therefore to speak of Arab objectives in that case. President Nasser's policy had been to soften up Israel to the point where, at some date of the future, it would be practicable either to defeat the Jewish State in battle or, alternatively, to force it to its knees under the pressure of military superiority. He had pursued this, on the one hand, with the *fedayeen* organized, trained, and directed by Egyptian Intelligence, with their nightly excursions across the armistice lines and their record of terrorist acts which made Jewish life along the armistice lines uneasy and almost impossible and, on the other, through the tremendous influx into Egypt of Czech weaponry after the arms deal of 1955. The Israeli objectives in 1956 were flexible and adapted to the development of events. At the least, they were no more than a major retaliatory raid against *fedayeen* bases. The intermediate aim would have been the clearing up of those bases, and the opening of the blockaded Straits of Tiran and securing free navigation through them. A possible maximum objective would have been occupation of Sinai, as a bargaining counter in the event of peace negotiations. The Sinai Campaign was in the nature of a preventive strike, utilizing the international situation, and the unique conjuncture in which Great Britain and France were threatening to use force against Egypt in their own cause—namely, opposition to the nationalization of the Suez Canal.

As for 1967, even today it is difficult to determine precisely what were the aims of President Nasser. His defenders argue that he had been preparing nothing beyond a demonstration of force and had not really intended to employ it. And, indeed, it does not seem likely that he considered the destruction of Israel's army and the occupation of the whole of Israel as an attainable target at that stage. Judging from the disposition of his strength in May-June, it must rather be assumed that, in addition to drawing Israeli troops away from the Syrian border and thus lightening the burden on his ally, his purpose was to close the Straits of Tiran again and make sure that they would not be opened by Israel; to stop any navigation from Eilat southward and thus shut off Israel's oil supply, as a major step toward its economic strangulation. It is obvious that simultaneously he meant to sunder the Negev from the heartland of Israel and establish a land-bridge between Egypt and Jordan. The emphasis in Egyptian propaganda at the time on the Negev and on the "illegality" of its inclusion in Israel would point to that conclusion. Even so, while the destruction of Israel did not appear to be on the cards then, it was more than doubtful whether Nasser would have been satisfied with the realization of the "lesser". Success would have generated a momentum that would have made it impossible for him to stop there and then, even if he were inclined to do so.

From 1968 to 1970, during the War of Attrition, the Arab objective was clear: to bring the Government of Israel to the realization that continued occupation of Egyptian territory would entail more loss than gain, and thus oblige it to give up the area occupied.

The Arab objective in 1973 is again not entirely clear. Since politicians are still debating the subject, one hesitates to intrude, although ultimately this will become another historical problem. The most likely hypothesis is that Egypt's plan was, in Phase I, to cross the Suez Canal and occupy territory to the east of it, and thereby upset the *status quo*. The present writer has not seen any evidence that, at all events to begin with, the Egyptian army proposed to penetrate into the heart of Israel. The Egyptian Government probably assumed, as Israel has always assumed in the previous wars, that in any case there would be intervention in one form or another by the UN or the Great Powers, so that hostilities would in all likelihood be relatively short.

As far as the Syrians are concerned, there was a very interesting problem. No doubt their objective, immediate and unconditional, was to recapture the whole of the Golan Heights. That was a minimum; there is, however, evidence suggesting that they planned to go further. They had brought along bridging equipment which would have enabled them to cross the Jordan, possibly a repetition of the abortive strategy of 1948—a desire to amputate the "finger" of Upper Galilee and annex it to Syria. It must be remembered that the Syrians had never agreed to the Mandatory boundaries that had been fixed for Palestine; they had never accepted the fact that the headwaters of the Jordan were included within the boundaries of British Mandated territory (not to speak of "*Suriya junubiya*", a term which President Assad has used, referring to the whole of Palestine as Southern Syria). The Syrians, following in the footsteps of the French, regarded the determination of the Mandatory boundaries between Syria and Palestine as a fraudulent act by the British against the French.

Throughout all these years, ever since the battle-cry of "*Falastin biladna*" ("Palestine is our country") was heard in the streets of Jerusalem in the early 1920s, the declared aim of the fighting and the warfare invariably included the "restoration of the legitimate rights of the Palestinian Arabs." This nebulous phrase—nebulous not necessarily to those who employ it, but for those for whose ears it is intended— was used to egg on the fighters; as has now been shown, except for 1948 it was not translated into concrete objectives of military action by regular Arab forces. After 1967, it was plain that this translation would be relegated to a second stage, and that the first stage, a specifically Egyptian and Syrian interest, unrelated to any Palestinian Arab one, was to recapture the territories taken from Egypt, among them the Sinai Peninsula (possibly excluding the Gaza Strip), and from Syria— namely, the Golan Heights. At a third stage, the "legitimate rights of the Palestinians" would come to the fore; but this was, basically, a cause for the Palestinian Arabs themselves to champion, with the Egyptians and other Arab States affording political and other aid.

Although the impression may at times be created that the question of "territories" took on prominence only after 1967, the fact is that all the fighting was concerned with territories. Historically, the origins of that motif may be dated as early as 1911, when neighboring Arabs raided the settlement of Merḥavyah. This may have been the first Arab attack, politically inspired, which aimed at the capture of terri- tory—specifically, the territory of a Jewish settlement. In 1920–21, and 1936–39, the issue in military terms was the territory of one after another Jewish settlement which was attacked, whether well- established villages or of very recent foundation, such as Ḥanitah and Tirat Ẓevi. In 1947 the issue was the whole area allotted to the Jewish State. The only major difference, in this respect, between before and after 1967 is this: up to that point, the Arab States had supposedly warred against Israel to help the Palestinian Arabs recover territories which they considered to be theirs (although, in the event, Jordan held on to a large area of Palestinian territory after 1949 and incorporated it in its own: only Egypt created a separate status for the Gaza Strip). After 1967, territories were at issue which Syria and Egypt considered to be very much their own. To the extent that there was a qualitative rise in the combat standards of Egyptian and Syrian soldiers in 1973, it must be largely attributed to this factor— in 1973, the Egyptian soldier fought for Egyptian territory, and the Syrian soldier fought for what he held to be Syrian territory. In 1948 when Gamal Abdul Nasser, then an Egyptian colonel, was encircled by Israel troops in the Faluja Pocket in the Negev, he once said, accord- ing to one witness: "Actually, what am I doing here? Why am I fighting in this country? We have problems with the British in Egypt and here I am in [what, by implication, he deemed] a foreign country, fighting against the Jews." There is no doubt that a soldier fights better when he fights for territory which he considers his own, and his commanders are under more powerful motivation to make a maximum bid for victory. The reverse, incidentally, is true of the Israeli side: not that the individual Israeli soldier fought less well on the banks of the Suez Canal, but when Egypt had captured territory to the east of it, there was not so compelling a reason for the Israeli high command to embark upon a major effort to recapture what had been lost. In his talk to Israeli newspaper editors on 9 October 1973, Moshe Dayan said expressly that the Canal was not Deganyah, implying that it merited less of an effort.

Initiative

The question of who took the initiative will be treated together with the issue of surprise, although they are by no means identical. The strategic initiative can be taken by one side without achieving any surprise at all; even the reverse may sometimes be true, as we shall see.

In the first phase of the War of Independence, waged against the Jews by Palestinian Arabs and irregulars from neighboring countries, the initiative was in Arab hands. This phase has occasionally been described as a civil war; the present writer doubts whether the description is really apposite. There is a basic difference between, say, the Spanish Civil War, where one Spaniard fought another because of political and ideological divergencies, and the war of 1947–48 in Palestine between Jew and Arab, two different nationalities living side by side in the same country. And Arab initiative was not accompanied by surprise. Ben-Gurion had predicted over and over again that if the UN resolution were favorable to the Zionist viewpoint, the Arabs, from their viewpoint, would consider themselves compelled to employ violence and prevent its implementation. It was only subsequently, early in April 1948, that the initiative passed into Jewish hands, when Operation Naḥshon contrived to open the corridor to Jerusalem, and with the carrying out of Plan D the Palestinian Arabs and Kaukji's "Liberation Army" were thrown on to the defensive, and ultimately routed.

From 15 May onward, the initiative passed into the hands of the five regular Arab armies which invaded Israel on that day. That reversion of initiative was not accompanied by any surprise, either. Well ahead of zero hour, it was well known in Israel what was to be expected. Schools were closed; total mobilization was ordered; trenches were dug. The doubt which prevailed until a few days before, as to the possible entry or abstention of Transjordan, was dispelled when Golda Meir came back with empty hands from her mission to Emir Abdullah. Yigael Yadin, the Chief of Operations of the *Yishuv's* armed forces, in the historic session of the People's Administration where the decision was taken to declare the independence of the State of Israel, predicted precisely what was about to happen. The Arab initiative petered out toward the first truce, surviving only very partially in the south and in the north during the subsequent ten days' fighting. Already, at that juncture, the I.D.F. had gone over to the offensive, particularly in the central sector, where Operation Danny yielded the capture of Lydda and Ramleh and, in the north, in Operation Dekel and Brosh, aimed at Lower Galilee and the Mishmar ha-Yarden enclave, respectively. The last phase of the war saw the initiative monopolized by the I.D.F.

In 1956, both strategic initiative and surprise were on the Israeli side. Although it was no secret that Israel had mobilized reserves, everyone, including President Eisenhower, assumed that its intention was to undertake an offensive against Jordan, the base of many of the terrorist operations into Israeli territory. Thus, the strike launched against Egypt, with a parachute drop near the Mitla Pass and the subsequent linking up of Israeli forces with the parachutists, came utterly unexpected. The spectacular military success of Israel that followed was in no small measure a result of the combination of initiative and surprise. This is the only one of the wars in which that was the case. It must also be said that the disappointing political consequences of the war were also, to a large extent, due to the same factors. To achieve surprise, the prior political spadework had necessarily to be foregone. The U.S. Government was not consulted and that was one of the reasons—though by no means the only one—why it turned so decidedly against Israel in the diplomatic aftermath of the fighting; it is a matter of history that Israel was forced to withdraw within four months from all the territories it had taken.

In 1967, the war started on Arab initiative. At the time of the Independence Day parade on 15 May in that year, nobody in a responsible position in Israel believed that war was in the offing, or would in fact break out within a few weeks. Certainly no-one believed that Israel would start one. When Abba Eban, Foreign Minister of Israel, was questioned in January 1967 about his predictions for the year just begun, he said that he knew what would not happen: neither war nor peace. And when Yizḥak Rabin, Chief of the General Staff, was asked as late as April 1967 about his own expectations, he said that a war in which Egypt and Jordan would operate together in co-ordinated manner could be excluded. In other words, not only did Israel have no intention of commencing war: its leadership did not forsee one. Perhaps the most surprising aspect of the 1967 war is that the Israeli side did achieve surprise. It is almost impossible to understand how President Nasser, who a few days earlier had exclaimed: "I am waiting for Rabin, and if he wishes to come, *ahalan wesahalan*, let him be welcome"—could have been taken aback when the Israel Air Force struck early on 5 June. Yet that is a fact: on that day, the Israel Air Force brought off an operational surprise in a situation in which strategic surprise was virtually out of the question.

During the War of Attrition, from 1968 to 1970, the initiative was in Arab hands. It was not the Israeli side which started that war. But no surprise was involved. When the Israel Defense Forces took up positions along the east bank of the Suez Canal, it was general knowledge that the Egyptians, from their own standpoint, had to exert every possible effort to dislodge them, or at least prevent them from digging in solidly and permanently.

In 1973 it was not only the initiative which was in Syrian and Egyptian hands, but there was also a considerable element of surprise: not surprise on the Day of Atonement at 2:00 p.m., when the firing actually began—by which time it was evident that fighting was about to break out—but surprise at "zero minus 24", so that the normal interval required for the orderly mobilization and disposition of Israel's reserves, envisaged as necessary in the event of the outbreak of large-scale war, was lacking.

Big-Power Attitudes

From this viewpoint Israel's most fortunate hour came in 1948. The war of 1948 was the only one in which both the U.S. and the Soviet Union were basically identified with the political objectives of the State of Israel. It should not be overlooked, however, that in that year Great Britain was still the major Power in the Middle East, which it is not today. It still had very close defense arrangements with Transjordan; it had a defense agreement with Egypt, and a similar one with Iraq. There were British forces along the Suez Canal, and the Arab Legion was officered and commanded by British personnel. The fact that Great Britain was, to a very large extent, aligned politically on the Arab side meant a great deal. But the U.S., although at that time of far less importance to the Middle East than it now is, as well as the Soviet Union, in essence espoused Israel's objective.

The reverse was true in 1956, when Great Britain and France followed a line more or less parallel to Israel's (although it was France alone which supported Israel openly; Great Britian essayed a tactic of neutrality.) The U.S. and the Soviet Union went resolutely and decidedly against Israel, and not only did Bulganin threaten Tel Aviv with a bombardment of rockets: there was also American advice to take that threat seriously—counsel which, in any case, was enough to convince Israel leaders that the U.S. would not do anything actively to oppose it. If 1948 was the zenith of Big Power attitudes from the Israel viewpoint, 1956 was its nadir. The war in 1956 was too short for Big Power unanimity markedly to influence military events; it was, however, more than evident in its political aftermath—within a few months Israel had to withdraw from all the territories that it had taken during the Sinai Campaign.

In 1967 the Soviet Union was wholly identified with the Arab side; in fact, there is evidence that that war resulted from Soviet instigation. The U.S. was identified to a large extent with Israel, at least, insofar as responsibility for the beginning of the war was concerned, and a wish to prevent any possible Israeli reverse. In that year, President Johnson's message to the Soviet Union was clear: if you stay out, we stay out—and the Soviet Union had good reason to believe that the converse would also have proved true. The fact that the U.S. not only prevented the adoption of an anti-Israel resolution at the UN, but also used its influence with other delegations to convince them to vote with it, which was quite unusual in American practice in Middle East debates, may be credited in large measure to the personal share of Arthur Goldberg, then U.S. Ambassador to the UN.

From 1968 to 1970, again, the Soviets were completely identified with the Arab side. Moreover, they apparently not only supported the Arabs, but also encouraged them to embark upon military adventures; and when failure was imminent in such cases, there was evidence of their direct military intervention to defend the heartland of Egypt against Israel reprisals by air attack. American identification with Israel, on the other hand, was far more qualified. While the U.S.

continued to make exceptional efforts to keep Israel's armed strength
in balance with that of its Arab neighbors, it was Secretary of State
Rogers who negotiated the cease-fire in 1970, and as mediator he was
precluded from taking sides. Whereas the U.S. at the time agreed with
Israel that no unconditional withdrawal could be demanded of it,
nor any unilateral withdrawal without some form of permanent
settlement, it disagreed with the prevailing view in Israel as to the
extent of territorial concessions which would have to be made by
Israel to achieve such a settlement or—in other words—as to the
ultimate alignment of a permanent boundary between Israel and its
Arab neighbors.

In 1973, in the Yom Kippur War and its aftermath, the Soviet
Union once more identified itself absolutely with the military and
political effort of Egypt and Syria, The logistical and possibly the
operational preparations for the concerted Egyptian-Syrian attack
were actively supported by the Soviet Union; and during the war
Soviet supplies arrived in unprecedented quantities. When the tide of
battle had turned, and Israel's forces in the north had advanced
beyond the purple line to within 25 miles (40 km.) of Damascus,
and 45 miles (70 km.) from Cairo in the south, it was the Soviet
Union which took the initiative to bring about a cease-fire which
would allow the Egyptians and Syrians to extricate themselves without
losing face. The U.S. helped Israel logistically, on what was an unprecedented scale for America, although much smaller than the
corresponding effort of the Soviet Union on behalf of the Arabs.
On the political level, however, there was no complete identity:
the agreement arrived at in Moscow between Secretary of State
Kissinger and the Soviet authorities, respecting Security Council
Resolution 338, while taking vital Israel interests into account, was
prompted no less by a concern for détente on a worldwide scale,
and for American positions in the Middle East. In the ensuing negotiations on the separation of forces with Egypt, at the Geneva Conference,
and the negotiation for separation of forces with Syria, it was Dr.
Kissinger who discharged the pivotal role of mediator which, by its
very nature, rules out identification with one or the other side. There is
thus no symmetry between the Soviet attitude to the Arab side,
and the American attitude to the Israeli—complete identification
on the one hand, a much more sophisticated and differentiated attitude
on the other.

Number of Fronts

The War of Independence was the bitterest from this viewpoint as well. It was conducted simultaneously on four fronts, with the Iraqis for a while adding a fifth. Hostilities were waged along all the boundaries of Israel at one and the same time.

The war of 1956 was in this regard the easiest, with only a single front, the Egyptian, although forces had to be pinned down in a state of preparedness along the Jordanian front, too, and thus there were limitations on the strength that could be deployed against the Egyptians. But that was not the case as far as the Israel Air Force was concerned.

The war of 1967 by contrast, was fought on three fronts—Egypt, Jordan, and Syria. Major offensive operations were staggered, so that the Air Force could be free to support each one of them. The counterattacks which resulted in the capture of the Golan Heights started after the battles with Egypt and Jordan had more or less been settled. The War of Attrition of 1968–70 was conducted on the Egyptian front alone, with terrorist activities as a major support of the Egyptian effort.

The Yom Kippur War of 1973 was fought on two fronts—Egypt and Syria, with a high state of preparedness and concentration of forces along a third—the Jordanian, and with good reason. Although Jordanian armor was actually engaged in the battle in the north alongside the Syrians, President Assad of Syria subsequently blamed his ally, King Hussein, for not having opened a third front. "The road to Jerusalem was open," he claimed. 1973 was also remarkable for the number and variety of other Arab armies which sent contingents to the principal belligerents—Iraq, Morocco, and Jordan to Syria; possibly Algeria and Libya to Egypt.

Weaponry

There has been a constant escalation, accelerated greatly during recent wars, in the type, sophistication, and firepower of weaponry utilized during the long years of the conflict. Almost a century ago one of the first settlers of Petaḥ Tikvah, Yehoshua Stampfer, complained that he did not even possess a single revolver to defend his settlement, and had to use sticks and stones against Arab rifles. The riots of 1920–21 witnessed the use of mostly antiquated light arms; in 1936–39, mortars and machine-guns were added. 1947–49 was fought with World War II hardware on both sides, including artillery, tanks, fighter planes, and some bombers. 1956 introduced post-World War II planes—Mystères and MIGs, and tanks. 1967 was mainly the victory of a modern air force, the Mirage taking pride of place, and of modern tanks. 1973 exemplified the use of armor on a scale that no previous war could match. The number of tanks used by the Syrians against Israel on a relatively narrow front on the Golan Heights far surpassed that maneuvered by the Germans in Operation Barbarossa, the invasion of the Soviet Union in 1941. Even more were used by the Egyptians. In addition, a variety of missiles appeared in 1973—anti-tank, air-to-air—of the highest sophistication, and never previously tried out under battle conditions. The 1973 war—more than any previous war—was a testing ground not only for tactics and strategy, but also for weapon systems developed by the U.S. and the Soviet Union.

Balance of Forces

Israel has been outnumbered in practically every war. A ratio of three to one in favor of the Arab armies had come to be accepted as tolerable. However, there were times when the real ratio was far worse. The nadir in that respect, from the Israel viewpoint, was no doubt the period between 15 May and the beginning of June 1948. Never did the balance of forces slump more negatively than then. The regular Arab armies entered the fray with fighter planes, tanks, and elements of artillery. The tanks (primarily Locusts of Second World War vintage) and guns may look rather unimpressive today; but when the Israel side did not possess a tank, cannon, or fighter plane, the heavy armament in the hands of the other side bespoke an absolute superiority. It was only after a few days that the first four field artillery pieces arrived in Israel—without sighting equipment (which was brought on a different ship), and the guns had to be ranged in by instinct. They were ranged into the Sea of Galilee, and once they hit this outflung target, a few degrees right or left was supposed to bring them on mark. When these arrived on 14 May the Mandatory authorities were still in charge and the ship which carried them was seized by the Royal Navy, but the guns were not detected, thanks to the stench of the onions that covered them, and the ship was let go shortly after midnight on 15 May. The allocation of the four guns was a decision left to Ben-Gurion personally. People with experience in artillery claimed that it was impossible to divide four guns up among different fronts, but there was a clamor for them from the Latrun front, from the Deganyah front and from the Ashdod front.

Once the matériel bought in Europe and in the U.S., and from as far away as Hawaii and Mexico, began to arrive, the balance of forces changed rapidly, so that toward the end of the War of Independence it might be said that, in terms of actual combat strength and excluding the forces left by the Egyptians in their base in Egypt and by the Jordanians in Transjordan, there was nearly an equilibrium. Israel never had numerical superiority, but there was an element of parity, and at certain times and places (particularly during the major operations in the south and in the north nearing the end of the war) there was local Israel superiority. It is no doubt one of Ben-Gurion's greatest achievements that as early as 1946 he had predicted that, if the Arabs in the past had engaged in demonstrations of force, this time they would use force to decide the issues of the day. He therefore called on the Jewish Agency and the Haganah to prepare for war against regular Arab forces. His view was met with a good deal of skepticism, even in Haganah headquarters. He was asked: "Why should we need anti-tank guns? Will the Arabs of Kalkiliya use tanks against us?" Ben-Gurion insisted, and a good deal of máterial was purchased before 15 May; when it came, it had considerable influence on the outcome of the war and the destiny of the State of Israel.

Another low point shadowed the first hours or days of the Yom Kippur War. The over-all ratio of forces in the afternoon of 6 October 1973 was in the neighborhood of one to ten or one to twelve—a ratio which makes a successful stand impossible, even in the most favorable circumstances. In the south, along the Suez Canal, it was worse still.

Duration

The longest war was that of the War of Independence: it lasted for twenty months, from December 1947 to July 1949. These included at least sixty full fighting days against Arab armies: there were lulls in between engagements, and particularly toward the end, following the second truce, there was hardly an occasion on which fighting took place on more than one front. Nevertheless in the light of the forces in existence at the time, the War of Independence was a full-scale one. The sixty actual fighting days against regular Arab armies were more than all the days in the subsequent wars together, the War of Attrition excluded.

The shortest war was that of 1956—a hundred hours; the war of 1967 lasted for six days; the War of Attrition of 1968–70—about a thousand days. It was a war of gunfire and not of movement, but it was a heavy one. There is sometimes a tendency to forget the bitterness of static warfare, just because Israel has become accustomed to swift wars of gunfire and movement. A war of gunfire without movement can well be as costly as one which involves movement. That was shown in Jerusalem in 1948; and again in the War of Attrition between 1968 and 1970; and once more in the War of Attrition that followed the Yom Kippur War. The Yom Kippur War itself lasted for eighteen fighting days, from 6 to 24 October 1973. Its aftermath, a mini-war of attrition accompanying the negotiations for separation of forces, continued intermittently in the south until the signature of the agreement with Egypt on 24 January 1974, and in the north up to the signature with Syria in Geneva on 30 May 1974.

Casualties

The War of Independence cost 6,000 Israel lives—about 1% of the entire population—including over 4,500 soldiers. The dividing line between soldiers and civilians, at a time when the army was in the process of formation, was faint. The war of 1956 cost about 200 lives; the war of 1967 close to 800; the war of 1968–70 cost some 400 lives; and the Yom Kippur War over two thousand five hundred. Its aftermath of attrition cost another 30 lives in the South, and 60 in the North.

Termination

It can be averred that each war stopped when the Arab side came to the conclusion that stoppage was in its interest. This does not imply that the halt was always against the wishes of Israel. On the contrary, in view of Israel's extreme sensitivity to bloodshed and to casualties, and particularly since its basically defensive objectives were achieved in most cases with its territory intact—whereas offensive strategic objectives, such as the destruction of enemy forces or the occupation of enemy territory or headquarters with a view to dictating terms, were considered politically unattainable—the Israel side would normally have been prepared to stop the fighting even earlier. Nevertheless, Israel's wishes were in no instance decisive in ending any of the wars.

Each war was ended by some means of international intervention. At the same time, with all respect for the myth which has grown up about the two Nobel Peace Prize winners, Ralph Bunche and Lester Pearson, it was never international intervention that led to cessation of hostilities, although that was a convenient pretext for the Arabs to stop, when in any case they were inclined to. The fact that two Nobel Peace Prizes have been given on account of this unhappy Middle East, which has had so little peace, is one of the ironic footnotes to the history of our times.

In 1949, the Egyptians agreed to armistice negotiations in Rhodes when the I.D.F. was deep in Egyptian territory, close to El Arish, with no organized Egyptian military forces between them and the Suez Canal, and the famous Egyptian brigade was encircled in the Faluja Pocket. The Egyptians did not agree to the negotiations because the Security Council had ordered them to do so. The order of the Council had been in unheeded existence for two months, in a Resolution adopted in November 1948, calling upon all sides to enter into negotiations for an armistice agreement. But the Egyptians would not agree to negotiate as long as they thought that they were still able to stand and fight. It was only after Israel's Operation Horev and the break-up of their dispositions when they had been militarily defeated, that they agreed.

In 1956, the Egyptians accepted a cease-fire when their forces in Sinai had been utterly routed, and once more, there was no significant fighting force left to continue the war. The same is true of 1967—the Egyptians, Syrians and Jordanians only accepted a cease-fire after a thorough military defeat. In 1970, there was no clear-cut defeat, but with the Israel Air Force's deep penetration into the heart of Egypt, the Egyptians reached the conclusion that the War of Attrition was more costly to them than to Israel and that they were being more ground down than their enemy.

And in 1973, when Israel had agreed to a cease-fire on 9 October, Egypt refused, and the Security Council was therefore not in a position to adopt a unanimous resolution on that subject; any such Resolution would have been vetoed by the Soviet Union. The Council adopted a unanimous resolution—No. 338—only when Israel forces seemed to endanger both Cairo and Damascus; in other words, when both the Egyptians and the Syrians had arrived at the conclusion that they had lost all the advantages which they had possessed at the beginning of the war. No longer was there an element of surprise on their side; they had forfeited the initiative; they were now on the defensive—and not very successfully so.

Thus, each of the wars was stopped by virtue of an international political act—an act which did not bring about the situation, but which put the international stamp of recognition on it. If there had been no Security Council resolutions in any one of the wars, it is likely that in any case they would all have petered out, to be renewed—as in fact they were—at some other time and place.

It has been said that Security Council resolutions have in fact prevented Israel from obtaining complete victory in 1949, 1956, 1967 and 1973. From a purely regional military viewpoint, that theory has a good deal to recommend it. In 1949, when the Egyptians finally agreed to armistice negotiations, there was no organized Egyptian military force left between Israel forces in Sinai, and Cairo. But there was a considerable British garrison along the Suez Canal, and the U.K. still had a mutual defense treaty with Egypt. Had this been invoked by Egypt, Great Britain would undoubtedly have pounced on Israel which, under these circumstances, could not have counted on any U.S. support; quite the contrary. British fighter planes did, in fact, patrol the battle area during the last stages of fighting, and five of them were brought down by the Israel Air Force.

Similarly, in 1956, the combined wrath of the U.S. and U.S.S.R. would have prevented Israel from further exploiting its military success into the heartland of Egypt, although here, too, the road to Cairo was open. (Concerning 1967, Nasser subsequently declared that there was nothing to prevent the I.D.F. from advancing to Cairo.) However, in 1967, during the War of Attrition, and again in 1973, direct Soviet intervention, in line with tacit or express commitments to prevent total Arab defeat and the capture of Arab capitals, was a possibility to be seriously considered, particularly since such further advance would have occurred against the advice of the U.S., whose restraining influence on the Soviet Union would have been withdrawn. The Soviets participated actively in the War of Attrition, and four planes piloted by Russians were downed at the time. Thus, it was not the UN instruments but the Big Power relationships, as expressed in their involvement in the Middle East conflict, that repeatedly prevented Israel from exploiting success, and turning victory in a single campaign into victory in a war.

Certain significant differences between the several international acts terminating the wars must be pointed out. In 1949, the unilateral intervention of the Security Council was followed by negotiations in which delegations of military and diplomatic representatives took part. Negotiations, while formally indirect, between the acting UN mediator and each one of the delegations separately, inevitably entailed face-to-face confrontations. In the case of Jordan, the real negotiations took place at the Emir's palace, in Transjordan, without UN presence. The resulting agreements, although far from constituting peace agreements (in fact, in each there is a preamble that it is a transition toward peace, and that the boundary lines therein agreed upon were determined without prejudice to the position of either side when peace was to come), were the closest that the sides ever came to a peace treaty. They were signed by diplomatic and military representatives of both sides, without any third party signature. This was the outcome of the military effort, and the political constellation. In territorial terms, the 1948 cease-fire and the subsequent 1949 Armistice Agreements meant total evacuation by Israel of all territories occupied beyond the Palestinian Mandatory boundary— the eastern part of Sinai and fourteen villages in the Lebanon up to the Litani River. Syria evacuated the Mishmar ha-Yarden bridgehead, but Israel forces were not permitted to enter it. Jordan handed over a slice of territory along the hills facing the coastal plain, along Wadi Ara, and the Tel Aviv-Jerusalem railway line; as a token compensation Israel ceded to Jordan some territory on the southern slopes of the Hebron Hills, along the road to Beersheba.

After the 1956 fighting, there was no direct agreement between Israel and the Arabs. There was a Security Council cease-fire resolution, and a call to all concerned to evacuate territories captured in the campaign. It was only a few months later that "an understanding" was achieved between the U.S. and Israel, and possibly one between the U.S. and the UN and Egypt. These understandings implied that no Egyptian regular forces would return to the Gaza Strip or to the other territories to be evacuated by Israel, and that the Straits of Tiran would be considered an international waterway, in which free and innocent passage would be permitted to ships of all nations, Israel included; but they involved no direct contact between Israel and the Arabs. Such was the ultimate political achievement of the 1956 war. The fate of the understanding is well known. Egyptian regular

forces returned to the Gaza Strip almost as soon as Israel withdrew
from it; and, when in 1967 Egypt challenged Israel's right to free
navigation through the Straits of Tiran, the understandings were of
no avail to prevent it.

The cease-fire resolution of 1967 did not include any call for Israel
to withdrawal; this was a basic difference. It was not that withdrawal
was not intended by any of the members of the Security Council;
it was just that the gap between the Russian insistence on unconditional
withdrawal and compensation, and the American position, which
would make withdrawal conditional on the attainment of a full and
final peace settlement, was so wide that it would have taken overlong
to negotiate. In view, therefore, of the urgency of the cease-fire
for the Arab side, the idea of withdrawal was dropped altogether.
It was not until November 1967 that Resolution 242 was adopted,
with withdrawal of Israel forces from "territories"—not from "*the*
territories"—as one of its requisites, but by no means the only one.

The War of Attrition came to an end in 1970 in an instrument
consisting of a set of parallel letters between Secretary of State Rogers
and the Egyptian Government on the one hand and the Israel Government on the other. There were no direct negotiations, nor was any
territorial change envisaged as part of that cease-fire.

The war of 1973 was stopped by a cease-fire resolution unanimously
adopted by the Security Council. The resolution—No. 338—did
not prescribe any immediate withdrawal, but by incorporating
Resolution 242 it also introduced the element of withdrawal. To
that extent the separation of forces with Egypt, and that with Syria,
fall within the compass of Resolution 338.

At the time of writing the Middle East is still in the aftermath of the
October war. The opening of the Geneva Conference, while it signifies
a more direct face-to-face negotiation than ever before, has yet to
proceed to tangibles. The two separation of forces agreements with
Egypt and the one with Syria were negotiated primarily through a
third party, Dr. Kissinger, only military details being worked out
directly between military officers of the two sides. Any signatures
of both sides on one document were limited to the military document,
and to military signatories in the case of the 1974 agreements. The
1975 agreement with Egypt was also signed by diplomats. The 1974
agreements were co-signed by representatives of the U.S. and the
U.S.S.R. Governments, as co-sponsors of the Geneva Conference.
The Soviet Government refused to sign the 1975 agreement, which
it considered as detrimental to its interest and as giving undue advantage

to the U.S.; as a result the U.S. representative also abstained from signing. In a way, the agreements of 1974 and 1975 bring us back to 1949. In both cases documents of a basically military nature were signed, not political agreements. Yet these are the only two cases in which an international dictum was followed by bilateral agreements, whatever their character.

Terrorism

Beginning as the outstanding feature of the 1936–39 Arab riots, terrorism became an almost ongoing phenomenon after 1948. Although it was but one type of attack against Israel, along with political, diplomatic, and economic warfare, its influence on the outcome of the wars described in this book was negligible. In fact, during those wars, terrorism came to an almost complete stop, not least because the terrorist organizations realized that they were not in a position to play a significant role in full-scale modern warfare.

Terrorism came to the fore in the intervals between the regular wars. The leaders of its organizations wished to remind the world, and the Arab governments above all, that they were still in existence, that they were a factor to be reckoned with in any political negotiation, and that they constituted an independent and meaningful element within the Arab world. Mostly in co-ordination with Arab governments, it was their task to keep the issue alive, to prevent the freezing of any *status quo*, however favorable to the Arab side. In addition, individual ambitions of this or that terrorist leader, normally supported by one or other Arab government, also played their part. In strategic terms, the business of terrorism was to soften up Israel militarily and materially, but primarily from the point of view of morale, in preparation for a military onslaught launched by regular armies or a political offensive. Although they caused grievous casualties from time to time, and demanded vigilance and an allocation of forces which were not without impact on the general state of preparedness of Israel's armed forces, terrorist operations as such could never claim military results of consequences.

However, they were not without a triggering effect. The invasion by regular armies in 1948 was preceded by local Arabs employing basically terrorist tactics; the war of 1956—by *fedayeen* raids; the war of 1967—by increasing activity of El-Fatah, founded in 1965; the war of 1973—by terrorist activity, climaxed by the hijacking of

planes outside the Middle East, and attacks against Israel-linked
objectives in Europe and elsewhere.

1973 in Perspective

The above comparisons should enable us to view the Yom Kippur
War, although fresh in our hearts and minds, in perspective. This
war, particularly grievous in terms of casualties—all casualties are
grievous, and for Jews "the saving of one life is as the salvation of
the world"—was not the most bitter one. The casualties in 1948
were far greater in absolute terms and, needless to say, in relative
terms. In 1948, the *Yishuv* lost 1% of its total, as against less than
one tenth of that ratio in 1973.

The war of 1973 was characterized by three particular features.
First, in this war alone, both initiative and surprise were in Arab
hands. The first Arab successes, which were very substantial, can
be ascribed to that. The Arabs had much more substantial successes
at the beginning of the 1948 war. In May 1948 the Ezyon Bloc, Neveh
Ya'akov, Atarot, and Beit ha-Aravah and Kalia, at the northern end of
the Dead Sea, fell to the Arab Legion; in the north—Massadah,
Sha'ar ha-Golan and Mishmar ha-Yarden fell to the Syrians; and
in the south—Niẓanim and Ne'ot Mordekhai, and subsequently
Kfar Darom. In 1973, the Arabs gained no such victories.

Second, two Arab armies, those of Egypt and Syria, had coordinated
not merely their strategies, but also their precise tactics, including
the meticulous coordination of zero hour; and finally, the Syrians and,
particularly the Egyptians, enjoyed the advantage of short lines.
It was they who fought close to their bases, while Israel had far more
extended lines of supply, with the related difficulties in switching
ground forces from one front to the other.

The crossing of the Suez Canal, an operation for which the Egyptian
army had been training over many years, was carried out when
only light Israel forces were on the east bank. The balance of forces
at the moment of crossing was one unprecedented in military history.
An entire army opposing almost nothing: 350 soldiers and three
tanks on the waterline, as against five divisions. The operational
achievement in crossing the Canal, therefore, is not something out
of the ordinary; the intelligence success—the success of the total
deception—is of course a different story. In the north, at the moment
when the fighting started, the ratio was one to ten or to twelve;

although this was somewhat more favorable than in the south, lacking the momentous physical barrier of the Suez Canal, the conditions were not basically different.

Against this background, it can be claimed that the success of the I.D.F. in the following phase of the war may have been the greatest triumph which it has yet achieved—a fact that does not seem to be sufficiently clear yet either in Israel or abroad. The Egyptians and the Syrians enjoyed tremendous advantages at the beginning—of surprise, and of short lines. Even so, the I.D.F. was able to turn the tide of war, to seize the initiative and to cross the Suez Canal to its west bank under conditions where no surprise was possible, for the Egyptians had every reason to expect such a crossing once a war began. And in the north, the Syrians were not only driven back from all the territory which they had captured on the Golan Heights, but yielded a good deal of territory beyond the purple line (the 1967 cease-fire line). All this taken together adds up to a tremendous military victory.

If Egypt and Syria should be retrospectively convinced, partly on account of self-critical statements made in Israel, that they won a massive victory, and now enjoy a vast military superiority—such a conviction might serve as an invitation to a fresh military initiative on their part, something which should surely be averted in the interest of all concerned.

10

Conclusions

As long as the Israel-Arab conflict continues, it may be premature to summarize. However, some concluding remarks may be in order, whose main points can be found in the accompanying table. Does any pattern emerge from them? The most striking feature may be the almost regular time interval of six to ten years between wars (the War of Attrition excluded). In fact, this is the continuation of a phenomenon witnessed in the twenties and thirties—1920–21; 1929; 1936–39; 1947–49; 1956; 1967; 1973. Is this accident, or intention, or predetermination? The beginning of each war (or campaign) is to be sought in the specific circumstances of the time, yet the pattern must not be dismissed lightly. Possibly the regular time lag may be explained in psychological terms—it takes about seven years for the high command of armed forces to renew itself; for a new generation of officers to come to office who, with increased self-confidence, are willing to try again where their predecessors have failed; alternatively, a logistical interpretation may suggest itself—to the extent that faulty equipment may be blamed for one failure, the introduction of new types of equipment, including purchase, reorganization and training, is also a process taking several years. Both explanations are open to criticism—but they cannot be dismissed lightly.

While the military outcome of war is largely determined by military factors, its diplomatic aftermath is more influenced by Great Power attitudes. The most blatant example of this truism is 1956—a resounding Israel victory followed by a diplomatic defeat.

While the number of fronts varies, there has been a steady widening of the circle of Arab states involved, politically and militarily. In 1936–39 governments of neighboring Arab states (as well as Saudi Arabia) were involved in the diplomatic process on British initiative. Their troops did not participate in actual fighting—only irregular volunteers participated, under the command of Kaukji. The same pattern emerged at the beginning of the War of Independence; but from May 1948 onward, the regular armies of five Arab states, including Iraq, were the main bearers of the burden of war. Subsequently, Arab contingents from further afield entered the fray. The war of 1973, although fought on two fronts only, witnessed the active participation of Moroccan and Iraqi troops, in addition to Jordanians. In the diplomatic aftermath, up to the agreements on the separation of forces, Algeria on the one hand, and Saudi Arabia on the other, played a significant part. With Arab involvement becoming more intense and varied, Moslem involvement was stagnant, or receded. As early as 1931 the Mufti of Jerusalem had organized the first Moslem Conference on Palestine; by 1973 the Moslems had not gone beyond the verbal support enunciated at that time.

A similar development—perhaps the most ominous—is that of arms utilized. From village pistols at the beginning to sophisticated missiles; from antiquated armament to equipment never used elsewhere—this is the line with least zigzags, reaching to the outer limits of conventional warfare. The possibility that this line may be extrapolated must not be excluded. Already it is evident that the Yom Kippur War has, in a way, fulfilled the function of the Spanish Civil War, in that it served as a testing ground for weapon systems developed by outside powers, in this case the Soviet Union and the U.S.

As has been seen, the use of violence for political ends was not a part of the Zionist concept. Theodor Herzl had not envisaged the possibility of resort to arms, for any purpose whatever. The instruments of Zionist policy were—for political Zionists—diplomacy, and—for practical Zionists—settlement and development of the land. When, by force of circumstances in Palestine, it was found necessary to establish a self-defense organization, "Haganah" (meaning "defense") was not only its name: it was its mission, and its operational and tactical doctrine. For many years it was defense in the strictest, most orthodox sense: static, passive, waiting for the enemy to strike. As late as 1937 there was a debate in the higher echelons of the Haganah as to whether Arab attacks against Jewish property, as opposed to persons, justified the resort to arms, and the decision at the time was in the negative. Restraint—havlagah—was practiced and preached. While the same cannot be said about the I.Z.L., that organization, too, was opposed to any armed initiative against the Arab population of Palestine. When the Haganah finally decided on a more mobile, active defense posture, "to move beyond the fence," it took great care to hit only the "guilty ones." As late as the spring of 1948, at the height of the War of In-

NAME OF WAR	DATE	DURATION	FRONTS	ISRAEL CASUALTIES		BIG POWER
				Number	Percentage of Population	During Fighting
Independence	1947–49	20 months	4	6000	almost 1%	US, USSR basically sympathetic to Israel; UK to Arabs (Jordan)
Sinai	1956	100 hours	1	200		US, USSR in sympathy with Egypt; UK neutral; France sympathetic to Israel
Six-Day War	1967	6 days	3	800		US in sympathy with Israel; USSR with Arabs
War of Attrition	1968–70	1000 days	1	400		As above.
Yom Kippur	1973	18 days	2	2522	almost 1‰	As above.

dependence, Haganah men, having penetrated into an Arab village which had served as a base for terrorist gangs, were severely reprimanded when, rather than hitting the gang leader, they had hit a man sitting next to him in a café.

Until April 1948, three decades after politically motivated violence had dominated the Palestinian scene, four months after the beginning of the War of Independence, the Haganah never attempted to capture Arab territory. Land was to be bought, not captured. Finally, in April 1948, with the *Yishuv* torn to pieces and political support for

ATTITUDE	OUTCOME	TERRITORIAL RESULTS	
After fighting		Of Military Operations	Of Diplomatic Follow-up
Unchanged	With 4 Arab countries; directly or quasi-directly negotiated; signed bilaterally, by military and diplomatic representatives.	Area allotted to Jewish State (—Mishmar Hayarden salient) plus additional areas inside and outside Mandatory Boundaries (Sinai—El Arish; Lebanon—Litani).	Israel relinquishes control of territories captured (Lebanon, Egypt) beyond Pal. Mandatory Boundaries; maintains control of territories captured within Mandatory Boundaries, except for area South of Hebron which is exchanged for territory in Jerusalem corridor, foothills, triangle.
US relents negative attitude to Israel objectives	Establishment of UNEF; understanding between Israel—US; Israel—UN.	Capture of Gaza; Sinai (up to 10 miles from Suez Canal).	Withdrawal from all territories.
Unchanged	Council Resolution 242; Jarring Mission.	Capture by Israel of Golan Heights; Sinai; West Bank.	No change.
	Egyptian missiles moved forward immediately after signature.	No change.	No change.
USSR in support of Arabs; US undertakes mission of mediation.	Separation of Forces Egypt (Jan. 74), Syria (April 74), negotiated indirectly through Dr. Kissinger; details directly through military representatives; signed Geneva, military representatives; UN, US, USSR witness; opening Geneva Conference, Egypt, Jordan Diplomatic representatives.	North: Israel recaptures area lost on Golan Heights and salient 400 sq. km. in Syria; South: Egypt in possession of narrow strip East of Canal, North and South end; Israel salient up to 100 kms. from Cairo.	South: Israel relinquishes all territory captured; Egypt remains in control East Bank Canal. North: Israel relinquishes all captured territory and Kuneitra, narrow strip adjoining.

the establishment of a Jewish state crumbling, particularly in the U.S., the Haganah undertook its first strategic offensive, to gain control of the area allotted to the Jewish state and access to the settlements beyond. Even then the directive was not to expel Arabs from their lands and places of abode.

Once the State was established it had to resort to force, frequently, almost continually. Yet the Israel Defense Force was true to its name, and its implied inherited mission: defense of the territory of the State, denying victory to the enemy.

When terrorist attacks became unbearable, it engaged in retaliation. There may have been cases of over-reaction; but as the word retaliation indicates, Israel reacted to acts of violence: it did not initiate them. There is no doubt that had there been no *fedayeen* attacks in 1955, there would have been no attack against Gaza; without El-Fatah attacks in 1968, there would have been no battle of Karame; without hijackings of planes, no attack against the Beirut airport. Even when the Israel government decided to take the initiative, the guiding concept was one of defense: against intolerable *fedayeen* attacks from Egyptian territory, and the threat of an all-out attack by Egypt with the help of massive Russian arms, in 1956; against huge Syrian and Egyptian concentrations, and the threat of strangulation through the closure of the Straits of Tiran, in 1967. Israel's strategic objectives were always put in negative terms: deny something to the enemy, prevent the enemy from accomplishing his aim. This is not a moral evaluation, it is a statement of fact; Israel's national objectives—the building of its state, society and culture, the creation of conditions for peaceful and neighborly relations with Arabs—cannot be achieved by force. Force is necessary to prevent others from destroying what has been built, to ensure the conditions for developments and growth.

When using force, Israel chose military targets, and only those. Civilians were hit in many Israel operations—regrettably, unavoidably, because of the proximity of military objectives to civilian concentrations, or by sheer error. Never in the history of the Haganah and I.D.F. were civilians deliberately killed.

This "purity of arms"—a motto and a doctrine that the I.D.F. inherited from the Haganah and inculcated in all its recruits—is not merely a moral category: it is a political guideline. Israel's objective was and is peaceful co-existence with its Arab neighbors. All of its successive governments have been convinced that the murder of civilians would perpetuate hatred, and hatred is not conducive to the achievement of that aim.

Israel's treatment of POWs has on the whole been exemplary. Here, again, the motive was not just humaneness or morality, nor even legal obligations under the Geneva Convention. It was the way Israel considered its enlightened self-interest. POWs were shown around the country and invited to Israeli homes, in an attempt— sometimes seemingly naive, almost pathetic—to educate today's enemies to become tomorrow's good neighbors.

The same cannot be said of the Arab side. Violence as a political instrument to combat Zionist settlement of Palestine was advocated almost from the beginning of this century, though the doctrine of violence preceded its actual application by several years. When organized violence was first employed, after World War I and the Balfour Declaration, Jews were the military target, Great Britain was the political one. The purpose of employing violence against Jews was to change British policy. The *Yishuv*, the Zionist movement, the State of Israel were never considered as the political partners to the conflict. They were—and are—not credited with a political will of their own. The assumption was—and is—that without outside support they would just wither away. The identity of Israel's patron has changed Until 1947 it was the Mandatory Government; in 1948, the UN; subsequently, the Big Powers; in 1973 and since, the U.S. The doctrine that Israel owes its survival to a patron has remained remarkably consistent. Ironically, when Herzl engaged in the first steps of his Zionist diplomacy, he turned to the Sultan of Turkey for a charter. He did not credit the Arabs with a political will of their own, and did not think of them as political partners. In his time there was some justification for that attitude; the Arabs, in fact, did not constitute a political factor. Needless to say, Herzl did not envisage the use of force to obtain the Charter: the incentives he offered the Sultan were political, economic and technological.

Except for relatively brief periods—from 1936 to 1939, when Arab arms were turned directly against the British Government, and in the years beginning 1969, when foreign planes became legitimate objects of hijacking—violence instigated by Palestinian Arabs and by Arab states was employed against a second party (the *Yishuv*, Israel) in order to change the policies of a third. It is this characteristic which explains many of the peculiarities of the conflict, which at times are at discrepancy with doctrines of war. It is this which explains why victory, in the orthodox sense, was not always important. In fact, most violent Arab adventures ended in defeat, or at best, in stalemate— from 1920 to 1973. Yet the instigators were often quite satisfied with the outcome. The White Papers of Churchill, Passfield and MacDonald, successively limiting the British commitment to the establishment of the Jewish National Home to a point where that commitment was effectively reversed, were attributed by Arabs, with considerable justification, to their show of force, even though that show had inflicted only marginal damage on the *Yishuv*.

The U.S. reversal of its position on partition, in March 1948; U.S.-Soviet co-operation against Israel following 1956 in spite of the Egyptian defeat in the Sinai War; the Rogers Plan of 1969, regardless of the losing War of Attrition; and certain U.S. actions and attitudes following the Arab defeat in the Yom Kippur War—may all be similarly explained. In fact, Saadat declared the aim of the war to have been to unfreeze the status quo, and to induce the U.S. to put pressure on Israel, or—as his journalistic mouthpiece Haikal put it—to squeeze the Israeli lemon. For such a purpose the fact of war was often more important than its military outcome, the show of force more telling than its actual impact.

A parallel—and complementary—dimension is to be found in third party interest in, and support for, Arab use of violence against the *Yishuv*, and Israel. Throughout the period of the British Mandate there were senior British officials in Palestine who disagreed with the policy laid down in the Balfour Declaration. Powerless themselves to change that policy, they aided and abetted Arab violence by omission or commission, by turning a blind eye or by giving active assistance, as a means of changing that policy. By the same token, there are many indications that attempts to reach an understanding between the Zionist Movement and moderate Arab opinion were frustrated by British officials.

In the late thirties, and during World War II, Italian and German aid to Arab rebels was evident: creating turmoil in British colonies, and pinning down forces in them, was considered in the Axis' interest.

From the Egyptian-Czech arms deal of 1955 onwards, the U.S.S.R. has to a large extent based its policy of gaining influence and possibly supremacy in the Middle East on the supply of arms and military equipment to Arab countries. The omnipresent possibility of war is of course a *sine qua non* for such a policy: once that possibility diminishes or disappears, the importance of arms supplies is proportionately reduced.

For their part, the continuing debate among Arab strategists is not whether, but how force should be employed. It concerns the relative importance and the distinctive roles of irregular warfare, conducted mainly by Palestinian Arabs with the support of Arab governments, and regular warfare, the domain of the Arab states. The legitimacy of force has never been questioned as a primary instrument of policy to combat the "evil" of Zionism and of Israel. The mission was not to change Israel's policy: Israel itself is the target, and to achieve that, force is used to change the attitudes of its "sponsors".

The often brutal and inhuman treatment of POWs, particularly by the Syrians—in addition to indicating a moral code—is in line with that thinking. What Israelis think of them is of little concern to Syrian rulers; they do not envisage them as tomorrow's good neighbors, at best as reluctant subjects.

Similarly, the deliberate killing of civilians consistently engaged in by terrorists from the earliest days, from Jaffa 1920 to Ma'alot 1974 follows the same pattern. If by and large Arab regular armies have desisted from such killing, it was primarily because of fear of retaliation, or the desire for respectability in the eyes of third parties, not out of any concern for public reaction in Israel itself.

That is why the refusal to negotiate directly with Zionist and subsequently Israeli leaders has taken on a doctrinaire, almost theological significance in Arab eyes. From the refusal of Sheikh Kassem al-Husseini, the relative of both the Mufti of Jerusalem and Yasser Arafat, to sit down with Zionist leaders in the 1920s, through the similar situation at the St. James Conference of 1939, to the refusal of President Saadat to sign a political agreement with Israel, there runs a continuous thread: the assumption that Israel is not an independent entity but rather a satellite, a stooge. Hence negotiations should be conducted, if at all, with its principals; commitments, if unavoidable, given to them, and promises extracted from them. It would then be their responsibility to make Israel adhere to the arrangements made. It is more than doubtful whether the beginning of the Geneva Conference augurs a change of attitude in this respect. So far, the Arab side has usually been able to achieve acceptable terms in spite of, or because of, this attitude.

The different attitudes to the use of force are the result of the basic asymmetry of the conflict. Israel's aim is survival and acceptance, as a permanent, integral and ultimately constructive part of the Middle East. The Arab aim is that of liquidation of the Jewish state; *Israel esse delendam*. Arab moderates are at best willing to acquiesce in the *de facto* existence of a quarantined, isolated, truncated Jewish state, leaving the future open to look after itself. It is this basic difference in outlook which dictates a defensive policy to the former, and an offensive one to the latter.

The Israel-Arab conflict is still far removed from any final solution. Clausewitz has said that where there are hostile emotions, there are hostile intentions. And hostile emotions will abide for a long while to come. Moreover, there will be those who will exploit them for their own purposes; leaders who will feed their ambitions upon them; Arab governments which will encourage them, for reasons of their own; and outside powers which will consider it in their interest to lend them support. The conflict is an "inevitable conflict," and as long as it is unresolved, it will be necessary to live with it, reducing violent outbursts and warfare to a minimum.

Quincy Wright, the political scientist, has described a curve according to which relations between states descend "toward war as tensions, military preparations, exchanges of threats, mobilizations, border hostilities and limited hostilities increase, and it moves toward peace as tensions relax, arms budgets decline, disputes are settled, trade increases and cooperative activities develop." By these criteria, the relations between Israel and its Arab neighbors are still close to the bottom of the curve, at the time of writing. However, the Israel-Arab conflict does not exist in a vacuum. Throughout most of recorded history this part of the world has been at the crossroads, the intersection of powerful interests whose center of gravity was beyond the boundaries of the Middle East. This is still true today. The attitude—actual or expected— of major outside powers in the case of war, the likelihood of their separate or joint intervention in favor of one or the other participant, are of considerable weight, in the Middle East curve, in the decision to start a war.

Whether the Yom Kippur War was the last in the bloody series, or just one in a chain of wars; whether the Middle East will now progress toward peaceful co-existence between Israel and its neighbors, or stumble from one rush of violence to another—is still in the balance. The issue depends on the emotions and visions, the fears and the hopes of people in many lands, on the decisions of statesmen in the area and beyond. The Big Powers bear a special responsibility; how they perceive their interests, and how they pursue them, are factors of cardinal importance in the complex equation of the destiny of the Middle East. Most people on both sides of the barricade, Arabs and Jews, however profound their differences, yearn for peace; they need it, want it, deserve it. Perhaps this record will strengthen their resolve to achieve it; for if there is anything to be learned from this history of half a century of violence, it is this: that nothing has been resolved by war.

11
Postscript

As this book was about to go to press, on June 27, 1976 at 1 p.m., Israel radio announced that Air France flight no. 139, en route from Ben-Gurion Airport, Tel-Aviv, to Paris, had been hijacked, with 247 passengers and 12 crew on board, shortly after a brief stopover in Athens. Although the identity of the hijackers was not immediately clear, it was obvious that after an interval of well over a year, one of the many Palestinian organizations had once more resorted to hijacking, the strategy that had proven in the past to bring maximum publicity to the cause, with minimum effort. No better way had yet been found for a handful of people to gain worldwide attention. Although subsequently it appeared that a splinter group of Habash's Popular Front for the Liberation of Palestine was responsible, and the P.L.O. sanctimoniously condemned the operation, the timing seemed logical from the viewpoint of the latter organization. Hard pressed by the Syrian army and the Christian Falange in the Lebanese Civil War; with one of its major bases in Lebanon having been captured by the Falange and another engaged in a desperate struggle; in short, with its Lebanese basis of operations, the only one which enjoyed considerable freedom of action, in dire peril; reduced to the humiliating circumstance of having to beg assistance from Egypt, which the P.L.O. had publicly condemned but a short while before as a traitor for having signed the second interim agreement with Israel—the P.L.O. had reached another nadir in its trajectory, and the image of its leader, Yasser Arafat, was sadly tarnished.

Some time later it was reported that the plane had landed at Benghazi, Libya; after a brief stop for refueling, it took off again, to an unknown destination. At 4 a.m. on Monday, June 28, it was announced that it had landed at Entebbe Airport, Uganda.

Israel was disconcerted. Field Marshall Idi Amin Dada, the President of Uganda, had not only broken off relations with Israel (as had most other African states), he had openly aligned himself with the P.L.O. P.L.O. pilots were granted training facilities by the Ugandan Air Force, and the Ugandan Army—ironically, trained largely by an Israel team in other, different times—had gone so far as to practice the "capture of the Golan Heights," during its maneuvers.

The Government of Israel at first put the entire onus for the safety of the passengers on the French government, which publicly assumed that responsibility. A major international effort was launched to secure the release of the hostages, with appeals being sent to all political and spiritual authorities, from the Pope to the Secretary General of the United Nations, and even to the Secretary General of the Arab League.

As time dragged on, it became clear that the terrorists, who had boarded the plane during the stopover in Athens (where security arrangements were notoriously inadequate), included both Palestinians and German anarchists. On Wednesday, the hijackers announced their conditions for the release of the hostages: the immediate release of 39 persons detained in Israel, including Kozo Okamoto, one of the perpetrators of the Lod Airport massacre, and Archbishop Hilarion Capucci, formerly head of the Greek Catholic Church in Israel, who had been convicted of smuggling arms and explosives in his vehicle, abusing his ecclesiastic immunity; of six persons detained in the Federal Republic of Germany, five detained in Kenya, one in Switzerland and one in France.

Idi Amin's personal role in the affair was pivotal. Although in his frequent contacts with the hostages he assured them that he was doing everything possible to rescue them, and—indeed—their accomodation and their food were adequate under the circumstances, it soon became clear that far from being an honest broker, he was negotiating *ex parte*. Additional armed Palestinians were permitted to join the hijackers at Entebbe; for a while, Ugandan soldiers were detailed to guard the hostages, thus relieving the hijackers from fatigue and psychological pressure, which in the past had proven an important factor in similar negotiations. Moreover, Idi Amin made public statements urging acceptance of the hijacker's demands, and blaming Israel's obstinacy for anything that might happen.

The French government had stated, early on, that it would not agree to any discrimination between Israeli and other passengers. On June 30 a batch of 48 hostages, all non-Israelis, and most non-Jews, was released, after a process of selection, carried out by one of the German hijackers, reminiscent of the worst episode in Jewish history. One day later, another group of 101 was released. By now, besides the

12 man crew, only 93 were left at Entebbe Airport, all Jewish, mostly Israelis. The hijackers had issued an ultimatum to the effect that if, by Thursday, July 1, 2 p.m. no satisfactory reply was received to their demands, they would blow up the terminal and the plane with all the hostages. Dynamite had, indeed, been placed around both objectives, and Ugandan soldiers had been warned to remove their positions 200 meters from both. As the hour of the expiration of the ultimatum approached, tension reached a climax.

The relatives of the hostages in Israel, who had organized themselves, put pressure on the Israel government to accede to the hijackers' demands. At about 11 a.m. on Thursday, July 1, Israel radio interrupted its broadcast to announce that the Government of Israel, in consultation with the leaders of the major opposition party in the Knesset, had unanimously decided to enter into negotiations with a view to the release of the detainees held in Israel. Unofficially, it was explained that the distance from Israel, almost 4,000 km., and the overt collaboration between host government and the hijackers, left Israel no other choice. In response, the hijackers postponed their ultimatum until Sunday, July 4, at 1 p.m.

All through Friday and Saturday the negotiations dragged wearily on. The hijackers, flexing their muscles, insisted that all detainees should be flown to Entebbe before the release of the hostages; there was absolutely no certainty that additional demands would not be made at that time—but the hour of the expiry of the ultimatum was approaching.

And then, at 3 a.m. on Sunday, July 4, the incredible news was broadcast by the Israel Army Network: the hostages had been released by Israeli forces, and were on their way home. All hijackers had been killed.

At the time of writing, it is still too early to give a precise description of Operation Entebbe, which throughout the free world—even where governments were reticent—evoked admiration and applause for Israeli courage and ability. Already on Tuesday, June 29, the Chief of the General Staff, General Gur, had advised the Cabinet that there was a "military option," and special planning teams had been set up. Planning continued throughout Wednesday and Thursday, but there were still aspects of the plan which appeared "reckless"; the risk to the hostages was too great. Finally, some time on Friday July 2, on the basis of intelligence obtained from different sources, the General Staff had concluded that the operation, although risky, was feasible. The Air Force declared that the approach, in total radio silence to avoid detection, was possible. The Ground Forces advised that if the first plane could touch down at Entebbe at a given distance from the terminal, it would be possible to reach the building and overpower the hijackers and the Ugandan troops before they would be able to blow the building up, although a number of casualties, both amongst passengers and troops, must be taken into consideration.

On Saturday, following a full-scale dress rehearsal, whilst some troops were already on the move to the points of departure, the Cabinet gave the green light. Four planes took off for Entebbe. The flight took 7 hours, partly because stormy weather necessitated a change of course near the target, but the planes arrived there on the minute. Within seconds, the commando force was off the plane and moving towards the target. The force was headed by a young veteran Sgan Aluf (Lt. Col.), who was killed in the operation by a bullet fired from the control tower. The force encountered two Ugandan soldiers who were on guard near the old terminal building, and hit them near the target, which was lit up. The force fanned out ready to burst in from all entrances simultaneously. When the first terrorist walked out of the building, the force's deputy commander opened fire, hit him and broke into the building. The two Germans were killed near the door and a third terrorist was killed ten meters further away. A fourth terrorist, who was injured and fell, tried to open fire but he too was killed. The troops ordered the hostages in Hebrew over loud-speakers to lie on the floor and keep their heads down, but even so several passengers were hit. Other forces overran the second floor, killing two terrorists who were hiding in a restroom. A seventh terrorist was killed in the northern wing of the building. Three terrorists were not accounted for.

One force guarded the surroundings of the building. Several Ugandan airforce Mig planes parked nearby were destroyed during the operation.

Within 45 seconds of the raiders breaking into the building, the hostages had been set free. The plane with all the hostages took off 53 minutes after the troops had arrived, although the raiders remained in Entebbe half an hour longer. During the dress rehearsal the operation had taken 55 minutes, 2 minutes longer.

On their way back, the planes stopped at Nairobi for refuelling, and unloading wounded who needed immediate treatment. At 3 a.m., when Idi Amin talked on the phone to Israel to an Israeli friend, he had been unaware of what had happened. When subsequently he found out, he accused the Kenyan government of collusion. The Government

of Kenya vehemently denied the allegation, and Israel announced
that it had imposed its planes on Kenya, which had agreed, for humanitarian reasons.

One officer, and three passengers had lost their lives in the operation.
An elderly woman, hospitalized in Entebbe, disappeared, presumably
killed in an act of blind, barbaric revenge.

Air France Flight 139 will long be remembered, as a manifestation
of the internationalization of terror, of the impotence of conventional
diplomacy in the face of a collaborationist government, but above
all—because of the daring and precise execution of Operation Entebbe,
its denouement. It has given IDF a new prestige and confidence,
obliterating the dire memories of the first days of the Yom Kippur War.
It may have provided an impetus towards a more determined national
and international effort to combat terrorism in general, hijacking
in particular. However, it is unlikely to terminate the role of terrorism
as a powerful means to keep the conflict alive, and maintain it in the
public eye. And it certainly cannot be considered as the end of the war.
The war goes on.

Selected Bibliography (English)

CHAPTER 1.

Herzl, Theodor, *Altneuland*.
Mandel, Neville, *Turks, Arabs and Jewish Immigration into Palestine 1882–1914* (Oxford 1965).
Middle East Affairs, No. 4 (London 1965), pp. 77–108.
Lawrence, T. E., *The Seven Pillars of Wisdom* (London 1935).
Meinhertzhagen, Richard, *Middle East Diary, 1917–1956*, (London 1959).
Jabotinsky, V., *The Story of the Jewish Legion* (New York 1945).
Allon, Yigal, *Shield of David* (London 1970).
Bauer, Yehudah, *From Diplomacy to Resistance; A History of Jewish Palestine 1939–1945* (New York 1970).
Middle Eastern Studies 2(1966).
Begin, Menachem, *The Revolt, Story of the Irgun* (New York 1951).
Golomb, Eliyahu, *The History of Jewish Self-Defence* (Tel Aviv 1946).
Ingrams, Doreen, *Palestine Papers, 1917–1922* (London 1972).
Palestine Disturbances in May 1921 (London 1930).
Report of the Commission on the Palestine Disturbances of August 1929 (London 1930).
Palestine Royal Commission: Report (London 1937).

CHAPTER 2.

Lorch, N., *The Edge of the Sword* (New York 1961; Jerusalem 1968).
Kimche, Jon and David, *Both Sides of the Hill* (London 1960).
Kurzman, Dan, *Genesis 1948* (New York 1970).
Joseph, Dov, *The Faithful City; The Seige of Jerusalem 1948* (New York 1960).

CHAPTER 3.

Eytan, W., *The First Ten Years* (New York 1958).
Eban, A., *My Country* (1972).

CHAPTER 4.

Henriques, Robert, *One Hundred Hours to Suez* (New York 1957).
Safran, Nadav, *From War to War, The Arab-Israeli Confrontation 1948–1967* (New York 1969).
Dayan, M. *Diary of the Sinai Campaign* (New York 1967).
Barker, A. J., *Suez, The Seven Day War* (London 1964).
O'Ballance, Edgar, *The Sinai Campaign 1956* (London 1959).

CHAPTER 5.

Yaari, Ehud, *Strike Terror* (Jerusalem 1970).
Harkabi, Y., *Palestinians and Israel* (Jerusalem 1974).

CHAPTER 6.

Churchill, Randolph S. and Winston S., *The Six-Day War* (London 1967).
Marshall, S. L. A., *Swift Sword* (New York 1967).
O'Ballance, Edgar, *The Third Arab-Israeli War* (London 1972).

CHAPTER 8.

Herzog, Chaim, *The Yom Kippur War* (1975).
Sunday Times, "The Yom Kippur War"